Communications in Computer and Information Science 571

More information about this series at http://www.springer.com/series/7899

Eric Ras · Desirée Joosten-ten Brinke (Eds.)

Computer Assisted Assessment

Research into E-Assessment

18th International Conference, CAA 2015
Zeist, The Netherlands, June 22–23, 2015
Proceedings

Springer

Editors
Eric Ras
Luxembourg Institute of Science and Technology
Esch/Alzette
Luxembourg

Desirée Joosten-ten Brinke
Open University of The Netherlands
Heerlen
The Netherlands

ISSN 1865-0929 ISSN 1865-0937 (electronic)
Communications in Computer and Information Science
ISBN 978-3-319-27703-5 ISBN 978-3-319-27704-2 (eBook)
DOI 10.1007/978-3-319-27704-2

Library of Congress Control Number: 2015957089

Printed on acid-free paper

This Springer imprint is published by SpringerNature
The registered company is Springer International Publishing AG Switzerland

Preface

Technology in assessment is a growing area for research and practice. The objective of the International Computer-Assisted Assessment Conference (CAA) is to bring together researchers and practitioners working in this field. This volume of conference proceedings provides an opportunity for readers to engage with refereed research papers that were presented during the 18th edition of the CAA, which took place in Zeist, The Netherlands. All the more practical-oriented contributions are available on the website[1]. Each paper was reviewed by at least three experts and the authors revised their papers based on these comments and discussions during the conference. The 15 selected research papers published here show excellent examples of current developments in technology-enhanced assessment. The subject of the contributions varies from research on automatic item generation, computer-adapted testing, the use of multimedia in assessment to e-assessment policies, etc. Formative as well as summative assessment approaches are subject of empirical studies in different learning domains. The papers will be of interest to educational scientists and practitioners who want to be informed about recent innovations and to obtain insights into e-assessment. We thank all reviewers, contributing authors, and the sponsoring institutions for their support.

June 2015

Eric Ras
Desirée Joosten-ten Brinke

---

[1] http://caaconference.co.uk/

Organization

CAA 2015 was organized by the Welten Institute - Research Centre for Learning, Teaching and Technology of the Open University of The Netherlands in cooperation with SURFnet, the collaborative organization for ICT in Dutch higher education and research and by the Embedded Assessment Research Group of LIST, the Luxembourg Institute of Science and Technology.

Executive Committee

Conference Chairs

Eric Ras	Luxembourg Institute of Science and Technology, Luxembourg
Desirée Joosten-ten Brinke	Open University of The Netherlands/Fontys, The Netherlands

Local Organizing Committee

Desirée Joosten-ten Brinke	Open University of The Netherlands/Fontys, The Netherlands
Eric Ras	Luxembourg Institute of Science and Technology, Luxembourg
Mieke Haemers	Open University of The Netherlands, The Netherlands
Annette Peet	SURFnet, The Netherlands
Johan van Strien	Open University of The Netherlands, The Netherlands
Ellen Rusman	Open University of The Netherlands, The Netherlands

Program Committee

Jorik Arts	Fontys University of Applied Sciences, The Netherlands
Geoffrey Crisp	RMIT, University of Melbourne, Australia
Silvester Draaijer	Free University of Amsterdam, The Netherlands
Hendrik Drachsler	Open University of The Netherlands, The Netherlands
Gerry Geitz	Open University of The Netherlands, The Netherlands
Mark Gierl	University of Alberta, Canada
Lester Gilbert	University of Southampton, UK
Davinia Hernandez-Leo	University Pompeu Fabra, Spain
Mieke Jaspers	Fontys University of Applied Sciences, The Netherlands
Marco Kalz	Open University of The Netherlands, The Netherlands
Kelly Meusen	Open University of The Netherlands, The Netherlands
George Moerkerke	Open University of The Netherlands, The Netherlands
Annette Peet	SURFnet, The Netherlands
Peter Reimann	University of Sydney, Australia
Peter van Rosmalen	Open University of The Netherlands, The Netherlands

Ellen Rusman	Open University of The Netherlands, The Netherlands
Venkat Sastry	Cranfield University, UK
Jos Speetjens	Fontys University of Applied Sciences, The Netherlands
Johan van Strien	Open University of The Netherlands, The Netherlands
Bill Warburton	University of Southampton, UK
Denise Whitelock	Open University, UK
Gary Wills	University of Southampton, UK

Sponsoring Institutions

MapleSoft, Amsterdam, The Netherlands
Teelen Kennismanagement, Wilp, The Netherlands
European Association for Technology-Enhanced Learning (EA-TEL), Hannover, Germany
Open University of The Netherlands, Heerlen, The Netherlands
SURFnet, Utrecht, The Netherlands
Luxembourg Institute of Science and Technology, Esch/Alzette, Luxembourg

Contents

The Psychometric Evaluation of a Summative Multimedia-Based Performance Assessment

Sebastiaan De Klerk[1,2(✉)], Bernard P. Veldkamp[2,3], and Theo Eggen[2,4]

[1] eX:plain, Amersfoort, The Netherlands
s.dklerk@explain.nl
[2] Research Center for Examinations and Certification, Enschede, The Netherlands
b.p.veldkamp@utwente.nl, theo.eggen@cito.nl
[3] University of Twente, Enschede, The Netherlands
[4] Cito, Arnhem, The Netherlands

Abstract. In this article, a case study on the design, development, and evaluation of a multimedia-based performance assessment (MBPA) for measuring confined space guards' skills is presented. A confined space guard (CSG) supervises operations that are carried out in a confined space (e.g. a tank or silo). Currently, individuals who want to become a certified CSG in The Netherlands have to participate in a one day training program and have to pass both a knowledge-based MC test and a practice-based performance-based assessment (PBA). Our goal is to measure the skills that are currently being assessed through the PBA, with the MBPA. We first discuss the design and development of the MBPA. Secondly, we present an empirical study which was used for assessing the quality of our measurement instrument. A representative sample of 55 CSG students, who had just completed the one day training program, has subsequently performed in the MC test, and then, depending on the condition they were assigned, the PBA or the MBPA. We report the psychometric properties of the MBPA. Furthermore, using correlations and regression analysis, we make an empirical comparison between students' scores on the PBA and the MBPA. The results show that students' scores on the PBA and the MBPA are significantly correlated and that students' MBPA score is a good predictor for their score on the PBA. In the discussion, we provide implications and directions for future research and practice into the field of MBPA.

Keywords: Performance-based assessment · Multimedia-based performance assessment · Psychometric evaluation · Design and development

1 Introduction

The growing capabilities and availability of technology enable a whole new generation of technology driven assessments, far more elaborated than computer-based transformations of formerly item-based paper-and-pencil tests [4, 10]. The new generation of technology-based assessments both expand and deepen the domain of assessment [9].

E. Ras and D. Joosten-ten Brinke (Eds.): CAA 2015, CCIS 571, pp. 1–11, 2015.
DOI: 10.1007/978-3-319-27704-2_1

Technology makes more flexible and context driven presentations of tasks and environments in CBA possible, which can lead to a broader and better understanding of what students have learned [4].

In this article, we discuss the design, development, and evaluation of a technology-based assessment that incorporates images, animations, and videos for the purpose of creating complex and interactive tasks in a simulation of a real-world setting. We call this type of technology-based assessment *multimedia-based performance assessment* (MBPA), because the tasks in the assessment are for a large part constructed of multimedia and are used to measure student skills that were previously being measured by a PBA. The purpose of the MBPA we discuss here is to measure the skills of confined space guards (CSG) after they have performed in vocational training. The CSG skills consist of 19 actions that a student has to take during the performance-based assessment (e.g., test the walkie-talkie, check the work permit, assess the wind direction, and register the number of people going in and out of the confined space).

Although PBA has been discussed and supported as a valuable tool for formative and diagnostic assessment of students [8, 11], the research is less supportive in cases where PBA was used as a summative assessment. This is foremost because PBAs are found to be prone to measurement error resulting from several sources; task, occasion and rater sampling variability [5, 6, 12]. Above that, task sampling and occasion sampling are confounded, which means that their combined effect strongly raises measurement error [13]. These findings indicate that students' scores resulting from performance in a PBA do not solely represent students' proficiency in a particular skill, but are influenced by the specific task they were assigned, the occasion of the assessment, and the raters judging their performance. Therefore, the purpose of the current study is to design, develop, and evaluate a multimedia-based equivalent of the PBA, for credentialing confined space guards in Dutch vocational training.

The first part of the paper focuses on design and development and in the second part of the paper an empirical study is presented that focuses on the psychometric functioning of the MBPA, and especially the empirical relationship between the MBPA and the PBA. We compared test scores resulting from the MBPA with students' test scores on the PBA, a paper-and-pencil (P&P) knowledge-based MC test and student ratings on questionnaires about computer experience and the usability of the MBPA. In the experiment, a random, yet representative, sample of students either first performs the PBA and then the MBPA, or vice versa. The central question of our study is: Is it possible to develop a multimedia-based performance assessment that produces valid and reliable estimates of the proficiency of confined space guards? We have the following hypotheses:

Hypothesis 1: The scores of students on the PBA will be positively correlated with the scores of students on the MBPA.
Hypothesis 2: The scores on the MBPA will not be correlated with students' background characteristics (i.e. age, education and ethnicity).
Hypothesis 3: The scores on the MBPA will not be correlated with students' answers on a computer experience questionnaire.
Hypothesis 4: The scores on the MBPA will be positively correlated with students' answers on a usability questionnaire.

Hypothesis 5: The group of students who do not pass the PBA will score significantly lower on the MBPA than the group of students who pass the PBA.
Hypothesis 6: The group of students who first do the PBA will score significantly higher on the MBPA than the group of students who first do the MBPA.
Hypothesis 7: The group of students who first do the MBPA will score significantly higher on the PBA than the group of students who first do the PBA.

2 Design and Development

The start of building an MBPA is to determine the purpose of the assessment. As said, the MBPA was built to measure the skills of CSG's as defined by subject matter experts in the "final attainment objectives" so that it can be used as an assessment for certification of CSG's.

The design phase was started by determining the constructs and attributes that we wanted to measure and analyzing them for translation into the MBPA's tasks. This was done in collaboration with subject matter experts (SMEs) through multiple rounds of consultation. Of course, a lot about the tasks of CSG's was already known through the instruction material and final attainment objectives of the performance-based assessment. Furthermore, the first author took part in a one day course and performed the PBA to become a certified CSG. We used this material and knowledge to further work out the constructs and attributes for the MBPA.

Based on this knowledge, the tasks in the assessment could be designed and developed in collaboration with the SMEs. We first build what we have called an *assessment skeleton,* in which the general flow of the assessment was laid out, including the multimedia and the tasks. This was done on a relatively abstract level but it ensured that all constructs, final attainment objectives, and primary observables are incorporated in the tasks. In validity terms: the demands for content validity were met through the use of the assessment skeletons. Because the assessment skeleton is still a rather coarse-grained representation of the assessment it is not sufficient for actually building the assessment. Therefore, we further elaborated the assessment skeletons into *assessment templates.* In the assessment templates we showed – screen by screen – what was presented during the course of the assessment. The assessment templates enabled us to collect the multimedia (video and photo material) in one day at a reconstructed job site in The Netherlands that is used for practice and performance-based assessments. In addition, the templates served as a primary input for the designer to design the buttons needed in the assessment.

We hired a professional ICT system designer who was very experienced in designing intuitive, usable and efficient interfaces for interactive websites. Furthermore, the templates in combination with the buttons provided the necessary materials for the programmer to build the structure of the assessment on the online assessment platform. The next step was to test the assessment; first on its technical functioning and then on its psychometric functioning in an empirical study. The assessment is administered via the internet and through multiple test rounds we were able to solve the technical bugs, thereby ensuring that the assessment was technically functioning. We will now present our experiment.

3 Method

3.1 Participants

The participants in the pilot study were 55 confined space guard students (1 female, 54 male, mean age: 40.4 years ($\sigma = 11.5$), age range: 19–64 years). They were requested to do the MBPA after they had completed their training.

3.2 Materials

Multiple-Choice knowledge-Based test. Immediately after the training, the students did a knowledge-based P&P test, consisting of 21 MC questions with 3 alternatives.

Performance-Based Assessment. In the PBA, students perform a CSG's job tasks in a reconstructed, yet realistic situation. Figure 1 gives an impression of a PBA for measuring CSG skills.

The rater uses a rubric consisting of 19 criteria to evaluate the student's performance. All 19 criteria can be judged as *insufficient* or *sufficient* by the rater. From the 19 criteria (e.g. "tests the walkie-talkie"), 9 are considered to be a knock-out criterion (e.g. "recognizes and reacts to an emergency situation") which means that if a student's performance

Fig. 1. Performance-based assessment

on one of these criteria is insufficient he or she does not pass the PBA. Besides the 19 criteria rubric that focuses on 19 individual actions that a student can take during the PBA, a second rubric was used for assessing the communicative and behavioral skills of the student. For the second rubric, the rater scores students' communicative skills, proactivity, environmental awareness, and procedural efficiency. Raters were asked to rate students on a scale ranging from 0 (e.g. "Student does not demonstrate any communication skills") to 3 (e.g. "Student communicates very strong"). Hence, students could get a minimum of 0 points and a maximum of 12 points on this rubric and a minimum of 0 points and a maximum of 19 points on the original rubric and both rubrics were filled out by the rater.

Multimedia-Based Performance Assessment. Clearly, another primary instrument in the study was the multimedia-based performance assessment. The scenario that students went through was the cleansing of a tank on a petrochemical plant by two workers, which was built in the online environment using multimedia. Students started in an office situation where the contractor handed the CSG and one of the workers the work permit. In this setting, students had to ask for explanation of the work permit by the contractor, check the work permit for blanks or errors, ask for a walkie-talkie and test the walkie-talkie. Then the setting changed to the confined space itself. In this setting, students were required to determine the right escape route in case of an emergency, students had to ensure that the environment was safe for the workers to work in and that there were no irregularities between the work permit and the actual situation at the confined space. In a next phase, students had to supervise two workers who were cleaning the interior of the confined space. Finally, students had to act upon a plant alarm. Students were required to watch the multimedia elements and to answer several types of questions (e.g. multiple choice, rank order, fill in the blank, etc.) during the administration of the MBPA. We also included so-called

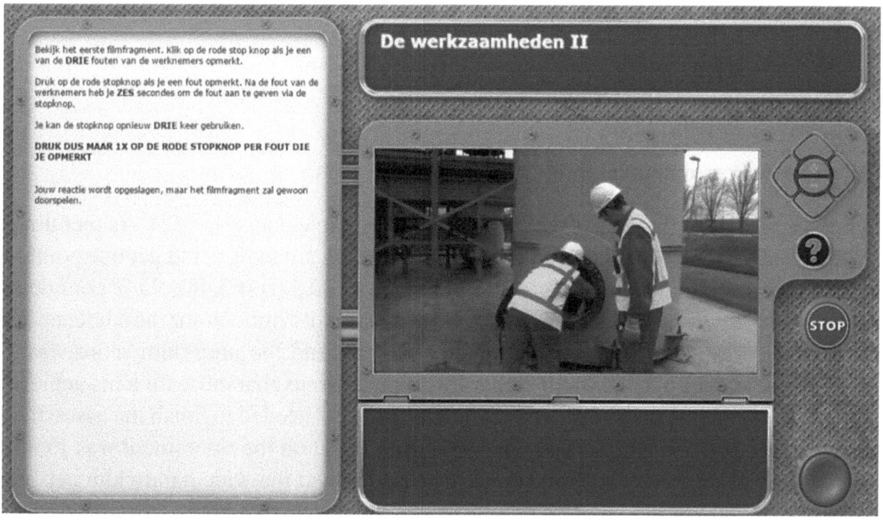

Fig. 2. Multimedia-based performance assessment screenshot.

intervention tasks. The intervention tasks required students to intervene in two videos of workers performing cleansing tasks in a tank whenever their actions were incorrect. Students could intervene by clicking on a big and red "stop" button that was presented right beside the video screen. Students were told that they only had three possibilities to click on the stop button. That is, if they clicked the stop button when there were no faulty actions of the workers, then they had one less chance to press the button. The MBPA consisted of a total of 35 tasks. Figure 2 gives an impression of the MBPA.

Questionnaire. After students had performed in the MBPA they were requested to fill out a questionnaire comprised of items (N = 15) addressing their background characteristics (e.g. "What is your highest level op completed education?"), computer use (e.g. "On a scale ranging from 1 (never) to 5 (every day) - How often do you play videogames on a computer?"), and MBPA interface (e.g. "On a scale ranging from 1 (strongly disagree) to 5 (strongly agree) - I was comfortable with the interface of the MBPA"). The questionnaire was based on a translated version of the System Usability Scale [1] and a questionnaire on the use of Internet and the computer at home, developed by Cito [3].

3.3 Procedure

Students participated in their training and completed the P&P test immediately afterwards. Then, depending on the condition they were randomly assigned, students either first performed the PBA and then the MBPA (N = 27) or reversely (N = 28). The students were not allowed to confer between both administrations, so that it was impossible that they exchanged knowledge regarding the MBPA. For the MBPA, students were seated behind a laptop or PC. All assessments were administered under supervision of the first author. Students logged in with a personal login on the assessment platform. There was no time limit imposed on students; neither for the individual tasks nor for the whole assessment. After students finished the assessment they had to fill out the questionnaire that was upside down on their table.

4 Results

4.1 MBPA Performance

In this section, we will discuss the analysis of the sample data (N = 55). As mentioned above, the assessment is composed of 35 items. In total, students could get one point for each correct answer. The mean score on the test was 22.5 ($\sigma = 3.44$), 95 % confidence interval [21.6, 23.6], which indicates that the test was quite difficult for the students. The maximum score obtained (by two students) was 30, and the minimum score was 14 (N = 1). The standard deviation is rather low which means that most students achieved a score around the mean. The average time that students needed to finish the assessment was 29 min ($\sigma = 8$). The minimum amount of time spent on the assessment was 19 min, the longest was 58 min. The high standard deviation and the wide bandwidth between minimum and maximum indicate that there is a lot of variance between students' time spent on the assessment.

The reliability of the MBPA is high (GLB = 0.94). We have looked at the best indicator of the reliability, the Greatest Lower Bound [16]. The GLB is the best indicator because the bias of the estimate is rather small [15], and compared to Cronbach's alpha, for example, the GLB is closer to the true reliability of the test [14]. The distribution of the test scores is not skewed (0.014), but many scores are distributed around the mean, thereby increasing kurtosis (0.488). Of course, the number of observations is limited, making it difficult to interpret these indices.

4.2 Hypotheses Testing

Our first hypothesis states that students' PBA score will be positively correlated with their MBPA score. Spearman's rho is used as a correlation index because the measures do not meet the assumptions of normality and linearity, while there is more of a monotonic relationship between the variables. For example, on the 19-point rubric, most students score 17 to 19 of the criteria as correct. The correlations are listed in Table 1.

Table 1. Correlations, means and standard deviations of measures (1000 sample bootstrapping performed)

Measure	1	2	3	4	5	6	7
1. MBPA							
2. PBA (19)	0.39†**						
3. PBA (12)	0.38†**	0.68***					
4. PBA (total)	0.43†**	0.84***	0.96***				
5. MC Test	0.30*	0.2	0.21	0.23			
6. MBPA (time)	0.01	−0.13	−0.2	−0.22	−0.05		
7. Q-Computer exp.	0.09	0.12	0.15	0.16	−0.01	0.1	
8. Q-MBPA usability	0.18†	0.15	0.09	0.16	−0.06	−0.18	0.42**

Note. *p < 0.05, **p < 0.01, ***p < 0.001, † (one-tailed)

The correlation between the MBPA and the rubrics used in the performance assessment is 0.38 ($p < 0.01$) and 0.39 ($p < 0.01$), respectively for the 19-point rubric and the 12-point rubric, which are both significant and thereby support our first hypothesis. We have also combined students' scores on both rubrics to get a *total rubric score*. The correlation between the total rubric score and the MBPA score is strongly significant ($r_s = 0.43$ ($p < 0.01$)). Of course, there is also a strong significant correlation between both rubrics used in the assessment ($r_s = 0.68$, $p < 0.001$). Furthermore, we also performed a linear regression analysis to see to what extent the performance in the MBPA can predict performance in the PBA. To correct for the negative skew of the distribution of the 19-point rubric, we performed a log transformation [7]. For correct analyses, we did this for both the 12-point rubric, the 19-point rubric, and the total rubric score. The regression analysis for the 19-point rubric showed a significant effect ($F(1,53) = 4.365$, $p < 0.05$), which indicates that the MBPA score can account for 7.6 %

of the variation in the PBA score. We performed the same analysis for the 12-point rubric, which was also significant ($F(1,46) = 5.544, p < 0.05$), with an explained variance of 10.1 %. Finally, we also performed a regression analysis for the total rubric score, which was also significant ($F(1,46) = 5.905$, $p < 0.05$), with an explained variance of 11.4 %. The total rubric score is the best predictor for performance in the MBPA. Unfortunately, the rater forgot to fill out the 12-point rubric on one assessment occasion, which explains the declined number of students in the second analysis. Furthermore, when we look at misclassifications at the 60 % cutoff percentage (as established by experts) for the MBPA, we see that 7 out of 8 students that failed their PBA also fail the MBPA. This indicates that the PBA score is a good predictor for the MBPA score.

We expected to observe no correlation between students' background characteristics and their score on the MBPA (H_2). The background characteristics are age, education, and ethnicity. Age was not correlated with assessment score ($r_s = 0.00$, $p > 0.05$). We calculated the biserial correlation coefficient for education. The biserial correlation coefficient is used when one variable is a continuous dichotomy [7]. First, we made two groups of students (low education vs. high education). The low education group consisted of students who have had education up to high school or lower vocational education ($N = 26$, $M_{\text{MBPA}} = 21.83$) and the high education group consisted of students who have had education from the middle level vocational education and upwards ($N = 27$, $M_{\text{MBPA}} = 23.08$). We calculated the point-biserial correlation (which is for true dichotomies [7]), and then transformed it into the biserial correlation. Although education and students' MBPA score were positively correlated, this effect was not significant ($r_b = 0.19, p > 0.05$). For ethnicity, we were especially interested in two groups: students with a Dutch ethnicity ($N = 40$, $M_{\text{MBPA}} = 22.8$) and students with another ethnicity ($N = 15$, $M_{\text{MBPA}} = 22.78$). Now, we calculated the point-biserial correlation between ethnicity (0 = Dutch, 1 = other) and the students' MBPA score. Again, we did not find a significant correlation ($r_{\text{pb}} = -0.01$, $p > 0.05$). These findings support our second hypothesis; there were no significant correlations between students' background variables and their score on the MBPA. Also, there was no significant correlation between the time spent on the MBPA and the score obtained ($r = 0.07, p > 0.05$).

We also found support for our third hypothesis, because there is no significant positive correlation between the students' MBPA score and their computer experience questionnaire ($r_s = 0.09$, $p > 0.05$). We could not find support for the fourth hypothesis, because there is no significant correlation between the MBPA score and usability questionnaire ($r_s = 0.14, p > 0.05$).

Our fifth hypothesis reflected our expectation that students who had failed their PBA would score significantly lower on the MBPA than students who had passed their PBA. Unfortunately, the group of students is rather small ($N = 8$), which makes it quite difficult to interpret the results and draw definitive conclusions. The group of students who passed the PBA had a mean score of 23.2 ($\sigma = 0.46$) and group of students who failed the PBA had a mean score of 20.1 ($\sigma = 1.1$). We used an independent samples t-test to check whether the groups differed significantly, which was the case ($t(53) = -2.563$, $p < 0.001$). We then performed a logistic regression analysis to check to what extent the MBPA score can predict whether a student will pass or fail in their PBA. The MBPA score is treated as a continuous predictor in the logistic regression analysis and the dependent variable (success in PBA) is a dichotomous outcome variable (0 = failed, 1 = passed). The analysis demonstrated that the MBPA score is making a significant contribution to the prediction of students failing or passing their PBA ($\chi^2(1, 55) = 5.09$, $p < 0.05$). Furthermore, the odds ratio (e^{β}) for the BPA score is 1.39 with a 95 % confidence interval [1.04, 1.86]. This suggests that a one unit increase in the MBPA score increases the probability of being successful in the PBA (i.e. passing the PBA) with 1.39. The results of the logistic regression analysis are presented in Table 2.

Table 2. Logistic regression analysis of passing performance-based assessment

Predictor	β (SE)	Wald's χ^2 (df = 1)	p	e^{β}	e^{β} (95 % CI)	
					Lower	Upper
Constant	−5.4	3.05	0.08	0.00		
MBPA Score	0.33	5.09	0.02	1.39	1.04	1.86

Hypothesis six and seven state that students' condition would positively influence the score on the second assessment they performed. However, students who first did the MBPA did not score higher on the PBA than students who started with the PBA [$F(1,53) = 0.96$, $p > 0.05$], and vice versa for the score on the MBPA [$F(1,53) = 0.05$, $p > 0.05$]. This indicates that there is no learning effect between both assessments.

5 Discussion and Conclusion

New forms of technology driven assessments are increasingly becoming part of the modern assessment culture. The aim of this study was to empirically investigate the design, development and evaluation of a multimedia-based performance assessment for credentialing confined space guards in Dutch vocational education. This study is one of the first endeavors in empirically determining the (psychometric) quality of an innovative computer-based assessment that aims to assess constructs normally associated with performance-based assessments.

The reliability of the MBPA is good; the GLB [16] is the best estimate of the reliability and gives the greatest lower bound of the reliability. That means that the reliability of the test is at least as high as the GLB indicates. In our case, the GLB is 0.94.

Students' scores on the PBA (rubrics independently and total rubric score) moderately correlated with their scores on the MBPA. The fact that the correlation is not stronger may be because of several reasons. First, the rubrics used for rating students' performance on the PBA do not show much variance in sum score. We had foreseen this problem already for the 19-point rubric and therefore developed the 12-point rubric; to induce more variation in students' PBA scores. Indeed, it does produce slightly more variance in students' scores, yet it might be too less to really make a difference. It is statistically difficult to establish strong relationships between two variables when one of the variables almost has no variance.

Thereby, we might have found the reason why there isn't a stronger relationship between PBA and MBPA. As discussed in the introduction, performance-based assessments generally suffer from measurement error. This might also be the case for the PBA in our study. In a future study, generalizability theory could be used to determine the psychometric quality of the PBA. Future research in this area should also try to find criteria that are out of the assessment domain. An external criterion could for example be students' future job appraisals, made by their managers. Also, a future study on the subject could include a strong analysis on the quality of the PBA, for example through generalizability theory [2].

Of course, there are some limitations to our study. First, the sample size is rather small. It was difficult to get a substantial number of students to participate in the study, because many assessment locations do not have internet or computers and the locations itself are spread all over The Netherlands. Also, the assessment itself takes place, on average, 15 times per year per location. Sometimes, a group consists of less than five students, which indicates that it can be quite difficult to get a sufficient number of students to participate. On the other hand, because there are not many students per year, we can say that we have included a substantial amount in our study. Furthermore, if we look at background, the sample does not systematically differ from the population.

As already mentioned, another limitation is the quality of the performance-based assessment. Although the PBA is professionally organized, only one rater is being used, who is also playing a part in the assessment (the operator). The 19-point rubric, used for rating a students' performance, shows little to no variance at all, which makes it difficult to draw firm conclusions regarding the MBPA – PBA comparison. Furthermore, another limitation is that this is a first version of the MBPA. If we look at the test and item characteristics presented, then there is room enough for qualitative improvement.

To conclude, with this study we make strong theoretical and practical contributions to advanced technology-based assessment. To our knowledge, we are the first to make an empirical comparison between a computer-based assessment and a practical or manual performance-based assessment in vocational training.

References

1. Bangor, A., Kortum, P.T., Miller, J.T.: An empirical evaluation of the system usability scale. Int. J. Hum.-Comput. Interact. **24**, 574–594 (2008)
2. Brennan, R.L.: Generalizability Theory. Springer, New York (2001)
3. Cito: The use of internet and the computer at home questionnaire. Dutch version (2014). http://toetswijzer.kennisnet.nl/html/internetvaardigheid/vragenlijst.pdf
4. Clarke-Midura, J., Dede, C.: Assessment, technology, and change. J. Res. Technol. Educ. **42**(3), 309–328 (2010)
5. Cronbach, L.J., Linn, R.L., Brennan, R.L., Haertel, E.H.: Generalizability analysis for performance assessments of student achievement or school effectiveness. Educ. Psychol. Meas. **57**(3), 373–399 (1997)
6. Dekker, J., Sanders, P.F.: Kwaliteit van beoordeling in de praktijk [Quality of rating during work placement]. Ede: Kenniscentrum handel (2008)
7. Field, A.: Discovering Statistics Using SPSS, 3rd edn. SAGE Publications Inc, Thousand Oaks (2009)

8. Gulikers, J.T.M., Bastiaens, T.J., Kirschner, P.A.: A five-dimensional framework for authentic assessment. Educ. Technol. Res. Dev. **52**(3), 67–86 (2004)
9. Levy, R.: Psychometric and evidentiary advances, opportunities, and challenges for simulation-based assessment. Educ. Assess. **18**(3), 182–207 (2013)
10. Quellmalz, E.S., Pellegrino, J.W.: Technology and testing. Science **323**, 75–79 (2009)
11. Roelofs, E.C., Straetmans, G.J.J.M. (eds.) Assessment in actie [Assessment in action]. Cito, Arnhem (2006)
12. Shavelson, R.J., Baxter, G.P., Gao, X.: Sampling variability of performance assessments. J. Educ. Meas. **30**(3), 215–232 (1993)
13. Shavelson, R.J., Ruiz-Primo, M.A., Wiley, E.: Note on sources of sample variability in science performance assessments. J. Educ. Meas. **36**(1), 56–69 (1999)
14. Sijtsma, K.: On the use, the misuse, and the very limited usefulness of Cronbach's alpha. Psychometrika **74**(1), 107–120 (2009)
15. Ten Berge, J.M.F., Sočan, G.: The greatest lower bound to the reliability of a test and the hypothesis of unidimensionality. Psychometrika **69**, 613–625 (2004)
16. Verhelst, N.D.: Estimating the reliability of a test from a single test administration. Measurement and Research Department Reports 98-2. National Institute for Educational Measurement, Arnhem (2000)

A Method for Generating Nonverbal Reasoning Items Using n-Layer Modeling

Mark J. Gierl[1(✉)], Marita MacMahon Ball[2], Veronica Vele[2], and Hollis Lai[3]

[1] Faculty of Education, University of Alberta, Edmonton, AB, Canada
Mark.Gierl@ualberta.ca
[2] Australian Council for Educational Research, Melbourne, Australia
{Marita.MacMahonBall,Veronica.Vele}@acer.edu.au
[3] School of Dentistry, University of Alberta, Edmonton, AB, Canada
Hollis.Lai@ualberta.ca

Abstract. Automatic item generation is the process of using item models to produce assessment tasks using computer technology. An item model is comparable to a template that highlights the variables or elements in the task that must be manipulated to produce new items. When a small number of elements is manipulated in the item model, the generated items look similar to one another and are often referred to as clones. The purpose of our study is to describe a method for generating large numbers of diverse and heterogeneous items using a generalized approach called n-layer item modeling. When a large numbers of elements is manipulated in the n-layer item model, diverse items are generated. We demonstrate the method by generating 1,340 nonverbal reasoning items that would be appropriate for a high-stakes medical admission test.

Keywords: Test development · Automatic item generation · Item writing · Technology and assessment

1 Introduction

Automatic item generation (AIG) [1–4] is a rapidly evolving research area where cognitive theories, computer technologies, and psychometric practices establish a process that can be used to generate test items. AIG can be described as the process of using models to generate items with the aid of computer technology. It requires two general steps. First, content specialists create item models that highlight the elements in the assessment task that can be manipulated. An item model is similar to a template that specifies the variables or elements in the task that must be manipulated to produce new items. Second, the elements in the item model are varied using computer-based algorithms to generate new items. The purpose of this study is to describe and illustrate a method where one item model can be used to generate many test items. The focal content area for item generation in this study is nonverbal reasoning.

E. Ras and D. Joosten-ten Brinke (Eds.): CAA 2015, CCIS 571, pp. 12–21, 2015.
DOI: 10.1007/978-3-319-27704-2_2

2 Item Modeling and the Problem with Cloning

Item modeling provides the foundation for AIG [5, 6]. An item model is comparable to a template, mould, rendering, or prototype that highlights the elements in an assessment task that must be manipulated to produce new items. Elements can be found in the stem, the options, and/or the auxiliary information. The stem is the part of an item model that contains the context, content, and/or the question the examinee is required to answer. The options include the alternative answers with one correct option and one or more incorrect options. For selected-response item models, both stem and options are required. For constructed-response item models, only the stem is created. Auxiliary information includes any additional content, in either the stem or option, required to generate an item. Auxiliary information can be expressed as images, tables, diagrams, sound, or video. The stem and options are further divided into elements. Elements are denoted as strings which are non-numeric content and integers which are numeric content. Often, the starting point is to use an existing test item. Existing items, also called *parent items*, can be found by reviewing previously administered tests, by drawing on existing items from a bank, or by creating the parent item directly. The parent item highlights the structure of the model, thereby providing a point-of-reference for creating alternative items. Then, content specialists identify elements in the parent that can be manipulated to produce new items. They also specify the content (i.e., string and integer values) for these elements.

One drawback of item modeling in the current application of AIG is that relatively few elements can be manipulated because the number of potential elements in any one item model is small. For example, if a parent item contains 16 words in the stem, then the maximum number of elements that can be manipulated is 16, assuming that all words in the stem can be made into elements. One important consequence of manipulating a small number of element is that the generated items may be overtly similar to one another. This type of item modeling can pose a problem in the current application of AIG because many content specialists view this process negatively and often refer to it pejoratively as "cloning".

Cloning, in a biological sense, refers to any process where a population of identical units is derived from the same ancestral line. Cloning helps characterize item modeling if we consider it to be a process where specific content (e.g., nuclear DNA) in a parent item (e.g., currently or previously existing animal) is manipulated to generate a new item (e.g., new animal). Through this process, instances are created that are identical (or, at least, very similar) to the parent because information is purposefully transferred from the parent to the offspring. Our current approaches to item modeling yield outcomes that are described by content specialists as clones. Clones are perceived by content specialists to be generated items that are overly simplistic and easy to produce. More importantly, clones are believed to be readily recognized by coaching and test preparation companies which limits their usefulness in operational testing programs. Hence, cloned items has limited practical value.

3 n-Layer Item Modeling: A Method to Address the Limitations of Cloning

AIG is the process of using an item model to generate items by manipulating elements in the model. When a small number of elements is manipulated, the generated items look similar to one another and, hence, are referred to as clones. Cloning is synonymous with *1-layer item modeling*. The goal of item generation using the 1-layer model is to produce new test items by manipulating a relatively small number of elements at *one layer* in the model. A generalization of the 1-layer item model is the *n-layer item model* [7]. The goal of automatic item generation using the n-layer model is to produce items by manipulating a relatively large number of elements at *two or more layers* in the model. Much like the 1-layer item model, the starting point for the n-layer model is to use a parent item. But unlike the 1-layer model where the manipulations are constrained to a set of generative operations using a small number of elements at a single level, the n-layer model permits manipulations of a set of generative operations using elements at multiple levels. As a result, the generative capacity of the n-layer model is substantially increased and, in the process, the number of content combinations also increase thereby producing more diversity and heterogeneity among the generated items.

The concept of n-layer item generation is adapted from the literature on syntactic structures of language where researchers have reported that sentences are typically organized in a hierarchical manner [8, 9]. This hierarchical organization, where elements are embedded within one another, can also be used as a guiding principle to generate large numbers of diverse test items. n-layer modeling serves as a flexible method for expressing structures that permit many different but feasible combinations of embedded elements. The n-layer structure can be described as a model with multiple layers of elements, where each element can be varied at different levels to produce different combinations of content and, hence, items.

A comparison of the 1- and n-layer item model is presented in Fig. 1. For this example, the 1-layer model can provide a maximum of four different values for element A. Conversely, the n-layer model can provide up to 64 different values using the same

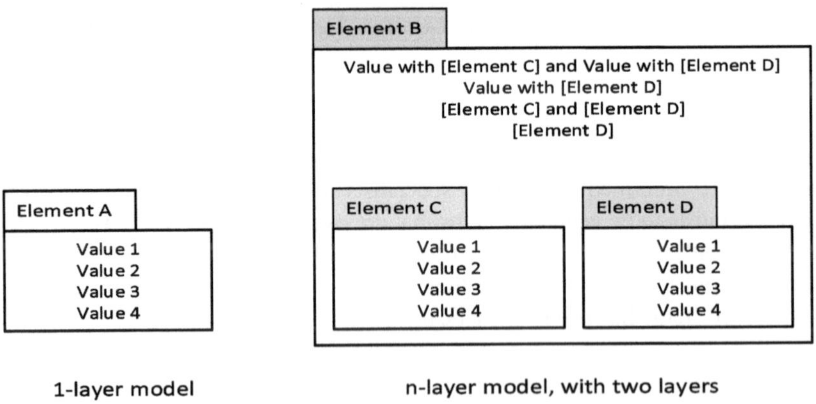

Fig. 1. A comparison of the elements in a 1-layer and n-layer item model.

four values for elements C and D embedded within element B. Because the maximum generative capacity of an item model is the product of the ranges in each element [10], the use of an n-layer item model will always increase the number of items that can be generated relative to the 1-layer structure.

The key advantage of using the n-layer structure is that more elements can be manipulated within the model resulting in generated items that appear to be different from one another. Hence, n-layer item modeling can be used to address the problem of cloning. The disadvantage of using an n-layer structure is that the models are challenging to create given the complexity of combining elements in an embedded fashion. Also, the effect of embedding elements in multiple levels, while useful for generating large numbers of diverse items, may make it challenging to consistently identify the correct solution for every generated item. Hence, constraints are required to ensure that content in the elements and layers are combined in a meaningful way so useful items can be generated. The importance of constraint programming will be illustrated later in our study.

4 Purpose of Study

The purpose of this study is to describe and illustrate a methodology for n-layer item modeling as it applies to generating nonverbal reasoning items. 1-layer item modeling dominates the current application of AIG. The n-layer item model serves as a generalization of the 1-layer approach. n-layer item modeling permits a large number of elements to be manipulated at multiple layers and, as a result, the generated items are more heterogeneous and, therefore, less susceptible to the limitations associate with cloning. We will also demonstrate how this method can be used to generate large numbers of diverse nonverbal reasoning items.

5 Method

The method section is presented in three parts. First, we describe the nonverbal reasoning item type. Second, we present the procedures used to implement the n-layer model. Third, we summarize the item generation process by describing the IGOR software program.

5.1 Nonverbal Reasoning Item Type

To demonstrate the application of the n-layer item modeling method, the nonverbal reasoning item format called "middle of the sequence" was used. A middle of the sequence parent item was selected because it is a format used by the Australian Council for Educational Research on an undergraduate admission test. Scores from the test are used in the selection of students for health science undergraduate programs. Middle of the sequence is one of three item formats used in the nonverbal reasoning section of the test. To solve this item type, examinees are required to reorder five figures to form the simplest and most logical sequence. Then, they select the alternative (A, B, C, D or E) that is in the middle of the sequence. This task is based on sequences of shapes designed to assess examinees' ability to reason in the abstract and to solve problems in non-verbal contexts.

An example of a middle of the sequence nonverbal reasoning item is shown in Fig. 2. To solve this item, examinees are first required to rotate the subfigure from each corner or vertex of the triangle to the middle position in the base image. Then, examinees are required to identify the most systematic order for the figures so the middle of the sequence can be specified. For our example, this order follows a clockwise rotation beginning in the bottom left corner of the triangle. Therefore, the correct sequence is CADBE and the middle of the sequence is figure D. The correct answer is indicated with an asterisk.

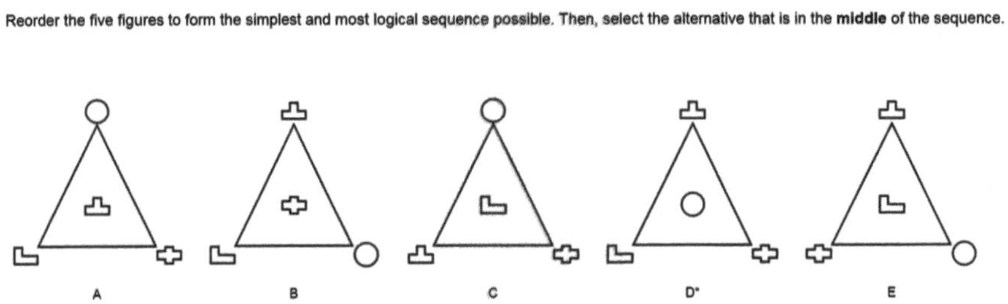

Fig. 2. A "middle of the sequence" nonverbal reasoning item.

5.2 n-Layer Item Modeling Procedure

The n-layer item model was created using the parent item presented in Fig. 2. Six layers were identified and manipulated to generate items. The layers are summarized in Fig. 3. Element 1 is the base image for the nonverbal reasoning item which corresponds to the central figure. Our example contains five base images (i.e., Element 1 = 5 values). Element 2 defines the number of positions for the subfigures located around the base image. Our example has two positions (Element 2 = 2 values). Element 3 specifies the number and shape of each subfigure. Our example has eight subfigures (Element 3 = 8 values). Element 4 specifies the type of rotation permitted by each subfigure around the base image. Our example allows for 12 rotational positions (Element 4 = 12 values). Element 5 highlights the shading pattern for the subfigures. We have nine shading patterns in our example (Element 5 = 9 values). Element 6 is the step logic required to rotate the subfigures from one base figure to the next in the sequence. Our example includes four different step logic sequences (Element 6 = 4 values). Taken together, our 6-layer item model has the element structure of 5*2*8*12*9*4.

5.3 Item Generation with IGOR

After the model is created, items were generated using IGOR [11]. IGOR, the acronym for Item GeneratOR, is a software program written in JAVA that produces all possible combinations of elements based on the definitions within the model. To generate items, a model must be expressed in an XML format that IGOR can interpret. Once a model is

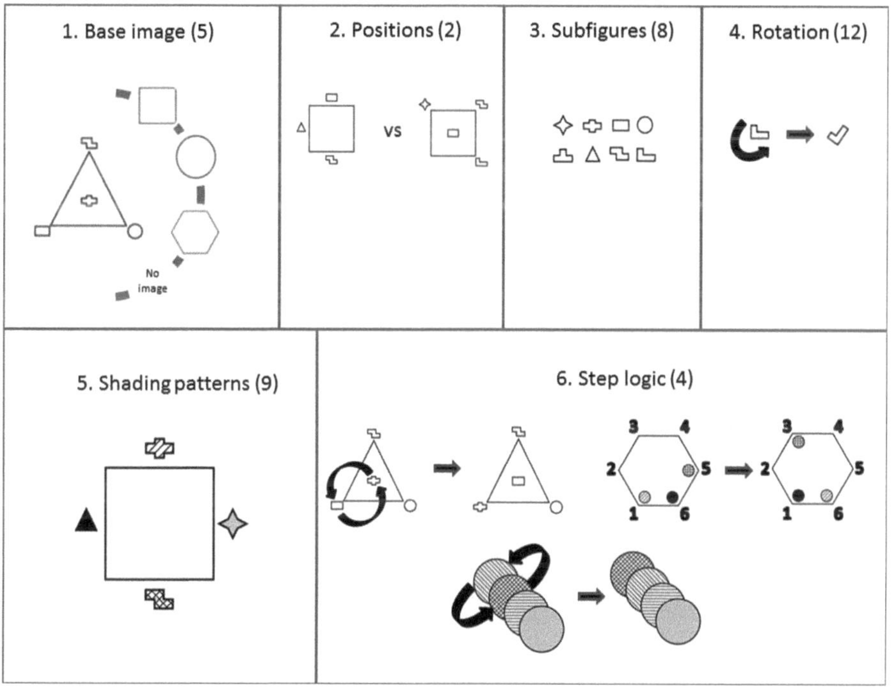

Fig. 3. A 6-layer nonverbal reasoning item model.

expressed in an XML form, IGOR computes the necessary information and outputs items in either a HTML or a Word format. Iterations are conducted in IGOR to assemble all possible combinations of elements subject to the constraints. Without the use of constraints, all of the elements would be systematically combined to create new items. For example, the 6-layer nonverbal reasoning item model in our example has 5*2*8*12*9*4 = 34,560 possible combinations. However, some of these items are not useful. Our goal was to generate middle of the sequence items that were comparable to the parent items found on the ACER admission test. As a result, constraints were used to ensure that the element and layer combinations only produced ACER-style nonverbal reasoning items. For instance, when the base image is a circle, the subfigure can only be a star. Or, when the base image is a polygon, the subfigure can only be a star or a circle. Constraints serve as restrictions that must be applied during the assembly task so that meaningful items are generated.

6 Results

IGOR generated 1,340 items from the 6-layer item model. A sample of five items with different combinations of elements in each of the layers is presented in Fig. 3. To increase generative capacity and to expand item diversity, elements and layers can be added to the existing model or new models can be created with different elements and layers. Hence, n-layer item modeling serves as a generalizable method for creating large numbers of diverse items and item types by manipulating the elements, layers, and models (Fig. 4).

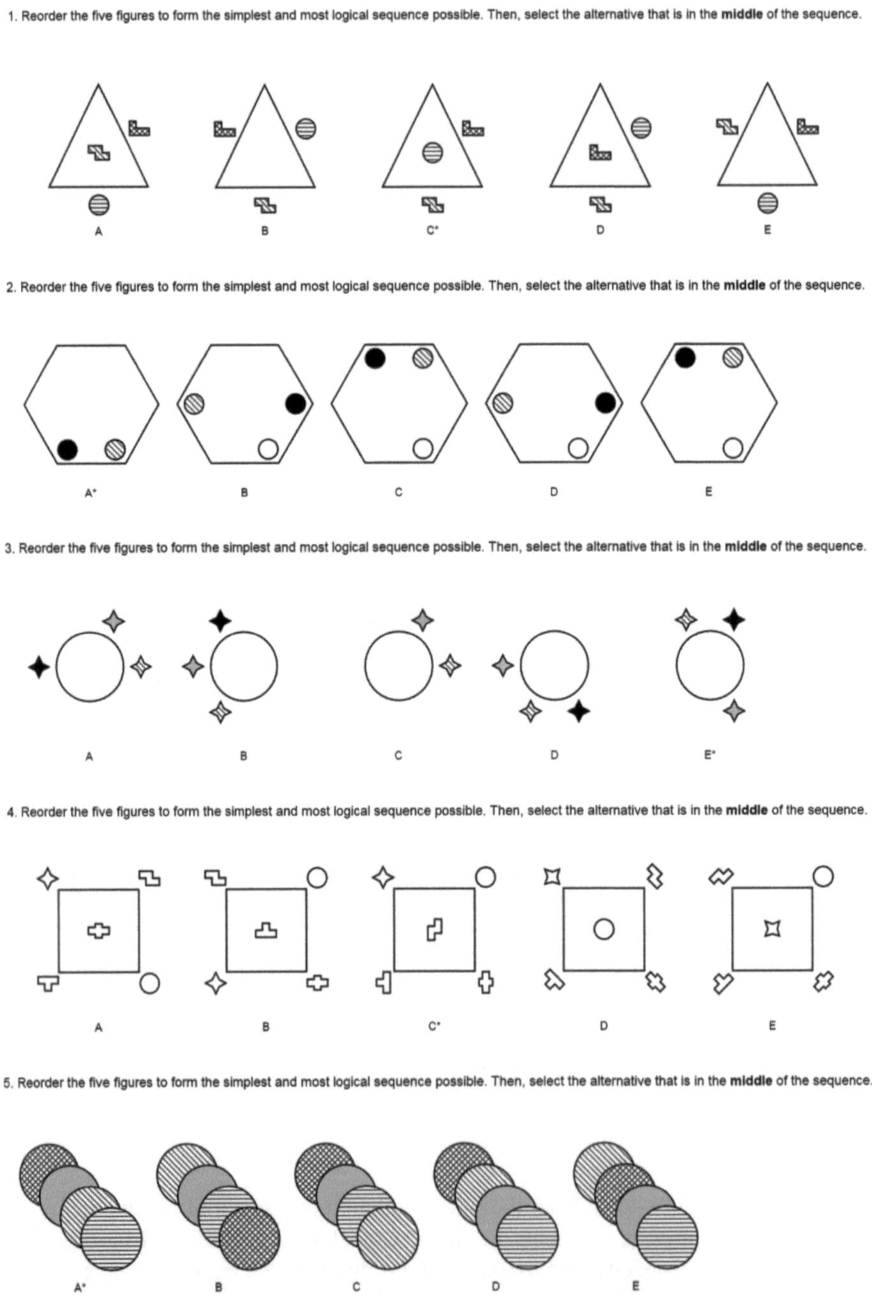

Fig. 4. A sample of five generated items from the 6-layer nonverbal reasoning item model.

7 Conclusions

Testing agencies like the Australian Council for Educational Research require large numbers of high-quality items that are produced in a timely and cost-effective manner. One approach that may help address these challenges is with automatic item generation. AIG is the process of using models to generate items using computer technology. It requires two steps. First, content specialists create item models. Second, the elements in the model are manipulated with computer-based algorithms. With this two-step process, thousands of new items can be created from a single item model, as we demonstrated in the current study. Not surprising, AIG is seen by many administrators in testing agencies as a "dream come true", given the laborious processes and high costs required for traditional item development. Unfortunately, many content specialists in these same testing agencies are not so enthralled by this dream because they find the quality of the generated items is still lacking.

This study was motivated by our desire to improve the quality of generated items given our discussions with content specialists. Simply put, content specialists dislike cloning because the generated items are too similar to one another for any practical use. We used biological cloning as an analogy for 1-layer item modeling, particularly when the generated items are designed to emulate the statistical properties of the parent. While item cloning has an important role to play in some AIG research [e.g., 12, 13], it is also important to recognize that these types of generated items may have limited value in operational testing programs, according to many content specialists, because they are easily produced, overly simplistic, and readily detectable.

In the current study, we described and illustrated a generalized method called n-layer item modeling. The n-layer model is a flexible structure for item generation that permits many different but feasible combinations of embedded elements and results in a diverse and heterogeneous pool of generated items. It can be used with any form of template-based item generation. It can be used to generate different item types. And, as was illustrated in our study, it can accommodate a wide range of elements at different layers within the model. We demonstrated the applicability of this method by generating 1,340 middle of the sequence nonverbal reasoning items that could be used by the Australian Council for Educational Research for the Undergraduate Medicine and Health Sciences Admission Test.

7.1 Directions for Future Research

In addition to generating more diverse and heterogeneous items, another application of n-layer modeling is generating multilingual test items. Different languages require different words, word orders, and grammatical structures. With a 1-layer model, these variables are not easily or readily manipulated because the generative operations are constrained to a small number elements at a single layer. However, with the use of an n-layer model, the generative operations are expanded dramatically to include more elements at multiple layers. Hence, language can serve as a layer that is manipulated during item generation. Therefore, one important direction for future research is to use n-layer item modeling to generate tasks in multiple languages by adding language as a layer in the model. A multilingual n-layer item model would permit testing agencies to generate large numbers of diverse items in multiple languages using a structured item development approach that is efficient and economical.

Acknowledgments. We would like to thank Vasily Tanygin for programming the nonverbal reasoning n-layer item model. We would also like to thank the Australian Council for Educational Research for supporting this research. However, the authors are solely responsible for the methods, procedures, and interpretations expressed in this study and these views do not necessarily reflect those of the Australian Council for Educational Research.

References

1. Drasgow, F., Luecht, R.M., Bennett, R.: Technology and testing. In: Brennan, R.L. (ed.) Educational measurement, 4th edn, pp. 471–516. American Council on Education, Washington, DC (2006)
2. Embretson, S.E., Yang, X.: Automatic item generation and cognitive psychology. In: Rao, C.R., Sinharay, S. (eds.) Handbook of Statistics: Psychometrics, vol. 26, pp. 747–768. Elsevier, North Holland, UK (2007)
3. Gierl, M.J., Haladyna, T.: Automatic Item Generation: Theory and Practice. Routledge, New York (2013)
4. Irvine, S.H., Kyllonen, P.C.: Item Generation for Test Development. Erlbaum, Hillsdale, NJ (2002)
5. Bejar, I.I., Lawless, R., Morley, M.E., Wagner, M.E., Bennett, R.E., Revuelta, J.: A feasibility study of on-the-fly item generation in adaptive testing. J. Technol. Learn. Assess. **2**(3) (2003). http://www.jtla.org
6. LaDuca, A., Staples, W.I., Templeton, B., Holzman, G.B.: Item modeling procedures for constructing content-equivalent multiple-choice questions. Med. Educ. **20**, 53–56 (1986)
7. Gierl, M.J., Lai, H.: Using automatic item generation to create items for medical licensure exams. In: Becker, K. (Chair), Beyond Essay Scoring: Test Development Through Natural Language Processing. Paper Presented at the Annual Meeting of the National Council on Measurement in Education, Vancouver, BC (2012)
8. Higgins, D., Futagi, Y., Deane, P.: Multilingual generalization of the model creator software for math item generation. Educational Testing Service Research Report (RR-05-02). Educational Testing Service, Princeton, NJ (2005)
9. Reiter, E.: NLG vs. templates. In: Proceedings of the Fifth European Workshop on Natural Language Generation, pp. 95–105. Leiden, The Netherlands (1995)
10. Lai, J., Gierl. M.J., Alves, C.: Using item templates and automated item generation principles for assessment engineering. In: Luecht, R.M. (Chair) Application of Assessment Engineering to Multidimensional Diagnostic Testing in an Educational Setting. Paper Presented at the Annual Meeting of the National Council on Measurement in Education, Denver, CO. (2010)
11. Geerlings, H., Glas, C.A.W., van der Linden, W.J.: Modeling rule-based item generation. Psychometrika **76**, 337–359 (2011)

12. Sinharay, S., Johnson, M.S.: Statistical modeling of automatically generated items. In: Gierl, M.J., Haladyna, T. (eds.) Automatic Item Generation: Theory and Practice, pp. 183–195. Routledge, New York (2013)
13. Gierl, M.J., Lai, H., Fung, K., Zheng, B.: Using technology-enhanced processes to generate items in multiplc languages. In: Drasgow, F. (ed.) Technology and Testing: Improving Educational and Psychological Measurement. Routledge, New York (in press)

Computer Adaptive Assessment for Learning in a Virtual Learning Environment

Maaike Heitink(✉) and Bernard P. Veldkamp

University of Twente, Postbus 217, 7500 AE Enschede, The Netherlands
{m.c.heitink,b.p.veldkamp}@utwente.nl

Abstract. In this project, five European countries are working together on the development of an online learning environment through which students can enhance key information processing skills (literacy, numeracy and problem solving in technology rich environments). This paper regards the numeracy learning unit that uses formative computer adaptive testing to offer learning tasks tailored to the students' ability level. In these formative testing activities students can use hints and feedback to complete the learning tasks. The use of feedback and hints will influence the students' response behavior. Therefore, for estimating the ability accurately, an IRT model will be used in which the use of these hints and feedback are taken into account. The learning modules are piloted with 900 students from Italy, Portugal and Norway.

Keywords: Formative assessment · Computer adaptive testing · Feedback · Online learning environment

1 Research Goal and Theoretical Framework

In the European project called LIBE "Supporting Lifelong learning with ICT Inquiry-Based Education" (REF. NO.543058-LLP-1-2013-1-IT-KA3-KA3MP–LIBE) partners from Italy, Great Britain, Norway, Portugal and The Netherlands work together on the development of an online learning environment intended for low educational achievers (16-24 years old). The online learning environment intends to enhance key information processing skills (literacy, numeracy, and problem solving in technology rich environments).

A crucial aspect in every learning environment is assessment. Assessment can have a formative and a summative function. Where summative assessment only focuses on assessing learning outcomes, formative assessment provides feedback to support learning and to gain insights in learning processes. Based on this support and insight, the learning process can be guided in the right direction [1–3]. Assessment not only allows constant monitoring of learners' progress and verification of course effectiveness, but can also be used as the main instrument to tailor education to students' needs.

Several kinds of formative assessment are stated in literature which all have different strategies to assess and support learning. This paper is focused on a study that regards to Assessment for Learning (AFL). AFL is part of 'everyday' learning practices [4] and

E. Ras and D. Joosten-ten Brinke (Eds.): CAA 2015, CCIS 571, pp. 22–26, 2015.
DOI: 10.1007/978-3-319-27704-2_3

focuses on the quality of the learning process [5]. Feedback is incorporated to guide future learning. AFL can be approached from a measurement perspective or an inquiry perspective [6]. In this paper we concentrate on the measurement perspective. AFL approached from a measurement perspective is characterized by the use of quantitative data to formulate feedback and to inform decisions on assessment activities that aim to determine to what extent a predetermined level has been achieved. Consequently, in this approach AFL concerns marking, monitoring and showing an ability level.

As noted before, an essential aspect in formative assessment is feedback. Feedback is defined as information provided by an agent regarding aspects of one's performance or understanding [7]. In the context of e-learning, formative feedback can be defined as (1) information specifically relating to the task or process of learning that fills a gap between what is understood and what is aimed to be understood [8], (2) information providing insights into learners' learning which can be used to adapt instruction to the learners' needs or (3) help learners in making choices regarding the future learning path they are going to take. Next to these cognitive and metacognitive functions of feedback, feedback can also have a motivational function encouraging learners to maintain their effort and persistence [9].

Feedback has been used in a large variety of types, defining their content and presentation (e.g. timing and scheduling/attempts) [7, 9, 10]. Several studies have focused on the effects of these different feedback types and its characteristics. Studies shows that elaborate feedback that is given directly after answering a question and can be used in a second attempt leads to positive learning results [10–12]. Elaborate feedback consists of information regarding the correctness of the response and additional hints/clues, worked out examples, or information resources that suggest what is still needed for the correct answer. Offering feedback that can be used in a second attempt means the student can complete a learning task correctly even though he or she did not know the answer at the first try. This means that the incorporation of multiple attempts can influence the response behavior of a student.

A recent development within digital learning environments is computerized adaptive testing for learning. In computerized adaptive testing, the difficulty of the task is adapted to the level of the student. In this study, formative computer adaptive testing will be implemented on a large scale. This study focuses on the question: *"How can the effect of feedback that is used in a computer adaptive test be modeled with Item Response Theory? And what consequences does this have for estimating the students' ability?"* To answer this question, a polytomous IRT model will be presented that accounts for the amount of feedback received in answering the question.

2 Research Method

2.1 Respondents

The learning modules are being piloted in Italy, Portugal and Norway. In every country 300 students are participating which leads to a total of 900 participants. Participants are selected based on age (16-24) and educational level.

2.2 The Learning Modules and Learning Environment

Moodle is used as the basis for the online learning environment. When entering this environment, students can chose whether they are willing to 'take the challenge' or just want to choose the sequence of the six developed learning modules themselves. 'Taking the challenge' initializes the sequence according to learner's level of performance on numeracy, literacy and problem solving that are associated with the questions of an entrance test. The six learning units are based on situations relevant and recognizable for the age group. The numeracy learning module consists of two learning units. In the numeracy learning unit, computer adaptive testing is used both for the learning tasks as the pre- and posttests. The pretest is used to determine the students' starting level and collect demographic information. The posttest is used to measure students' ability after the learning module is completed.

To make sure students experience an appropriate challenge, learning tasks are offered at different difficulty levels by applying computer adaptive testing during the learning modules. Based on the response given during the learning tasks, students receive feedback. If the student completed the learning tasks with an incorrect answer, the student will receive feedback and has the opportunity to give another response.

2.3 Data Collection

Data are collected through the online learning environment. This study initially focuses on data from the numeracy learning unit. Students will start with an adaptive pretest followed by the learning unit in which learning tasks is offered adaptively and finish with an adaptive posttest. Response data of the pretest, posttest and learning unit's learning tasks are saved in a database. Additionally, background variables regarding demographics and response behavior (e.g. response time) are collected.

2.4 Analysis

Data will be analyzed using Item Response theory (IRT). Depending on the data collected, an IRT model will be selected that fits the data (Rasch or 2-parameter logistic model). The substantial feedback students receive to use can use in a second attempt after answering a question incorrectly, will influence their response behavior. The response pattern is, after all, not only based on responding correctly or incorrectly, but also on processing the feedback or hints. In order to take this into account when estimating the ability, a polytomous module named Partial Credited Model (PCM) is proposed (1) [13]. In this model, a score of 0 represents an incorrect answer after received feedback, a score of 1 means the question is answered correctly after feedback is used and a score of 2 means the question is answered correctly without feedback is used. After this, the polytomous estimates will be compared to ability estimates that follow from a standard IRT model in which only a distinction is made between correct and incorrect response to the question. Additionally pre and posttest will be compared to determine the learning unit's effectiveness.

$$P_{i_g}\left(\theta_n\right) = \frac{exp \sum_{g=0}^{l} \left(\theta - \beta_{i_g}\right)}{\sum_{h=0}^{m} exp \sum_{g=0}^{l} \left(\theta - \beta_{i_g}\right)} \quad (1)$$

In which:

θ_n is the ability level of the student
$P_{i_g}(\theta_n)$ is the probability of a randomly chosen user with ability θ responding in a category (g) to item i.
β_{i_g} is the location of items on the latent scale
h = 0,1,…g…, m and g represents a specific category
m + 1 is the number of response categories

3 Intended Results and Contribution to Practice

The most important results will be focused on estimating the ability while taking into account used feedback and hints and the effect of taking feedback usage into account when estimating the ability and the effectiveness of the learning unit. Innovative in this research is the use of an IRT model that takes into account feedback usage in a formative computer adaptive learning environment.

Results will be available after the pilots planned in October 2015. Figure 1 shows intermediate analysis with simulated data indicates that both the Rasch model and the PCM slightly overestimate students' ability, in which PCM overestimates less then Rasch (0,198 for PCM and 0.233 for Rasch). Furthermore a sloping trend was found in which the lower ability levels are slightly overestimated while the higher ability levels are slightly underestimated.

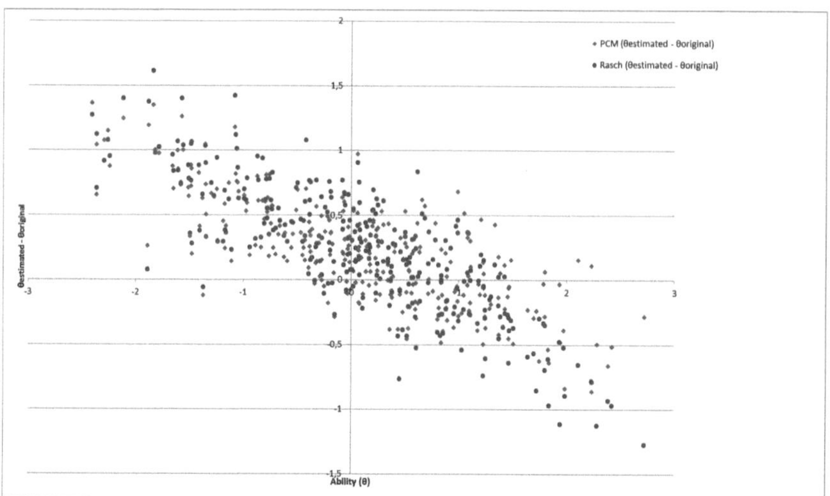

Fig. 1. Ability estimations for answer behavior with feedback (simulated data).

References

1. Van der Kleij, F., Vermeulen, J.A., Schildkamp, K., Eggen, T.: Towards an integrative formative approach of data-based decision making, assessment for learning, and diagnostic testing. In: International Congress for School Effectiveness and Improvement, Chili, January 2013
2. Bennett, R.E.: Formative assessment: a critical review. Assess. Educ. Principles, Policy Pract. **18**, 5–25 (2011). doi:10.1080/0969594X.2010.513678
3. Black, P., William, D.: Assessment and classroom learning. Assess. Educ. Principles, Policy Pract. **5**, 7–74 (1998). doi:10.1080/0969595980050102
4. Klenowski, V.: Assessment for learning revisited: an Asia-Pacific perspective. Assess. Educ. Principles, Policy Pract. **16**, 263–268 (2009). doi:10.1080/09695940903319646
5. Stobart, G.: Testing times: The uses and abuses of assessment. Routledge, Abingdon (2008)
6. Hargreaves, E.: Assessment for learning? thinking outside the (black) box. Camb. J. Educ. **35**, 213–224 (2005). doi:10.1080/03057640500146880
7. Hattie, J., Timperley, H.: The power of feedback. Rev. Educ. Res. **77**, 81–112 (2007). doi: 10.3102/003465430298487
8. Sadler, D.R.: Formative assessment and the design of instructional systems. Instr. Sci. **18**, 119–144 (1989). doi:10.1007/BF00117714
9. Narciss, S.: Feedback strategies for interactive learning tasks. In: Spector, J.M., Merrill, M.D., van Merrienboer, J.J.G., Driscoll, M.P. (eds.) Handbook of Research on Educational Communications and Technology, 3rd edn, pp. 125–144. Lawrence Erlbaum Associates, Mahaw (2008)
10. Shute, V.J.: Focus on formative feedback. Rev. Educ. Res. **78**, 153–189 (2008). doi: 10.3102/0034654307313795
11. Van der Kleij, F.M., Feskens, R.C.W., Eggen, T.J.H.M.: Effects of feedback in a computer-based learning environment on students' learning outcomes: a meta-analysis. In: Annual Meeting NCME, San Francisco (2013)
12. Narciss, S.: Designing and evaluating tutoring feedback strategies for digital learning environments on the basis of the interactive tutoring feedback model. Digit. Educ. Rev. **23**, 7–26 (2013)
13. Ostini, R., Nering, M.L.: Polytomous Item Response Theory Models. SAGE Publications, London (2006)

Testing Competences Worldwide in Large Numbers

Complying with ISO/IEC 17024:2012 Standard for Competence Testing

Marianne Hubregtse[1(✉)], Stefanie Moerbeek[1], Bernard P. Veldkamp[2], and Theo Eggen[3]

[1] EXIN Holding B.V., Utrecht, The Netherlands
{marianne.hubregtse,stefanie.moerbeek}@exin.com
[2] University of Twente, Enschede, The Netherlands
b.p.veldkamp@utwente.nl
[3] Cito B.V., Arnhem, The Netherlands
theo.eggen@cito.nl

Abstract. The ISO/IEC 17024:2012 describes best-practices regarding competence assessment. The standard emphasizes validity and sound processes to create high-quality competence assessments. The question is how to comply with the ISO/IEC standard when creating large-scale, worldwide assessments. In addition, the competence framework describes competences that require years of experience as part of the competence. We determine to what extent of mastery candidates need to master the competence to start working. We assess this by testing the requisite knowledge with a multiple-choice exam and the required minimum level of mastery of the competence with a Practical Assignment. This assignment is assessed by trainers, which creates the need for supervision and accreditation of the trainers. This paper shows an example of a certification scheme to explain how we comply with the ISO/IEC standard. The creation of the certification scheme and the accreditation of the trainers are described. The compliance with the ISO/IEC standard is explained.

Keywords: Competence assessment · ISO/IEC 17024:2012 · Assessment quality · Large-scale assessment · Worldwide assessment · Validity · e-Competence framework

1 Introduction

1.1 Testing Competences

Competences are a combination of knowledge, skills and attitudes [1, 2]. Testing *knowledge* can be done fairly easily, by using multiple-choice exams. Testing *competences* is more complex.

Proving that a candidate masters a competence is difficult. Some competence frameworks describe a competence by defining the knowledge, skills and attitude of a professional working in that area for a longer period of time. The e-CF framework for ICT competences [3] that we work with is one of those frameworks. Even though the competences are described for professionals with at least 5 years of experience, a professional

E. Ras and D. Joosten-ten Brinke (Eds.): CAA 2015, CCIS 571, pp. 27–39, 2015.
DOI: 10.1007/978-3-319-27704-2_4

starting out in a job is not completely void of any competence; rather they master part of the competence as described in the framework. Employers still want to know in which competences a professional has started working towards complete mastery. Therefore, exams can be designed in a way that allow candidates to show their partial mastery.

Sometimes, this means that the exams need to give the candidates the opportunity to show that they have the requisite background knowledge. In that case, we can show the partial mastery with a multiple-choice exam. In other cases, a professional needs to show that they master basic tasks, have the requisite background knowledge and have an adequate attitude, to work towards full mastery of the competence. Consequently, some certification schemes will incorporate only multiple-choice exams, while others will have a mix of both multiple-choice exams and practical assignments.

For example, when creating an exam for a starting Scrum Master, it must be determined to what extent a described competence must be shown by a starter. Suppose that a relevant competence states that the candidate: "Takes proactive action and develops organizational processes to address the development needs of individuals, teams and the entire workforce." (Manage, D.9. Personnel Development, level 4) [3]. It might be relevant for employers to attract a starting Scrum Master that has shown that she knows how to take action to help individual team members to develop their competences. The proactivity and the team needs could only be relevant for professionals with a few years of experience.

When testing partial mastery of competences, the test goal and exam specifications must specify exactly which competences are tested to exactly what extent. In addition, it must be explained why the experts judge the partial mastery to be enough for starting professionals. In some cases, it might be that showing the requisite knowledge is enough to start working. We take a pragmatists view to competence testing in this case.

For instance, suppose that we want to create an exam that shows that a Software Developer can start developing in PHP. It is judged enough to test whether the candidate has the necessary knowledge. Suppose that a relevant competence is: "Acts under guidance to develop, test and document applications." (Build, B.1. Application Development, level 1) [3]. The same competence asks for the following knowledge components: "The candidate is familiar with

- the appropriate software programs/modules;
- hardware components, tools and hardware architectures;
- [etc.…]" (Build, B.1. Application Development, Dimension 4, 1st 2 knowledge examples) [3]

In this case it is reasonable to test whether the candidate knows enough PHP to start coding under guidance of a more experienced coder.

1.2 Worldwide Examination

When assessing competences all over the world, a few challenges are introduced.

Firstly, the validity of the certification scheme must be proven in an international context. We do this by collaborating with international subject matter experts and training providers, but it stays important to test localizations for validity within that local context.

Secondly, when competences are tested, training and practical assignments are always part of the certification scheme. However, trainers and supervisors are not EXIN employees, so that we can maintain impartiality. As a certification body, we are responsible for assessing and scoring. By allowing the trainers and supervisors to act as assessors, we outsource part of our work. The challenge lies in ensuring that competent and honest trainers and supervisors do the assessments.

1.3 Large-Scale Assessments

We sell around 150,000 exams per year. Most of these exams are exams that only test the requisite knowledge of candidates to start their professional careers. These are multiple-choice exams. About 64 % of these exams are taken online using Online Proctoring. The candidate is required to log onto a secure web-environment, show proof of identification and to allow that for each exam sound and video are recorded. All videos are looked at fully (on high-speed) by an employee to signal any indication of fraud.

The other 36 % are paper-based exams. These exams have bubble-sheets that allow for automated scoring of the exams. The forms are read in by scanner and email, or by mobile application through a photograph. Only supervisors are allowed to send in the exam forms.

The scoring of practical assignments cannot be automated, because the criteria always need to be interpreted by an expert. However, we are in the process of allowing trainers or assessors to directly input their scoring of the individual candidates into our database. As of the writing of this paper, this is not fully done yet. Currently, supervisors and trainers score the candidates on paper, using the provided observation criteria, and only report the result (passed/failed) to our database. Changing this will involve training the supervisors and trainers to use the system correctly.

2 The ISO/IEC 17024:2012 Standard

The ISO/IEC 17024:2012 standard [2] describes best practices regarding assessing competences. As an exam institute, it is important for us to be ISO/IEC 17024:2012 certified. Not only does certification give us more credibility as an exam institute issuing certificates, we are also genuinely concerned with quality and think that the ISO/IEC standard reflects best practices.

In this paper we will define *certification scheme* as it is described in the ISO/IEC standard (Article 3.2) [2]: the "competence and other requirements related to specific occupational or skilled categories of persons". In a certification scheme, all requirements, that a candidate needs to fulfill before obtaining a certificate, are described.

For the purposes of clarity, *exam* is here defined as a multiple-choice test of the knowledge of candidates on a certain topic. *Assessment*, is defined as any test that allows a candidate to demonstrate their extent of mastery of a competence.

The ISO/IEC norms do not always specify exactly which processes you need to follow. While getting certified, additional questions were asked about the processes of creating the certification scheme, maintaining impartiality whilst working with a select few experts and ensuring high validity exams.

We will shortly discuss the ISO/IEC 17024:2012 papers that elicited questions, to show what auditors asked after most (in our case). A short definition of validity, that we can agree with, is given as well, since the ISO/IEC standard does not define the concept of validity.

The NEN-EN-ISO/IEC 17024:2012 standard [2] is a best-practices guideline when creating the certification scheme. However, although it gives recommendations on what elements regarding the certification scheme must be described (ISO 17024:2012, Paper 8) [2], it does not give practical guidelines or examples.

Specifically, there is no information in the standard on creating large-scale and worldwide competence assessments, nor on how to deal with testing partial mastery of competences. For us, it was difficult to justify exactly how we complied with the ISO/IEC standard, even though we felt we were on the right track. We show how one might argue this compliance. We show a real example of a certification scheme used for worldwide competence assessment. We also describe how we have solved the issue of taking full responsibility for the quality of the assessment, while outsourcing the assessment.

2.1 Compliance with ISO/IEC 17024:2012

The ISO/IEC 17024:2012 standard [2] is quite extensive and, therefore, this paper does not cover all parts of it. However, three of the papers are relevant here: Paper 8 regarding the validity of the certification scheme, Paper 5 regarding the impartiality of the certification body and Paper 6 regarding outsourcing work.

Validity. ISO/IEC 17024:2012 states that:

"A certification scheme shall contain the following elements:

(a) scope of certification;
(b) job and task description;
(c) required competence;
(d) abilities (when applicable);
(e) prerequisites (when applicable);
(f) code of conduct (when applicable)." (Paper 8.2) [2]

These elements in the certification scheme help build a validity argument (see also Sect. 2.1). These instructions also underline the importance of specifying the partial competences tested, complete with a specification of the knowledge and skill elements that need to be mastered (and thus tested). The example will show one way of building these elements.

We define a valid exam as an exam where the score yields information that you can use to make decisions about a candidate [4, 5]. Validity can be made plausible by showing the link between all tasks the candidate may encounter as a professional, the competences necessary for performing those tasks and the chosen questions and assignments for the certification scheme [5, 6] as described in the test goal and the exam specifications.

We ensure validity of the certification schemes by allowing professionals (often subject matter experts) and trainers to be involved in the creation of the scope, the job and task description, the required competences and abilities. In addition, we discuss the prerequisites and codes of conducts for certification with subject matter experts.

Impartiality. In order for candidates to be assessed fairly, it is often recommended to separate the training provider and the certification body [7–17]. EXIN is an independent certification body and does not provide training to candidates, which makes it easy to comply with the ISO/IEC 17024:2012 (Paper 5.2), which states that "Offering training and certification for persons within the same legal entity constitutes a threat to impartiality [2]."

Since we do not train candidates, there is absolute impartiality; we do not benefit from candidates passing or failing assessments. However, not training candidates also means that there are no opportunities for our employees to come directly into contact with candidates during their performances for their assessments. This means that we need professionals and trainers to help us ensure validity, and thus we need to outsource part of the work on a certification scheme.

Outsourcing Work. According to the ISO/IEC 17024:2012 standard, the certification body remains responsible for the outsourced work and thus must "ensure that the body conducting outsourced work is competent and complies with the applicable provisions of this International Standard;" (Paper 6.3.2.b) [2]. A challenge lies in ensuring that assessors that you rely upon to assess a candidate's performance are competent and comply with the rules you have set for the assessment.

We ensure that assessors comply with our rules by accrediting our training providers, training the trainers and auditing them on a regular basis. In order to ensure competence of the assessors, we ask for work experience in a relevant area, references that confirm the work-experience and the successful completion of the exam that they will assess. Trainers with ample work experience in a relevant area are exempt from the mandatory training and practical assessment. Other candidates never are.

3 Example: EXIN Agile Scrum Master

This part of the paper will give a description of the processes used to create the certification scheme for Agile Scrum Master. Please note that the certification scheme was still in development whilst writing this paper. All examples given are subject to change during the development, but they do reflect an example of what the final product could look like. The processes followed to create this certification scheme give insight in how we deal with maintaining impartiality, ensuring validity and outsourcing work regarding the creation of the certification scheme and the assessment of the candidates.

3.1 Certification Scheme

The Preparation Guide is our central documentation of the certification scheme. This guide is freely available to anyone on our website. It contains all elements for a certification scheme as listed by the ISO/IEC 17024:2012 standard. Candidates and trainers can refer to this document to prepare for the assessments.

Scope of Certification. Agile Scrum is a project management method for software development. A small team (3–9 people) works in short iterations of time, to deliver new functionality. Every new iteration, the list of requirements for the software is updated and prioritized. This creates great flexibility for the customer.

Scrum knows three major roles: Product Owner, Scrum Master and Development Team member. The team is self-managing. Therefore, there is no need for a traditional project manager. Instead, the Product Owner is the voice of the customer and helps prioritize features for the next iteration. The Scrum Master coaches the team to be self-managing through servant leadership and training. A Scrum Master also keeps track of the progress of the project.

Process. The scope of the certification is determined based on market research. A survey was sent out under 54 partners (mostly training companies) and candidates, to generate the scope of the exam. Allowing our partners and candidates to give input on new certification schemes shows the market value and adds to the validity.

Test Goal. The goal of the Agile Scrum Master certification scheme is to gather enough information on the competences of the candidate to determine whether a candidate is ready to perform the desired tasks to the desired level, and thus deserves a certificate. This means that a candidate with an Agile Scrum Master certificate must be able to function in the role of Scrum Master. The candidate is not expected to master the competences as a professional with a few years of experience would. Rather, the candidate must show that she has just enough competence to start working as a Scrum Master for the first time. In addition, the candidate must show that she has the requisite knowledge to perform the function.

Job and Task Description. In this case, there is already a solid framework that describes full competences: European e-Competence Framework (e-CF) [3]. Instead of defining our own competences for every single certification scheme, all EXIN certification schemes use the e-CF as a common framework. The complete e-CF represents the practice domain of the Agile Scrum Master. The selection of the competences represents the competence domain.

European e-Competence Framework. The practice domain is described in the e-CF [3]. The e-CF describes ICT competences in the five main areas Plan, Build, Run, Enable and Manage. The levels within each competence give an indication of the level of responsibility that is required: a higher level indicates more responsibility. In essence, the e-CF is a job and task analysis for the five main areas; professionals in the ICT work field collaborated to create the e-CF.

Process. EXIN employs exam experts, that are trained on best practices in assessment and exam creation. Since the certification portfolio covers a broad part of the ICT work field, we rely on subject matter experts for the content of the questions and practical assignments. Since we certify candidates worldwide, we work together with subject matter experts from all over the world. We use online authoring methods to work together on content and questions. The content of the job and task description is supplied by subject matter experts. We select the subject matter experts on the basis of their demonstrated or verified experience and earned certificates.

For Agile Scrum Master, two exam experts guided two international subject matter experts in building the job task analysis from the e-CF. Firstly, both subject matter experts individually selected the relevant competences from the framework. Then an online video conference was held under supervision of the exam experts, where the subject matter experts agreed on the relevant competences and level. The result is shown in Table 1.

Table 1. Example e-CF mapping for agile scrum master

Area	Competence name	e-Level	Extent
Plan	A.2. Service Level Management	4	Superficial
Plan	A.5. Architecture Design	3	Superficial
Build	B.2. Component Integration	3	Superficial
Build	B.3. Testing	3	Superficial
Enable	D.3. Education and Training Provision	3	Partial
Enable	D.9. Personnel Development	2	Partial
Manage	E.3. Risk Management	3	Partial
Manage	E.5. Process Improvement	3	Partial

Mastery of Competences. The e-CF mapping alone is not enough to start developing the assessment. In addition to the mapping, it must be decided to what extent the competence level should be represented in the certification scheme. Furthermore, it should be decided which knowledge components a candidate should be able to show.

Process. The extent to which a candidate must show mastery of a competence could fall into one of the following categories: general, partial or superficial. For each competence in the e-CF, we have developed a set of observation criteria. The full set of criteria for each competence is extensive, but when a candidate has shown that they can perform all tasks listed in the criteria (as a professional with experience often can), they are awarded credit for the full competence.

The extent of the mastery that is tested within a certain certification scheme is decided by the number of observation criteria that are assessed through the practical assignments. When 1 % to 29 % of the total number of criteria are assessed, the competence is regarded as covered superficially. Between 30 % and 69 % coverage of the criteria is regarded as partial. When 70 % or more of the criteria of a competence level are covered by the certification scheme, we regard the competence as generally covered. The subject matter experts, under guidance of the exam experts, decided which observation criteria are relevant for the scope of the exam and the test goal.

After this was decided, the subject matter experts and the exam experts agreed on the relevant knowledge components and translated these to the exam requirements, which form the basis for developing questions for the multiple choice exam.

Assessment Process. The Agile Scrum certification scheme consists of a multiple-choice exam, a mandatory training and successful completion of the Practical Assignments. The trainers are responsible for assessing whether the candidate has shown adequate competence, in the Practical Assignments. What is 'adequate' is determined by the chosen observation criteria. The trainers are provided with material and observation criteria that show under which conditions a candidate is eligible for successful completion of the Practical Assignments. The trainers must use the Practical Assignments issued, but they may adapt to their context, in order to allow candidates to show their mastery of the competences. Where possible, the assignments have a clear rating scale, to help the trainer assess.

As mentioned earlier, we keep control over the assessment by accrediting the trainers. In addition, the required multiple-choice exam ensures that we directly control at least half of the scoring of the assessment.

Skills and Attitude Assessment. As can be seen from Table 1, Agile Scrum Master does not cover any of the relevant competences generally. It is important to specify which observation criteria are seen as relevant for Agile Scrum Master, so that all trainers may assess candidates as uniformly as possible.

The observation criteria for the competence D.3. Education and Training Provision (level 3) are: The candidate can…

- address organizational skills needs and gaps
- *adapt training plans to address changing demands*
- promote and market training provision
- design curricula and training programs
- *establish a feedback mechanism*
- *implement continuous improvement of education and training delivery*
- *assess added value of training provision*

Of these criteria, the italicized criteria were chosen by the subject matter experts as relevant for a starting Agile Scrum Master. These are 4 out of 7 criteria, or 57 %, so we call the competence covered partially. The same process was repeated for all other competences in this certification scheme.

Knowledge Assessment. After determining the competences relevant for the certification scheme, we asked the subject matter expert to identify all the requisite knowledge for a starting Scrum Master. This list of requisite knowledge is captured in the exam blueprint, which is made available for trainers and candidates in the Preparation Guide. The resulting exam blueprint is shown in Table 2. The Agile Scrum Master exam consists of 40 multiple-choice questions, divided over the exam requirements. The questions allow the candidate to show that she possesses the requisite knowledge to start as a first-time Scrum Master.

Table 2. Example exam blueprint for agile scrum master

Exam requirements			# Questions
1. Agile Way of Thinking			
	1.1	Agile concepts	2
	1.2	Continuously improving the process	1
	1.3	Other Frameworks and other Agile frameworks	2
	1.4	Applying Agile principles to IT Service Managements	1
2. Scrum Master Role			
	2.1	Responsibilities and Commitment	3
	2.2	Coaching the Team and Mediating	3
	2.3	Other roles (Product Owner, Development Team)	3
3. Agile Estimating, Planning, Monitoring and Control			
	3.1	Writing and maintaining the Product and Sprint Backlog	3
	3.2	Agile Planning	2
	3.3	Agile Estimation	4
	3.4	Tracking and communicating progress	3
	3.5	Staying in control	1
4. Complex Projects			
	4.1	Scaling Agile Projects	2
	4.2	Suitability of Agile for different types of projects	2
	4.3	Agile administration in tooling and tool integration	1
5. Adopting Agile			
	5.1	Introducing Agile	3
	5.2	Self-organization	2
	5.3	Agile requirements and proper environment	2
Total			40

The subject matter experts individually brainstormed about the requisite knowledge and then agreed in a video-conference on the final blueprint, under guidance of the exam experts. Subsequently, the exam requirements were worked out into exam specifications.

For example, the exam specifications for the exam requirement 2.3 Scrum Master are: The candidate can…

- identify which tasks are related to the role of Scrum Master.
- explain the competences required for performing the role of the Scrum Master.
- explain the tasks, responsibilities and authorities of the Scrum Master.

As can be seen from Table 2, the exam includes 3 questions for this exam requirement, so that each of the exam specifications can be represented in the exam. We try to assure that there is an equal number of questions and exam specifications, to ensure consistent exams.

When there are more exam specifications than questions in the exam, the subject matter experts are asked to agree beforehand on the exam specifications that are interchangeable in the exam. When there are fewer exam specifications than questions in the exam, the subject matter experts must agree on which specifications are represented by more than one question.

As soon as the exam specifications and requirements are accepted by both the subject matter experts and the exam experts, other international subject matter experts are asked to create the content for the actual multiple choice questions, under the guidance of the exam experts. The question creation process includes a review by both a subject matter expert and an exam expert, to ensure validity and quality. By asking different subject matter experts to determine and create the content of the assessment, we ensure international relevance and validity.

Prerequisites and Code of Conduct. The Preparation Guide includes all the prerequisites for the exam. In this case, all exams that show that the candidate understands the Agile Scrum framework were accepted as prerequisites. The code of conduct is not applicable for this certification scheme. (It would be applicable for a certification scheme Ethical Hacking, for instance.)

4 Discussion

We use the European e-Competence Framework (e-CF) [3] to create certification schemes. Since this framework describes competences that require work-experience, we test whether candidates have adequate mastery of the competence to start working with a Practical Assignment. Additionally, we test whether they possess the requisite knowledge to start working with a multiple-choice exam.

The example certification scheme for Agile Scrum Master complies with the ISO/IEC 17024:2012 standard for certification of competences. We have shown the processes we use to create all elements that need to be present in the certification scheme according to Article 8.2 [2]. We use subject matter experts to create valid, internationally relevant exams. To ensure the competence of the subject matter experts, we ask them to prove their experience and expertise to us, by means of work history and earned certificates. In addition, we train the subject matter experts ourselves in item development best practices, using online training and self-study. In order to ensure impartiality, we always work with at least two experts, preferably from different countries, guided by at least one of our own exam experts.

We have shown how we determine the scope of the certification. By using both the e-CF and market research, we add validity and relevance to our exams. If we combine the scope of the exam with the input of at least two subject matter experts, we can create a very relevant, and thus valid, certification scheme. This combination is a form of the job and task description, as mentioned in the ISO/IEC standard.

We realize that there are other ways of conducting a job and task analysis. However, the main steps that need to be taken, are already undertaken in the creation of the e-CF: all competences have been described, complete with knowledge and skills examples. It seems efficient to use this information. We allow the subject matter experts to decide which competences of the e-CF enable the candidate to fulfill the scope of the certification. Nevertheless, we could have chosen to re-do that work, or to do the job and task analysis for all parts of the world separately.

We are also aware that adding more subject matter experts will change the outcome of discussions. In principle, the determination of the scope, as with any further work on the certification scheme, is not limited to two subject matter experts. In many cases, we work with more than two subject matter experts. However, we are bound by constraints of time and budget. We try to balance the implications of adding another expert to the development team with our constraints.

We have described a process of determining the extent to which we measure each competence. By using a fixed set of observation criteria for all competences to determine the extent, this is done in a repeatable way, making it less subjective and more comparable between certification schemes.

We realize that the fixed set of criteria does impose a limit. We could miss important criteria, by not allowing the subject matter experts to create new criteria for competences and abilities that fit the certification scheme better. However, we feel that the benefits of comparability and objectivity outweigh the consequences of the inflexibility. Furthermore, it is beneficial for candidates to work with a single framework and fixed criteria; it makes it easier to show the value of their certificate in an international context. (Or at least, where the e-CF is recognized.)

The Preparation Guide describes all these elements to the candidates and lists the pre-requisites and code of conduct, when applicable. This document, which is freely available, helps comply fully to Article 8 of the ISO/IEC standard.

We have a relative easy job of staying impartial, since we do not train the candidate. Therefore, we comply with the mentioned Article 5.2.1 concerning impartiality. However, being impartial creates a new challenge. We must outsource both part of the creation of the certification scheme to subject matter experts *and* outsource part of the assessment to trainers.

In keeping control whilst outsourcing part of the creation of the certification scheme, the solution is to keep a review by our own experts in the process. This ensures that an EXIN employee ultimately decides on the content of the certification scheme, giving us control.

The responsibility for the assessment part is a little more difficult. Outsourcing the authentic assessment is a threat to keeping full responsibility for the quality of the certification scheme (ISO/IEC standard Article 6.3.2) [2]. We solve this issue by accrediting the training organizations and the trainers. We ensure that the trainers are familiar with best practices for assessing candidates and we regularly inspect the assessments. To ensure that the work of the trainers is in compliance with the exam regulations, we audit the training organizations and we keep records of the audits.

By accrediting training organizations and trainers, we aim to keep high quality assessment and honest assessment. Since trainers are only allowed to change the context of assignments and not the assessment criteria themselves, we keep more control over the assessment, complying with Article 6.3.2. By demanding that the candidate not only shows skills (and is assessed in the training), but also shows their knowledge and insight in a multiple-choice exam, we keep grip on the certification.

The system is not water-tight and we are well aware of that. On the other hand, the system is affordable and easy to implement, even for large-scale assessments in an international context.

References

1. Mulder, M., Weigel, T., Collins, K.: The concept of competence in the development of vocational education and training in selected EU member states. J. Vocat. Educ. Train. **59**, 53–66 (2007). doi:10.1080/13636820601145549
2. NEN-EN-ISO/IEC. NEN-EN-ISO/IEC 17024:2012, IDT - Conformity assessment - general requirements for bodies operating certification of persons (2012)
3. CEN. European e-Competence Framework version 3.0 - a common European Framework for ICT Professionals in all industry sectors, 3rd edn. CEN (European Committee for Standardization) (2014)
4. Borsboom, D., Mellenbergh, G.J., van Heerden, J.: The concept of validity. Psychol. Rev. **111**, 1061–1071 (2004). doi:10.1037/0033-295X.111.4.1061
5. Wools, S. Evaluation of validity and validation. In: 9th Annual AEA-Europe Conference on Hisarya, Bulgaria, pp 1–9 (2008)
6. Brennan, R.L. (ed.): Educational Measurement, 4th edn. Praeger Publishers, Westport, Connecticut (2006)
7. Govaerts, M.J.B., Schuwirth, L.W.T., van der Vleuten, C.P.M., Muijtjens, A.M.M.: Workplace-based assessment: effects of rater expertise. Adv. Heal. Sci. Educ. **16**, 151–165 (2011). doi:10.1007/s10459-010-9250-7
8. Van Scotter, J.R., Moustafa, K., Burnett, J.R., Michael, P.G.: Influence of prior acquaintance with the ratee on rater accuracy and halo. J. Manage. Dev. **26**, 790–803 (2007). doi:10.1108/02621710710777282
9. Williams, R.G., Sanfey, H., Chen, X., Dunnington, G.L.: A controlled study to determine measurement conditions necessary for a reliable and valid operative performance assessment: a controlled prospective observational study. Ann. Surg. **256**, 177–187 (2012). doi:10.1097/SLA.0b013e31825b6de4
10. Engelhard, Jr., G., Myford, C.M., Cline, F. Investigating assessor effects in National Board for Professional Teaching Standards assessments for early childhood/generalist and middle childhood/generalist certification. Res. Rep. Educ. Test Serv. I–IV, i-77 (2000)

11. Pitts, J., Coles, C., Thomas, P., Smith, F.: Enhancing reliability in portfolio assessment: discussions between assessors. Med. Teach. **24**, 197–201 (2002). doi:10.1080/01421590220125321
12. Clauser, B.B.E., Margolis, M.J.M., Clyman, S.G., Ross, L.P.: Development of automated scoring algorithms for complex performance assessments: a comparison of two approaches. J. Educ. Meas. **34**, 141–161 (1997). doi:10.1111/j.1745-3984.1997.tb00511.x
13. Van der Schaaf, M.F., Stokking, K.M., Verloop, N.: Cognitive representations in raters' assessment of teacher portfolios. Stud. Educ. Eval. **31**, 27–55 (2005). doi:10.1016/j.stueduc.2005.02.005
14. Ryan, A.M., Daum, D., Bauman, T., Grisez, M., Mattimore, K., Nalodka, T., McCormick, S.: Direct, indirect, and controlled observation and rating accuracy. J. Appl. Psychol. **80**, 664–670 (1995). doi:10.1037/0021-9010.80.6.664
15. Eva, K.W., Rosenfeld, J., Reiter, H.I., Norman, G.R.: An admissions OSCE: the multiple mini-interview. Med. Educ. **38**, 314–326 (2004). doi:10.1046/j.1365-2923.2004.01776.x
16. Iramaneerat, C., Yudkowsky, R.: Rater errors in a clinical skills assessment of medical students. Eval. Health Prof. **30**, 266–283 (2007). doi:10.1177/0163278707304040
17. Shechtman, Z.: Agreement between lay participants and professional assessors: support of a group assessment procedure for selection purposes. J. Pers. Eval. Educ. **12**, 5–17 (1998). doi:10.1023/A:1007932515469

The Success Factor in Assessment: Motivation or Playing? A Case Study in Gamification

Desirée Joosten-ten Brinke[1(✉)], Niels Schultz[2], and Robin Platjouw[3]

[1] Open Universiteit of the Netherlands, Welten Institute, Fontys University of Applied Sciences, Postbus 2960, 6401 DL Heerlen, The Netherlands
Desiree.joosten-tenbrinke@ou.nl
[2] Amstelvlietsstraat 407, 1096 GG Amsterdam, The Netherlands
[3] Basisschool 't Slingertouw, Waterlinie 260, 5658 NS Eindhoven, The Netherlands

Abstract. A high educational value of computer games in formal learning seems to be an important reason to use gaming in the classroom. However, this value is not necessarily realized by the use of games and a conscious use is important. In this study, primary school students get the opportunity to play games related to the core objectives of education on the subjects of math, spelling and geography. It is investigated whether greater awards will change the decision behavior of the students in choosing games on specific subjects and the subsequent consequence on the assessment. Results show no significant relation between awarding and subject choice. Neither an effect has been found on the relation of practice time and learning outcomes. A large significant association is found between different practice times on the different subjects. A positive intrinsic motivation of the students has been found for learning in general and learning with games.

Keywords: Gamification · Formative assessment · Learning outcomes · Motivation

1 Introduction

A high educational value of computer games in formal learning seems to be an important reason for teachers to use gaming in the classroom (Frazer et al. 2014). Gamification can be seen as a stimulator for learning. It has the potential to enhance and support learning. Playing computer games is linked to a range of perceptual, cognitive, behavioral, affective and motivational impacts and outcomes (Connolly et al. 2012). Most often, games are used for learning and not for summative assessment purposes. If the game provides students with information about their mastery, the games can be useful for assessment *for* learning, in other words formative assessment. The increased motivation brought about by games may have the potential to increase the validity of formative assessments (McClarty et al. 2012). McClarty et al. emphasize the importance to provide the learner with an appropriate level of agency or autonomy. The steering principle in gaming for learning should be the awarding system. Children receive coins, batches and so on to stimulate playing. Unfortunately, if children are free to choose their own learning path, they might choose games for subjects they are already good at,

E. Ras and D. Joosten-ten Brinke (Eds.): CAA 2015, CCIS 571, pp. 40–46, 2015.
DOI: 10.1007/978-3-319-27704-2_5

because in that case the chance for awarding will be larger. The question is whether a voluntary use of computer games enhances the learning process?

In this study, primary school students got the opportunity to play games related to the core objectives of education on the subjects of math, spelling and geography. The default state of the game is that students can choose what they like to play. In that setting, teachers experience that their pupils especially choose topics that they find easy, because of the larger chance to quickly earn a lot of coins. However, choosing easy games is not stimulating for learning outcomes. It is investigated whether the choosing behavior of students can be directed by giving specific awards. It is expected that students will choose those subjects in which they can earn the most and that their choice increases the learning outcome for that subject.

This led to the main research question: 'To what extent change learning behavior (in terms of motivation to learn) and the learning outcomes when students within a game are encouraged to choose assignments on specific topics?'. This research question is divided into the following sub questions:

RQ1. Do students choose subjects that they are less good at, if the chance to get a larger award is higher?
RQ2. Do students perform better on a specific topic as they spend more time on that topic in the assessment game?
RQ3. What is the relation between intrinsic motivation and playing the games?

The expectation is that the choose of the games can be steered by the awarding system of the game. Students can be steered in the direction of the topics for which they perform less.

2 Method

Participants
The participants in this study were 117 primary school students (57 female and 60 male) from four 5th grade classes of two different schools. Mean age of the students is 10.2 years ($sd = .46$).

Materials
Questionnaire. A 23-item Intrinsic Motivation Inventory (IMI) (McAuley et al. 1989; Ryan et al. 1991) was used to assess participants' subjective experience related to learning in school in general and learning by gaming more specifically. The instrument assesses participants' intrinsic motivation and self-regulation via several sub scales: perceived competence, interest, perceived choice, pressure/tension and effort. Interest (example item 'I think the lessons are very interesting'), is considered as a direct measure of intrinsic motivation, while the other sub scales are positive indicators of intrinsic motivation: perceived competence (example item'I am satisfied with my school performance'), perceived choice (example item 'I may choose assignments by myself') and effort (for example 'I tried very hard when practicing'). Pressure is considered as a negative indicator of intrinsic motivation (example item 'I often feel nervous while practicing at school'). In the pre-test the items concern learning in general, in the post-test the items are

more specified towards use of games for learning. Participants had to answer the items on a 7-point Likert scale (1 = definitely not true; 7 = definitely true).

After the data had been collected, the questionnaires' reliability is measured. The internal consistency of the intrinsic motivation subscales, determined via the Cronbach's alpha coefficients, are presented in Table 1. As the reliability of the subscale Effort is too low, this scale has been left out for further analyses.

Table 1. Reliability of the subscales (Cronbach's alpha) at pre-test

Scale	# items	Cronbach's alpha
Perceived competence	4	.77
Interest	6	.82
Perceived choice	4	.79
Pressure	5	.78
Effort	3	.49

Pre-test and post-test. For mathematics, spelling and geography an assessment was constructed based on items available in the computer games. The assessment of mathematics consisted of 40 items, the assessment of spelling consisted of 40 items and the assessment of geography consisted of 30 items. All items were multiple choice questions with four alternatives.

Computer game. The computer game is a web-based game, in which participants can choose different kind of games within eighteen different subjects. Subjects include math, spelling and geography, but also for example history, English, reading or social skills. The game logs information about playing time, games started, games ended completely, and scoring.

Procedure

The experiment took three month. All students from three classes, all belonging to one school, got accounts for a computer game that is aligned with the subjects of study. These students were ad random divided over two experimental conditions. Condition 1 provided students with double awarding for specific subjects. The double awarding directed mathematics in the first month, spelling in the second month and geography in the third month. Condition 2 made use of equal awarding over the subjects. Students in the fourth class served as a control group. Their school was not nearby the first school to prevent that students knew each other and discussed the gaming, and these children did not get accounts for the computer game.

In the first week of the experiment, all students filled in the questionnaire and made a cognitive assessment on math, spelling and geography (pre-test) After that, the students in the experimental condition received an account of the computer game and the teacher showed them how to use the game. Students were allowed to play the games whenever they wanted, they did not receive an assignment that obliged them to use the gaming.

Besides, they could choose every subject they wanted. During the experiment, the teacher informed twice whether the students were using the game and how they experienced playing the game. This was done, to stimulate use without giving directive instructions. After three month, the students again filled in the questionnaire and made again an assessment on math, spelling and geography (post-test). The students did not receive a figure on the assessments.

3 Findings

Preliminary findings

Over the three month, 59 students (= 68 %) logged in 1338 times and started 5121 games. The subjects math (31.0 %), geography (10.7 %), English (9.9 %) and spelling (9.6 %) have been chosen most often. Further analyses will focus on math, geography and spelling.

Pre-test and post-test results

Table 2. shows the results of the pre-test and post-test divided over the three conditions. Table 3. shows the results of the subscales of the intrinsic motivation questionnaires. A significant difference between the conditions is found on the pre-test for perceived competence. The control group ($M = 4.83$) scores significant lower than the experimental group with double coins ($M = 5.56$), $F(2, 114) = 3.68$, $p < 0.05$.

Table 2. Mean scores (*M*) and Standard deviations (*sd*) on pre-test and post-test for the three conditions.

	Control group		Exp. Group double		Exp. Groep random	
	M	*Sd*	*M*	*sd*	*M*	*sd*
pre spelling	25.31	5.45	26.15	4.40	26.07	4.47
pre math	25.70	6.96	25.05	5.07	24.33	6.49
pre aardrijks	40.34	4.59	41.43	4.17	40.81	5.49
post spelling	29.26	5.10	28.56	3.67	27.52	3.99
post math	29.80	7.00	26.53	7.78	28.90	6.82
post geography	41.70	5.55	43.00	4.87	43.07	7.97

RQ1. Do students choose subjects that they are less good in, if the chance to get a larger award is higher?

The hypothesis for this sub question was that students like to have as many coins as possible and therefore will choose the subjects for which they may receive the double coins, even if this subject is their weakest subject. Students could receive double coins for math in period 1, for spelling in period 2 and for geography in period 3. In these

Table 3. Mean scores (M) and Standard deviations (*sd*) on the subscales of the IMI questionnaire.

	Control group		Exp. Group double		Exp. Groep random	
	M	*sd*	*M*	*sd*	*M*	*sd*
Perceived competence_t1	4.83	1.36	5.56	1.05	5.34	1.08
Interest_t1	4.76	1.25	5.27	.97	5.08	1.24
Perceived choice_t1	4.24	1.48	4.42	1.33	4.47	1.31
Pressure_t1	5.59	1.21	5.69	1.38	5.80	1.21
Perceived competence_t2	5.02	1.18	4.79	1.26	4.96	1.17
Interest_t2	5.31	1.59	5.47	1.21	5.09	1.09
Perceived choice_t2	4.38	1.52	4.61	1.24	4.41	1.20
Pressure_t2	5.89	.95	6.15	0.97	5.98	.85

* t1 = pre-test; t2 = post-test

three periods, no significant associations have been found between the scores on respectively math in period 1, spelling in period 2 and geography in period 3 and the number of games played. For math a significant positive association has been found between pre-test and number of math games played in period 2 ($r = .47$, $p < .05$), meaning that students with a high score on math, played more math games than the lower scoring students. Only for spelling a significant negative association has been found in period 3 ($r = -.48$, $p < .05$) which means that the low scoring students on the pre-test choose to play spelling games. However, this was not related with double coins.

A comparison between experimental group 1 and experimental group 2 on the scores on the subjects in the period where double coins could be earned do not show significant differences.

RQ2. Do students perform better on a specific topic as they spend more time on that topic in the assessment game?

The mean time that students spend on the subsequent subjects are given in Table 4. Students who didn't play a game on a specific topic are left out.

Table 4. Time spending per subject (in minutes)

	N	*Minimum*	*Maximum*	*Mean*	*SD*
Geography	35	1.38	377.95	49.46	77.12
Mathematics	55	1.70	381.73	63.19	85.51
spelling	40	0.03	144.21	19.00	27.37

The hypothesis is that if students practice longer their assessment score will improve. Manova analyses show that only for geography the post assessment score can be explained by the play time on geography games. For all subjects the pre assessment score is predictive for the post assessment score. Besides the score on the post assessment for math is also explained by the perceived choice and the condition.

Looking further at the relation between practice time on the different subjects, for all relation a significant positive association is found: practice on geography correlates significantly positive with practice time for mathematic ($r = .54$, $p < .01$) and with practice time for spelling ($r = .41$, $p < .01$), practice time for mathematics correlates significantly positive with practice time for spelling ($r = .71$, $p < .01$).

RQ3. What is the relation between intrinsic motivation and playing the games?

A significant difference has been found on the subscale 'Perceived competence' and on the subscale 'Pressure'. Perceived competence of playing games is significantly lower than the perceived competence of learning in general ($t = 2.76$, $df = 109$, $p < .05$). Pressure for learning by gaming is significantly lower than pressure on learning in general ($t = -2.70$, $df = 109$, $p < .05$).

Perceived competence of playing games has a significant positive association with the post test score on mathematics ($r = 0.18$, $p < .05$). The effect of interest on the post test score on spelling is significant ($F = 1{,}99$, $df = 23$, $p < .05$).

4 Conclusion and Discussion

In this study, primary school students got the opportunity to play educational games related to the core objectives on the subjects of math, spelling and geography. We hypothesised that if we could steer the choice behaviour of students by giving an awarding, students should also choose subjects they less master. Therefore, the computer game had been adjusted and students in one experimental group received a message that they could earn bonus coins when they played games in a specific subject. The other experimental group didn't receive the message and their scoring did not depend on the subject they played. No significant effect has been found on the bonus awarding of students. They didn't change into subjects for which they could receive double coins. As we saw a significant association between the practice time on all three subjects, a conclusion might be that students do not have the intention to get better in the subject of the game, but that they just likes playing. Unfortunately, there was neither an effect of the practice time on learning outcomes. The scores on the pre-test were the strongest predictors for the post test scores.

In this study, we selected the subjects mathematics, spelling and geography. Although the results in general were comparable over the subjects, some subject specific results have been found. Students with a high pre-test score on mathematics played significant more mathematic games. This strengthens the conclusion that students do not have the intention to get better in the subject of the game, but that they like to play games they are already good at. Only in period 3 students with a low pre-test score on spelling choose to play more spelling games. Geography was the only subject in which play time is related with the post assessment score.

Based on this small study, a few tentative recommendations can be made. In this study, the student was autonomous in choosing the subjects he or she liked and the teacher only stimulated the students to use the computer game. This led to a behaviour in which, at least for mathematics, students chose for subjects they were already good at. A large portion of the started games was not correctly finished, meaning that students stop playing the game before the end of the game. As students in primary education are positively intrinsic motivated for learning in general and for learning with games specifically, it seems to be important that teachers guide their students in the use of the computer game. It has to be clear for students (and for their parents) why a computer game is used, if the intention is to learn from the game. As the use of the game was voluntary, just 68 % of the students used their account. This degree of voluntariness may have declared the results. The use of gaming as a formative assessment should be based on the key processes in learning and teaching: (1) Establishing where the learners are in their learning; (2) Establishing where they are going, and (3) Establishing what needs to be done to get them there (Black and Wiliam 2009; Wiliam and Thompson 2007).

References

Black, P., Wiliam, D.: Developing the theory of formative assessment. Educ. Assess. Eval. Account. **21**, 5–31 (2009)

Connolly, T.M., Boyle, E.A., MacArthur, E., Hainey, T., Boyle, J.M.: A systematic literature review of empirical evidence on computer games and serious games. Comput. Educ. **59**, 661–686 (2012)

Frazer, A., Recio, A., Gilbert, L., Wills, G.: Profiling the educational value of computer games. Interac. Des. Archit. J. ID&A **19**, 1–19 (2014)

McAuley, E., Duncan, T., Tammen, V.V.: Psychometric properties of the intrinsic motivation inventory in a competitive sport setting: a confirmatory factor analysis. Res. Q. Exerc. Sport **60**, 48–58 (1989)

McClarty, K.L., Orr, A., Frey, P.M., Dolan, R.P., Vassileva, V., McVay, A.: A literature review of gaming in education. Gaming in education (2012)

Ryan, R.M., Koestner, R., Deci, E.L.: Varied forms of persistence: when free-choice behavior is not intrinsically motivated. Motiv. Emot. **15**, 185–205 (1991)

Wiliam, D., Thompson, M.: Integrating assessment with instruction: what will it take to make it work? In: Dwyer, C.A. (ed.) The Future of Assessment: Shaping Teaching and Learning, pp. 53–82. Erlbaum, Mahwah (2007)

A Practical Procedure for the Construction and Reliability Analysis of Fixed-Length Tests with Randomly Drawn Test Items

Silvester Draaijer[1(✉)] and Sharon Klinkenberg[2]

[1] Faculty of Psychology and Education, Department of Research and Theory in Education, VU University Amsterdam, Amsterdam, The Netherlands
s.draaijer@vu.nl

[2] Faculty of Social and Behavioural Sciences, University of Amsterdam, Amsterdam, The Netherlands
S.Klinkenberg@uva.nl

Abstract. A procedure to construct valid and fair fixed-length tests with randomly drawn items from an item bank is described. The procedure provides guidelines for the set-up of a typical achievement test with regard to the number of items in the bank and the number of items for each position in a test. Further, a procedure is proposed to calculate the relative difficulty for individual tests and to correct the obtained score for each student based on the mean difficulty for all students and the particular test of a student. Also, two procedures are proposed for the problem to calculate the reliability of tests with randomly drawn items. The procedures use specific interpretations of regularly used methods to calculate Cronbach's alpha and *KR20* and the Spearman-Brown prediction formula. A simulation with R is presented to illustrate the accuracy of the calculation procedures and the effects on pass-fail decisions.

Keywords: Sparse datasets · Classical test theory · Educational measurement · P-value · Reliability

1 Introduction

As the demand for defensibility regarding the quality of online higher education assessment and testing increases, it is crucial that teachers have appropriate tools and guidelines to design and evaluate such tests.

Teachers in higher education can nowadays easily administer formative and summative online achievement tests [1] to student in which test items are randomly drawn from larger item banks. Because items are drawn randomly from an item bank, each student responds to a unique set of test items for the same test. In computer-assisted assessment (CAA) literature, this feature of computer-based testing (CBT) systems is mentioned as a distinctive characteristic of computer-based testing that makes it an attractive alternative to fixed, paper-based tests in view of being able to more systematically address

E. Ras and D. Joosten-ten Brinke (Eds.): CAA 2015, CCIS 571, pp. 47–60, 2015.
DOI: 10.1007/978-3-319-27704-2_6

item quality, prevent item exposure and cheating and provide the possibility of administering tests at multiple instances in time [2].

Teachers have expressed a need to know how many test items should be available in an item bank for test set-ups when such tests are used for formative medium stakes tests or for summative high stakes final examination purposes. In order to respond to that need, it is of importance to first establish the main criteria with which the quality of tests and test items can be judged and, accordingly, how typical set ups of a test and item bank should be designed. As will be suggested, besides content validity, the level of difficulty and reliability of such tests is of main importance.

Further, it is a psychometric challenge to address the issue of difficulty level and reliability with randomly drawn test items and the current CBT systems in use in higher education, such as Questionmark Perception, BTL Surpass, Blackboard, Moodle or Canvas. These systems have limited capabilities for calculating these properties of tests with randomly drawn items. In this paper, this problem will be discussed in more detail and practical procedures for analyzing such tests and estimating their reliability are proposed to optimize fair treatment of students with regards to pass-fail decisions.

First, the case is made to relate the number of test items in an item bank to the number of students taking a test and the number of responses per item required for an analysis with acceptable confidence levels for item and test characteristics. Second, the case is made to systematically adjust individual student scores based on the difficulty level of each individual test. For the latter, statistical procedures to estimate the mean difficulty of a test for students will be described. Finally, estimations for reliability based on classical test theory calculation methods and score adjustment will be presented.

1.1 Background

An important drawback of random item selection from an item bank for each student is that the content validity, reliability and difficulty level of these tests for each individual student are challenging to control. A solution to this problem could be the application of adaptive testing possibilities based on item response theory (IRT). In higher education, however, employing IRT-based approaches is very difficult because it requires advanced technologies and extensive test item development and analysis procedures to develop calibrated test item banks and IRT adaptive tests [3]. Resources and expertise for such applications are in general lacking [4]. Also, the understanding of such procedures by students and the general public is limited, which restricts their acceptability.

In higher education, teachers and support staff resort to better known methods derived from classical test theory (CTT) to assemble and analyze tests and test items. Veldkamp [5] described a procedure for assembling tests of equal difficulty based on CCT when test item banks are available with known values for the difficulty of the test items (p-value) and the correlation values of the test items with the test scores (r_{it}). Veldkamp suggested that item banks should then be structured so that tests could be drawn in a stratified manner to result in tests with equal difficulty and equal deviation. His method built on procedures described by Gibson and Weiner [6]. The main problem with the approach of Veldkamp is that the item characteristics obtained by CTT inherently are not independent from quality of instruction, quality of circumstances, level and distribution of the test-taker population's ability. This implies that his procedure has fundamental limitations and that an approach is needed that uses obtained item characteristics *after* instruction and administration to students.

2 A Proposal for a Testing Procedure in Higher Education

Teachers in higher education are limited to drawing test items randomly from item banks by the possibilities of the CBT systems at their disposal. These available CBT systems *are* capable of assembling and administering fixed-length tests [7] and of drawing test items randomly without sophisticated drawing algorithms from a pool of test items for each question *position* of a test. This starting point forms a first but feasible step to deploying a construction method that ensures content validity.

2.1 Assumptions

The first assumption for the construction of higher education achievement tests is that there is sufficient content validity: all learning objectives or topics are adequately represented in the test. Further, a rule of thumb in higher education is that summative achievement tests consisting of 4-option multiple-choice questions need at least forty test items of moderate difficulty and acceptable levels of discrimination to reach acceptable levels of measurement precision [8].

A second assumption is that in higher education, the most important decision resulting from an achievement test is whether a student passed or failed the test. For that reason, setting an appropriate cut-off score and ensuring sufficient reliability of a test to minimize false negative or false positive pass-fail decisions is of importance. As every student receives a test with different test items, each student has a test with a unique level of difficulty and reliability. In particular for students who score near the cut-off score, considerations that compensate students with relatively difficult tests are likely to be of importance.

2.2 Proposed Structure of an Item Bank

To ensure a representative selection of test items, a robust procedure is proposed in which, for each *position* in a test, test items are drawn from one specific pool of test items that closely reflects the intended topic and taxonomic cognitive level for that position. Drawing each item from one pool minimizes the chances that test items will be dependent on one another in the test as a whole and will ensure that items will be responded to in a much as possible equally distributed manner. Figure 1 shows this principle of item pool structure and item selection.

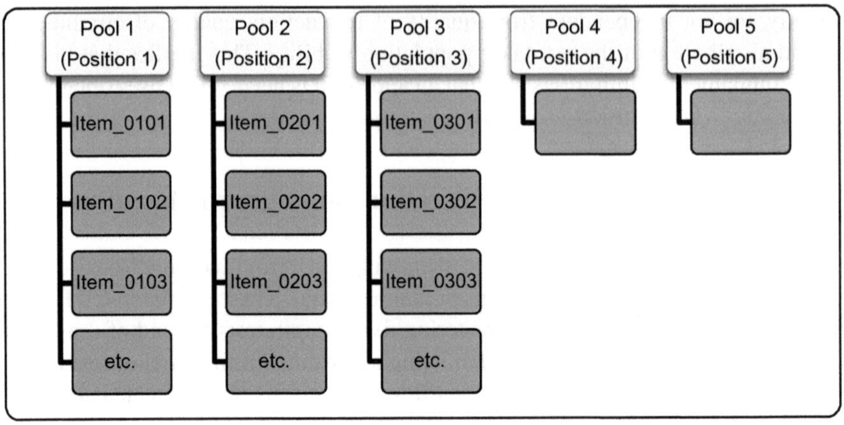

Fig. 1. Example of an item bank structure of an item bank as a reflection of the position of test items in a test

2.3 Number of Test Items for an Item Bank

Though many responses to test items are needed for stable parameter estimations of difficulty and correlation values [9], as a rule of thumb in higher education, 50 responses is regarded as a minimum to be acceptable for decision-making purposes. Taking this minimum as a starting point results in a recommendation for the number of items per position and items according to Eqs. (1) and (2), in which *N* is the number of students expected to take the exam.

$$n_{(items\,per\,position\,in\,pool)} = \frac{N}{50} \tag{1}$$

$$n_{tot(total\,items\,in\,bank)} = n_{(items\,per\,position\,in\,pool)} * positions\ in\ test \tag{2}$$

2.4 Level of Difficulty for Test Items

It is hard, if not impossible, for teachers in higher education to design test items with known difficulty [10, 11]. Findings from methods and research regarding procedures for item-cloning to control item difficulty are advancing [3, 12], but must be regarded as out of reach for teachers in higher education. Therefore, each student receives test items with different difficulty, resulting in a different level of difficulty for each test. The proposed selection procedure ensures that content validity requirements are met to quite an extent, but does not ensure fairness with regards to difficulty level. The next chapter will address that problem.

3 Estimating the Level of Difficulty for a Test

After construction of an item bank and administration of a test to students, a procedure with the following steps is proposed to estimate the level of difficulty for a test and the level of difficulty for individual students.

First, for each item in the bank, the percentage of students answering the item correctly is calculated. This yields the level of difficulty (proportion correct) p_i for each item. Most CBT systems provide this characteristic for test items and randomly drawn test items by default.

Second, the mean level of difficulty for the test $\bar{p}_{test}$ is calculated by summing the p-value for all items and dividing by the number of test items in the item bank, according to formula (3).

$$\bar{p}_{test} = \frac{\sum_{n_{tot}} p_i}{n_{tot}} \tag{3}$$

Third, according to formula (4), the level of difficulty for the test for each student $\bar{p}_s$ is calculated by summing the p-value for each item a student responded to divided by the number of test items n_s for each student.

$$\bar{p}_s = \frac{\sum_{n_s} p_{i_s}}{n_s} \tag{4}$$

3.1 Correction for Difficulty Levels Between Students

A correction can be made for the level of difficulty for each student in such a way that the level of difficulty of the test will be equal for each student. In the simplest form, this can be done using additive correction. Each student's proportion of correct answers on the test $Prop_{corr}$ will be corrected to $Prop'_{corr}$ as a function of the difference between the mean difficulty of all test items and the mean difficulty for the test of a particular student, as represented in formula (5).

$$Prop'_{corr_s} = Prop_{corr_s} + \left(\bar{p}_{test} - \bar{p}_s\right) \tag{5}$$

After establishing the final adapted score for each student, the cut-off score procedure can be applied. It will be obvious that for a number of students who achieved a score close to the cut-off score, a different decision regarding failing or passing could be made depending on the level of difficulty of their particular test.

A problem with simple additive correction is that students could achieve a proportion correct higher than 100 % if a student scored correct on all items and was provided with a relatively difficult test. In order to overcome this problem, more sophisticated procedures for correction could be applied. For example, correction of scores could be applied only for students with a relatively difficult test and a score close to the cut-off score to prevent false-negative decisions. Or, adjustments could be set so that the amount of adjustment of the scores runs linearly from zero at the maximum or minimum score to the total corrected score adjustment at the cut-off score. We refer to Livingston [13] for more sophisticated methods for test equating, also incorporating score variance and other considerations.

4 Test Reliability

Well-known methods are available for calculating the reliability of a fixed-length test with a fixed set of test items. The general approach is to calculate Cronbach's alpha α [14] for polytomous items, or *KR*20 (Kuder-Richardson 20 formula) for dichotomous items [15]. In such approaches, variances of item scores and test scores for all students and items are used.

However, in this paper the situation is staged for tests with randomly drawn test items in which the item bank holds more items n_{tot} than are presented to the students N. After administration, the result matrix with the scores for each item for each student is a so-called sparse dataset. The emptiness of these datasets can be in the order of 50 % or more. The large number of empty positions prevents a straightforward calculation of α or *KR*20, in particular because of different interpretations of the number of test items for which calculations need to be carried out and because of calculation procedures in which, for example, list-wise deletion of data occurs. A solution to this problem is to make an estimation of α or *KR*20 using the characteristics of the items in a sparse dataset.

4.1 Lopez-Cronbach's Alpha

The first method for making an estimation of reliability was described by Lopez [16]. In this paper, we refer to this measure as α. The advantage of the Lopez' procedure is that it can be used for both dichotomous and polytomous items. His method uses the correlation matrix of the item scores of items in an item bank. In his approach, the Spearman-Brown prediction formula is conceptualized as in formula (6).

$$\alpha_{tot} = \frac{n_{tot}\bar{r}}{1 + \left(n_{tot} - 1\right)\bar{r}} \tag{6}$$

In (6), $\bar{r}$ is the mean inter-item correlation of the items in the item bank. The procedure that Lopez suggested to calculate α_{tot} is to first calculate the correlation matrix for the items. Second, calculate the mean of the off-diagonal correlation values of the correlation matrix. Third, calculate α using formula (6).

A remaining problem, however, is that the calculated reliability now reflects the situation in which all items in the item bank are used. Based on the assumption of test homogeneity (items have comparable characteristics), a procedure for calculating the mean reliability of all the student's tests is to use the Spearman-Brown prediction formula [17] according to formula (7).

$$\alpha'_{tot} = \frac{k\alpha_{tot}}{1 + (k-1)\,\alpha_{tot}} \tag{7}$$

In formula (7), k is the factor for the relative increase or decrease in the number of items. In the case of items drawn randomly from an item bank, k will always be the proportion of items sampled from the bank divided by the number of items in the bank.

4.2 *KR*20

For dichotomous items, we use a conception of the standard deviation of a test SD_{test} based on Gibson and Weiner [6], using the item-test point-biserial correlation values r_{it_i} of each item i in the item bank and the level of difficulty p_i for each item according to formula (8). The reason for using this formula instead of the regularly used formula for determining SD_{test} is that in formula (8), characteristics of the items distributed to students are sufficient to calculate SD_{test}. Using the SD_{test}, $KR20$ (equal to α for dichotomous items) is calculated according to formula (9).

$$SD_{test} = \sum\nolimits_{i=1}^{n_{tot}} r_{it_i} \left[p_i\left(1-p_i\right)\right]^{\frac{1}{2}} \tag{8}$$

$$KR20 = \frac{n_{tot}}{n_{tot}-1}\left[1 - \frac{\sum_{i=1}^{n_{tot}} p_i\left(1-p_i\right)}{SD_{test}^2}\right] \tag{9}$$

The values for r_{it_i} and p_i are calculated mostly by default by current CBT systems and could be used to manually calculate $KR20$.

After calculating $KR20$ on the basis of the procedure described above, the Spearman-Brown formula parallel to formula (10) needs to be used again to calculate the mean estimate $KR20'$ for the students based on the number of administered items n_s per student.

$$KR20' = \frac{kKR20}{1 + (k-1)\,KR20} \tag{10}$$

4.3 Test Reliability for Individual Students

When assuming no homogeneity and with dichotomous scoring, the reliability for each *individual* student $KR20_s$ could also be computed by using only the data of the individual items administered to each student n_s, according to formulas (11) and (12).

$$SD_{test_s} = \sum\nolimits_{i_s=1}^{n_s} r_{it_{i_s}} \left[p_{i_s}\left(1-p_{i_s}\right)\right]^{1/2} \tag{11}$$

$$KR20_s = \frac{n_s}{n_s-1}\left[1 - \frac{\sum_{i_s=1}^{n_s} p_{i_s}\left(1-p_{i_s}\right)}{SD_{test_s}^2}\right] \tag{12}$$

4.4 Simulations for Estimating the Accuracy of Calculated Reliability Parameters

To provide evidence for the degree of accuracy of the procedures described, a simulation was set up using R [18]. In the simulation, two research questions were formulated:

1. To what extent does the correction procedure for the sum scores decrease incorrect pass-fail decisions?
2. How robust are the two presented procedures for calculating Lopez' α and $KR20$ for a typical sparse dataset on the basis of the proposed test construction set up?

In order to determine the robustness of the described procedures, a benchmark for reliability comparison is needed. For this purpose, we ran a simulation where data with known reliability (Cronbach's α) were generated. To achieve this, we sampled data from a multivariate normal distribution from a predefined covariance matrix. Cronbach's α was calculated from this covariance matrix, called sigma (Σ), resulting in a fixed alpha. The covariance matrix had properties that conform to the associated assumptions of homogeneity and equality of variance while also approximating real-world item parameters.

$$\Sigma = \begin{bmatrix} \sigma_{11}^2 & \sigma_{12}^2 & \cdots & \sigma_{1n}^2 \\ \sigma_{21}^2 & \sigma_{22}^2 & \cdots & \sigma_{2n}^2 \\ \vdots & \vdots & \ddots & \vdots \\ \sigma_{d1}^2 & \sigma_{d2}^2 & \cdots & \sigma_{dn}^2 \end{bmatrix}$$

From this matrix, Cronbach's α was computed using the ratio of mean variance and mean covariance according to formula (13).

$$\alpha = \frac{K\bar{c}}{\bar{v} + (K-1)\bar{c}} \tag{13}$$

Here, K is the number of items, $\bar{v}$ is the average variance for all items (the mean of the diagonal from the covariance matrix Σ), and $\bar{c}$ is the average of all covariances between all items (the off-diagonal from Σ).

By specifying the mean variance and mean covariance, the covariance matrix was used to simulate multivariate data where the underlying α is known. In this example, using $\bar{v} = 1.17$, $\bar{c} = 0.16$ and $K = 400$ results in $\alpha = 0.98$.

We created Σ by sampling the discrimination parameter a for each item from a uniform distribution $a \sim U(0.25, 0.55)$ and applying a residual variance of 1 as is a common assumption within item response theory. Applying this to Σ resulted in:

$$\Sigma = \begin{bmatrix} 1.22 & 0.22 & \ldots & 0.26 \\ 0.22 & 1.21 & \ldots & 0.25 \\ \vdots & \vdots & \ddots & \vdots \\ 0.26 & 0.25 & \ldots & 1.3 \end{bmatrix}$$

Using this covariance matrix, we generated multivariate data $x \sim N_k(\mu, \Sigma)$ consisting of 400 items and 500 students. For later analysis, it was desirable to generate responses based on known abilities θ's and item difficulties β's. We therefore sampled normal θ's $\sim N(0, 1)$ and uniform β's $\sim U(-2, 2)$. Multivariate normal responses were sampled using the mvrnorm() function from the R package MASS written by Ripley et al. [19]. From this, we calculated a response matrix where the binary response was determined by the difficulty, ability, discrimination and covariance structure. We categorized the continuous response by assigning values of 1 when it exceeded the item difficulty β and values of 0 when the continuous response was lower than β. For a detailed description of binary data modeling we refer to De Boeck and Wilson [20].

The following procedure was used for this simulation. We generated a binary response matrix with dimensions of 400 and 500 based on the above method, with a known $\alpha = 0.98$. We calculated Cronbach's α from the response matrix using the cronbach.alpha() function from the ltm package written by Rizopoulos [21], applied the $KR20$ and Lopez' method and then applied Spearman-Brown's formula to all methods. We also calculated $\rho_{xx'}$ by correlating the standardized known student ability θ's with standardized sum scores. This represented the real reliability. From the full response matrix, a sparse matrix was created by randomly sampling 40 responses for every student. The sparse matrix was used to again calculate Cronbach's α, $KR20$, and Lopez and apply the Spearman-Brown correction. In addition to calculating $\rho_{xx'}$ on the sum scores of the sparse matrix, we also calculated the corrected sum scores using the method described in formula (5). This procedure was repeated 10,000 times to get robust estimators and determine their lower and upper bounds based on a 95 % confidence interval. Confidence intervals were calculated using the 2.5 % and 97.5 % quantile scores. The full simulation code can be found in the GitHub repository by Klinkenberg [21].

Furthermore, we calculated the pass-fail rate based on a predefined cut-off score of 60 %. By comparing this to the true pass-fail rate, we created cross tables containing the amount of correct and incorrect decisions.

4.5 Results of the Simulation

The results of the simulation are graphically represented in Fig. 2. The figure shows the calculated reliabilities and the 95 % confidence interval for each method used. The true alpha on which the data were simulated is indicated at the bottom. The Spearman-Brown corrected reliabilities indicate the estimates for 40 sampled items. These should be compared to the lower bound of the correlations between the true θ's and the sum and corrected sum scores in the sparse data. The remainder of the reliabilities, also in the sparse set, estimated the reliability of the full item bank. Note that alpha for sparse data is missing because it could not be calculated with sparse data using R (or other programs), an essential point of this paper.

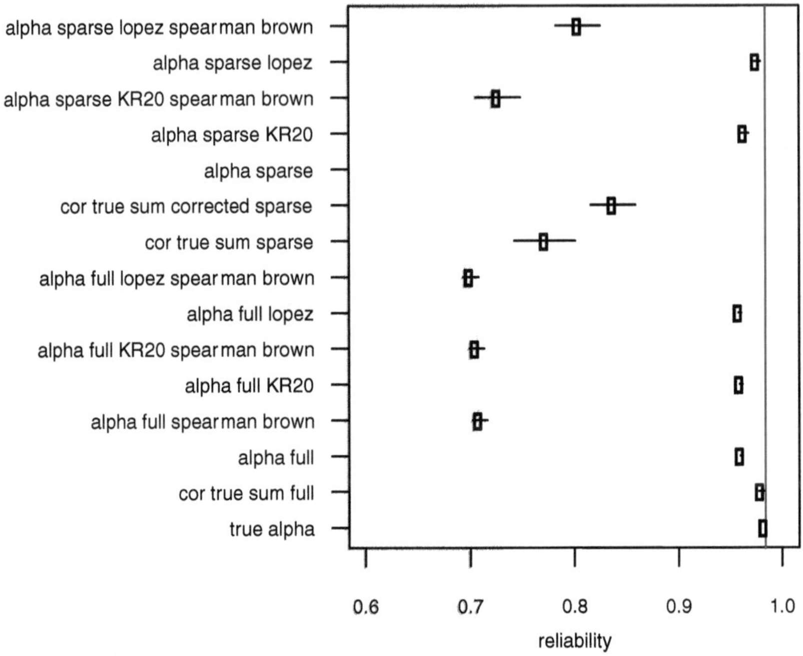

Fig. 2. Reliabilities plotted against true alpha of .98

In Table 1, the correlation between the true abilities and the ability scores $\rho_{xx'}$ shows the true reliability of the test based on a simulated alpha of .98. Further, the table shows the computed values for the different estimation methods using the simulation.

Table 1. Reliabilities as simulated with alpha .98

	Full data		Sparse data		
	Full	Spearman-brown	Sparse	Spearman-brown	Sparse corrected
$\rho_{xx'}$	0.98	.	0.77	.	0.84
CB α	0.96	0.71	.	.	.
*KR*20	0.96	0.71	0.96	0.73	.
Lopez	0.96	0.70	0.98	0.81	.

The table shows that the true reliability of the full dataset corresponds to the true alpha. Also, the true reliability ($\rho_{xx'}$) of the full dataset corresponds to the alpha used to generate the data. This seems a bit strange, as Cronbach's alpha is the lower bound of the true reliability [22]. It would be expected that the alpha used to simulate the data would be lower than the true reliability ($\rho_{xx'}$). We attribute this to the small variations in the estimations due to the large sample size, number of items, the random sampling error and rounding. The found reliability estimates for the sparse datasets after Spearman-Brown correction for test length show normal values for reliability obtained for achievement test with forty test items (0.77, 0.73, 0.81) and are an indication for the appropriateness of the proposed calculation procedures.

Table 1 further shows that the corrected proportion correct for individual students results in an increase in true reliability compared to the non-corrected sum scores, and a slight increase in true positives. Even when not using correction, the *KR*20 procedure does not result in an overestimation of reliability but in an underestimation (0.73 versus 0.77). Using the Lopez procedure results in an overestimation (0.81 versus 0.77). Further, when applying correction, the Lopez method still yields an underestimation (0.81 versus 0.84).

In Table 2, the sensitivity and specificity of the pass-fail decisions in percentage are given. Of particular interest are the differences in true pass decisions for the sparse and sparse corrected score procedures. This difference is 3 % (from 28 % to 31 %). Though this difference is not large, it has real-world implications; in our simulation, 15 students (3 % of the 500 students) would receive a true-positive instead of a false-negative pass-fail decision, and the number of false-positives would increase by 1 % (9 % instead of 8 %).

Table 2. Sensitivity and specificity of pass-fail decisions

		Full data		Sparse		Sparse corrected	
		Pass	Fail	Pass	Fail	Pass	Fail
True	Pass	37 %	3 %	28 %	12 %	31 %	9 %
	Fail	3 %	57 %	8 %	52 %	9 %	51 %

4.6 Conclusion of the Simulation

In answer to research question 1 regarding the effect of applying a correction procedure for pass-fail decisions, we conclude that correcting the sum scores for mean individual difficulty from sparse data yields a higher reliability (84 % versus 77 %) and lower percentages of false-negative decisions.

With regards to research question 2 concering the robustness of the two presented methods for calculating *KR*20 and Lopez' α, we conclude that the *KR*20 and Lopez methods with Spearman-Brown correction provide practical means for calculating reliability values. However, both methods overestimate the reliability in comparison with the Spearman-Brown correction of the full data matrix. In comparison to the true reliability of the sparse data, we conclude that the *KR*20 method is the most conservative.

5 Conclusion

In this paper, a procedure to construct a fixed length test with randomly drawn items from an item bank has been proposed. The procedure provides guidelines for the set up of a typical test as used in higher education regarding the number of items in the item bank and the number of items for each position in a test. The procedure tries to cater to the need for valid, reliable and fair assessment practices.

Procedures have been proposed for relatively easily obtainable item characteristics to calculate the relative difficulty of individual tests for students and to correct the obtained score for each student based on the mean difficulty of all tests and the difficulty of a particular test.

Two procedures have been presented for solving the problem of calculating the reliability of such tests. This problem needs to be addressed because the test analysis calculation algorithms of current CBT systems used in higher education do not have options for reliability calculation at all or have flawed algorithms for tests with randomly drawn test items. The recommended procedures used a specific interpretation of regularly used methods of calculating α and $KR20$.

The presented simulation showed that the methods described result in valid calculation methods and that the procedure using the $KR20$ approach with Spearman-Brown correction yielded the most conservative estimate.

5.1 Further Research

This study is a first exploration into developing practical means to assess the validity and fairness of achievement tests with randomly drawn test items in higher education using CTT. It answers questions regarding calculation and correction procedures for individual student scores. The study also elicits new research questions.

First, with respect to the estimation procedure of α for sparse data, our study showed different results compared to the original paper by Lopez. In particular, in our simulation, the estimation yielded an overestimation of reliability. Further research is needed to establish why and to what extent these differences occur and are dependent on variables such as number of responses, number of items in the bank and number of items drawn, parameters of student ability difficulty and discrimination distribution of items or use of corrected item-test correlations [23], etc. Obviously, studying the effects of these variables on other estimation methods is needed for further validation of the proposed procedures.

Second, as simulated data were used in our experiment, using real-life data would also provide more insight into the applicability and acceptability of the procedure and calculations.

Third, if tests are provided to students in smaller batches (or even at the level of the individual) running up to the total number of students expected to take the achievement test, methods could be implemented to use streaming calculations. That is, methods could be designed in which item parameters for difficulty and discrimination are set by teachers before test administration and the item parameters could be adjusted as new responses are recorded. The incoming data could then be used to make better estimations of the item parameters and, hence, better decisions for passing or failing students. This would imply using methods related, for example, to moving averages calculations [24, 25].

5.2 Practical Implications

As our paper has shown, the fairness of pass-fail decisions using randomly drawn test items is hampered because of differences in individual test difficulty. This results in two important implications.

First, when teachers or institutions of higher education design tests in which test items are drawn randomly from an item bank, they should be aware of the differences in individual test difficulty. Although drawing items randomly can be beneficial in view of practical considerations, it has a negative effect on individual students in the false-negative category. Interpreting test results for these tests should be done with caution, and consideration for failed students who encountered more difficult tests is appropriate. Also, attention should be given to evaluating the degree to which teachers and students understand the correction procedure for pass-fail decisions.

Second, a call is made for developers of the CBT software used in higher education to equip their products with features that enable fairer treatment with regard to analysis possibilities and scores correction possibilities when deploying tests with randomly drawn items. Designing such software with a user-friendly interface could be quite a challenge but does not have to be impossible. Our source code is freely available for inspection and further use and development under Creative Commons on Github. This would result in an increased understanding of the characteristics of achievement tests in higher education and in fairer treatment of students.

References

1. Draaijer, S., Warburton, B.: The emergence of large-scale computer assisted summative examination facilities in higher education. In: Kalz, M., Ras, E. (eds.) CAA 2014. CCIS, vol. 439, pp. 28–39. Springer, Heidelberg (2014)
2. Mills, C.N., Potenza, M.T., Fremer, J.J., Ward, W.C.: Computer-Based Testing, Building the Foundation for Future Assessments. Lawrence Erlbaum Associates, London (2002)
3. Glas, C.A.W., Van der Linden, W.J.: Computerized Adaptive Testing With Item Cloning. Appl. Psychol. Meas. **27**, 247–261 (2003)
4. Van Haneghan, J.P.: The impact of technology on assessment and evaluation in higher education. In: Technology Integration in Higher Education: Social and Organizational Aspects, pp. 222–235 (2010)
5. Veldkamp, B.: Het random construeren van toetsen uit een itembank [Random selection of tests from an itembank]. Exam. Tijdschr. Voor Toetspraktijk. **9**, 17–19 (2012)
6. Gibson, W.M., Weiner, J.A.: Generating random parallel test forms using CTT in a computer-based environment. J. Educ. Meas. **35**, 297–310 (1998)
7. Parshall, C.G., Spray, J.A., Kalohn, J.C., Davey, T.: Practical Considerations in Computer-Based Testing. Springer, New York (2002)
8. van Berkel, H., Bax, A.: Toetsen in het Hoger Onderwijs [Testing in Higher Education]. Bohn Stafleu Van Loghum, Houten/Diegem (2006)

9. Schönbrodt, F.D., Perugini, M.: At what sample size do correlations stabilize? J. Res. Personal. **47**, 609–612 (2013)
10. Cizek, G.J., Bunch, M.B.: Standard Setting: a Guide to Establishing and Evaluating Performance Standards on Tests. Sage Publications, Thousand Oaks (2007)
11. Impara, J.C., Plake, B.S.: Teachers' ability to estimate item difficulty: a test of the assumptions in the angoff standard setting method. J. Educ. Meas. **35**, 69–81 (1998)
12. Gierl, M.J., Haladyna, T.M.: Automatic Item Generation: Theory and Practice. Routledge, New York (2012)
13. Livingston, S.A.: Equating Test Scores (without IRT). Educational Testing Service, Princeton (2004)
14. Cronbach, L.J.: Coefficient alpha and the internal structure of tests. Psychometrika **16**, 297–334 (1951)
15. Kuder, G.F., Richardson, M.W.: The theory of the estimation of test reliability. Psychometrika **2**, 151–160 (1937)
16. Lopez, M.: Estimation of Cronbach's alpha for sparse datasets. In: Mann, S., Bridgeman, N. (eds.) Proceedings of the 20th Annual Conference of the National Advisory Committee on Computing Qualifications (NACCQ), pp. 151–155, New Zealand (2007)
17. Spearman, C.: Correlation calculated from faulty data. Br. J. Psychol. 1904–1920 **3**, 271–295 (1910)
18. Team, R.C.: R: A language and environment for statistical computing. R Foundation for Statistical Computing, Vienna, Austria (2015)
19. Ripley, B., Venables, B., Bates, D.M., Hornik, K., Gebhardt, A., Firth, D., Ripley, M.B.: Package "MASS." (2014)
20. De Boeck, P., Wilson, M. (eds.): Explanatory Item Response Models. Springer, New York (2004)
21. Klinkenberg, S.: Simulation for determining test reliability of sparse data sets (2015)
22. Woodhouse, B., Jackson, P.H.: Lower bounds for the reliability of the total score on a test composed of non-homogeneous items: II: a search procedure to locate the greatest lower bound. Psychometrika **42**, 579–591 (1977)
23. Cureton, E.E.: Corrected item-test correlations. Psychometrika **31**, 93–96 (1966)
24. Lucas, J.M., Saccucci, M.S.: Exponentially weighted moving average control schemes: properties and enhancements. Technometrics **32**, 1–12 (1990)
25. Wei, W.W.: Time Series Analysis. Addison-Wesley, Boston (1994)

Tomb of Osiris: Gamifying the Assessment of Collaborative Complex Problem Solving Skills on Tangible Tabletops

Bibeg Limbu[1], Valérie Maquil[1], Eric Ras[1(✉)], and Armin Weinberger[2]

[1] Luxembourg Institute of Science and Technology, Esch-sur-Alzette, Luxembourg
{bibeg.limbu,valerie.maquil,eric.ras}@list.lu
[2] Universität des Saarlandes, Saarbrücken, Germany
a.weinberger@edutech.uni-saarland.de

Abstract. "Tomb of Osiris" is a collaborative puzzle-based game on a Tangible Tabletop, with the aim to gamify the MicroDYN approach. MicroDYN is an approach to assess complex problem solving skills through tasks within micro-worlds. Gamifying MicroDYN proposes new solutions for fostering collaboration and maintaining users' motivation during assessment. This paper describes the game design, and in particular the different design decisions taken in order to support the MicroDYN procedure, game flow, collaboration, and tangible interactions. By following the design-based research approach, the project aims at exploring and manifesting guidelines for fostering collaboration and motivation in a collaborative game-based MicroDYN scenario.

Keywords: MicroDYN · Complex problem solving · Collaborative complex problem solving · Collaborative game · Tangible user interface · Tangible tabletop

1 The MicroDYN Approach with Tangible User Interfaces

MicroDYN is a psychometric approach for measuring complex problem solving (CPS). It is implemented by a series of independent tasks in microworlds of varying difficulty [1] and follows a formal framework to guarantee comparability [2]. A microworld is an isolated but a complete subset of phenomena. These phenomena are simulated through variables in a computer-supported environment in which one can learn through personal discovery and exploration by altering the variables. Microworlds should be simple, general, useful, and syntonic [3]. In MicroDYN approach, microworlds are embedded into fictitious semantics which are based on Linear Structural Equations (LSE) [2]. The variables are labelled without deep semantic meaning to avoid activation of prior knowledge during problem solving [1]. The assessment of complex problem solving is typically done in a prior knowledge free context, because the psychological construct of complex problem solving does not contain the assessment of prior knowledge, and therefore plays no relevant role. Nevertheless, in the context of formative assessment the activation of prior knowledge is crucial.

E. Ras and D. Joosten-ten Brinke (Eds.): CAA 2015, CCIS 571, pp. 61–68, 2015.
DOI: 10.1007/978-3-319-27704-2_7

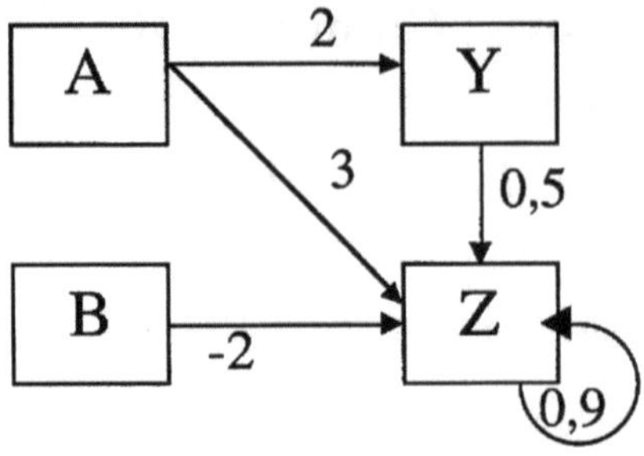

Fig. 1. Linear system

In a LSE (see Fig. 1), the user is allowed to manipulate variables A & B, however the relationship is not disclosed. One of the relation equations can be described as "Yt +1 = 2.At" where t is the time factor & Y is the output variable [2].

Kröner et al. [4] identified three main phases of CPS: rule identification, rule knowledge acquisition and rule knowledge application, which are a part of the MicroDYN approach. The problem solving procedure requires the user to pass through all three phases in a chronological order for each microworld.

Test takers usually face five to seven microworlds in a single test which takes around 45 min overall. Since CPS is a mental process [5], which is self-guided and requires users to constantly acquire knowledge, motivation is an integral part of it. MicroDYN must infer, situations that are completely new and do not allow previous knowledge activation as microworlds, during the course of 45 min with more or less limited methods of interaction which may lead to students losing motivation over the course of the test and thus increases the chances of unreliable data.

Beyond motivational limitations related to CPS assessment, technological limitations exist. Since complex problems are dynamic phenomena, computer-based approaches lend themselves to create CPS settings. However, even with the existing technology it's a challenge to measure collaborative CPS [6]. This project has chosen to use tangible user interfaces (TUI) to create a co-located collaborative setting for testing the CPS with MicroDYN.

TUIs allow users to directly manipulate bits of data by manipulating physical objects in a real space [7]. Tangible Tabletops were found to be enjoyable to use [8], encourage equity of participation [9], and promote learning [10]. Tangible objects can embody concepts to be learned, that users can directly manipulate in order to create and test relations among them [11]. It allows designers to create user interactions that are easy to use, and allow users to quickly adapt to the technological complexity, and focus on solving the microworld only.

This paper presents the implementation of a game-based design approach on a tangible tabletop following the MicroDYN approach. The proposed solution allows a group of users to solve a complex problem collaboratively by sharing the same workspace and enforces collaboration by using game design elements. The aim of the work is to explore the possibilities a game-based design can offer for enhancing collaboration and tackling the motivational issues in CPS settings, and, hence, to gain useful insights in collaborative complex problem solving.

2 Game Design

2.1 Overview

"Four Archaeologists are lost & trapped after a devastating accident in the Historical excavation site rumoured to be the tomb of the Osiris, God of Death. Countless explorers have perished in its labyrinth trying to escape. Nobody knows what surprise awaits them. But if they wish to make it out alive, they must work together. Will they make it out alive together or perish with their selfishness?"

The proposed game is a puzzle based collaborative game where each puzzle is a microworld. The game is set on a labyrinth of an Egyptian pyramid, where four archaeologists have been trapped. The game is played on a tangible table top where each player is stationed at one of the four sides of the table. Each player has access to his/her region and physical tangibles that he can use to explore the digital space in game, find clues and solve the puzzle while collaborating. Clues are hidden dispersed among the four player's individually accessible section. Players must work together to find the answer and solve the puzzle within the global time frame.

A tangible tabletop also allows users to have face-face interactions. To foster collaboration, guidelines have been issued, such as preserving Territoriality [12] in a shared space. Moreover, a shared digital space prohibits secret communication within the game and affords interdependence and individual accountability [13].

The game was designed to allow for flexibly administering additional microworlds as per need in the future. The microworlds are key puzzles in the game at each level that cannot be skipped. The user is required to explore the surroundings to look for key elements with help of a tangible avatar (see Fig. 1) and clues that are crucial to solve the problem during the implementation phase of the puzzle. The implementation phase of the microworld puzzle enforces a fixed number of allowed steps to create a challenge.

Fig. 2. Tangible avatar

Additional game elements such as competition with other peer groups and rewards have been implemented.

The first microworld (see Fig. 2) accepts user inputs through the physical tangible object, which manipulates the location of output (stars) based on LSE's. But the effect of inputs on the output is not explicitly shown and users have not only to figure out their weight of control on the star but also collaboratively find out their respective stars that they control. They also have to collaborate to put the pieces of puzzle together while negotiating with other team mates. In this case, the goal is divided into independent tasks that the players solve by controlling a variable each, while the second microworld is planned to implement a shared input system. That implies that all players must equally partake in solving each of the sub-goals. The players exercise a different weight of control over every output variable, and all users require to actively solve each of the sub-goals (Fig. 3).

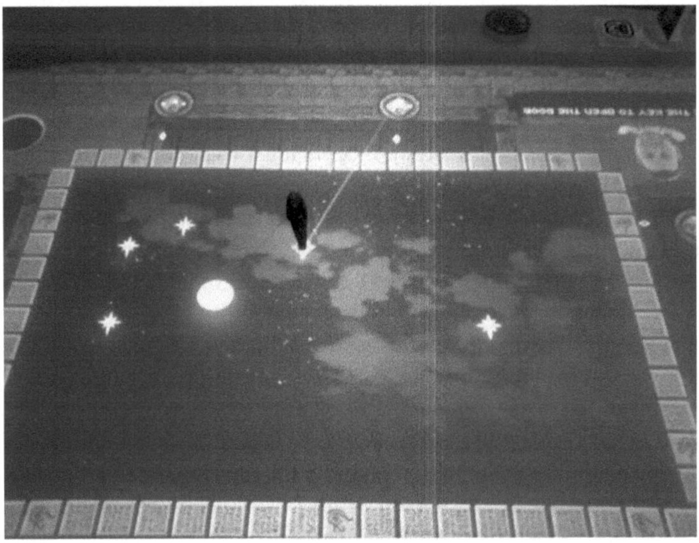

Fig. 3. In the first microworld, users need to collaborate in order to position the stars in a certain way

2.2 Elements of Game Flow

The project attempts to gamify the MicroDYN methodology by inserting gaming elements into the MicroDYN approach in order to foster users' motivation. Prensky [14] proposed six elements that define a game and create flow experience [15].

1. *Goals and objectives*: The main goal in the game is to solve the puzzle-based microworlds and make it out alive together. Puzzles are administered one after another as a set of the MicroDYN tasks.
2. *Outcome and feedback*: Feedback is generated by the MicroDYN output variables (star positions in the first microworld) based on user input collected by the help of

widgets. In order to make sure the users are able to collect rich information, real-time feedback, which is event driven are provided as player interacts with the game objects with help of tangibles. For example, instead of providing the feedback to the correct answer at the end, the correct answer is divided into parts that can be tracked as user attempts to make the correct answer and thus connect the information collected. Summative feedback is also provided by means of global time, rewards, and score. Group performance is measured in terms of number of steps required to solve the game while the game design in itself fosters peer feedback and decision making among the players.
3. *Interaction*: Tangible and touch-based interactions are implemented in the game. The game is collaborative and collocated, thus mechanisms to enforce collaboration have been included in the game play design as a part of interaction.
4. *Competition*: As in most MicroDYN the main constraint is to solve the task on time, nevertheless, the possibility to compete against another group using the total score at the end of the game is implemented in order to induce more fun and challenge.
5. *Story*: During the whole game the flow of the story is maintained and different microworlds are inferred in terms of puzzles. The story in the game is linear but challenges during the game play allow exciting social moments that are crucial in any collaborative game.
6. *Rules:* Semantics of microworld along with the game constraints make up the rules of the whole game. The game offers players opportunities to form social rules among the players themselves. For example in first puzzle players have to devise strategies to assist themselves to understand the semantics of puzzle faster.

2.3 Compromises Regarding Game Design

It should be noted that compromises had to be made to game design elements in order to preserve the MicroDYN elements. The project was primarily MicroDYN driven and all other aspects such as game and collaborations were add-ons to the MicoDYN approach. Some of the main compromises were as follows:

1. The Chronological order of the MicroDYN execution required players to explore the puzzle first, map it, and then implement their knowledge. On top of that, players did not have time constraints over the exploration phase which created difficulties in executing the game story smoothly. As such, no event can be implemented to trigger the end of exploration or mapping which leads the user astray from the story.
2. Mapping comes after or during the exploration phase and has no events attached. While rewards can be achieved it creates a sense of meaningless action in terms of game design. It gives no concrete feedback to the user and might create confusion.
3. Due to explorative nature of microworlds, competition against an artificial agent was not an option. Therefore, we decided to create competition against time. However, lack of balance of skills and challenge has been shown to disrupt flow. Similarly it also neutralized the risk v/s reward concept which is present in most games.
4. Puzzle solving and interactions were limited due to restrictions imposed by MicroDYN such as two to three inputs, linear relation and step-by-step execution.

Variations between the two puzzles were difficult to achieve which risked repetition in game play including lack of random unpredictable events which creates curiosity in players needed to foster motivation (Malone [16]).

Such compromises ensured that the comparability aspects of MicroDYN were preserved in an individual level. However, on a collaborative level game play, there lacks enough research on collaborative CPS or on MicroDYN to substantiate these design decisions.

3 Game Implementation

The game is being implemented using TULIP framework in java language 8.0. TULIP is a framework for building tangible tabletop applications [17]. A basic game flow diagram is presented below (Fig. 4).

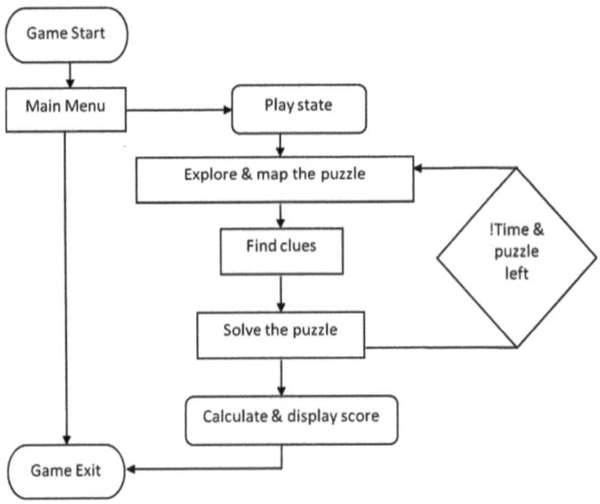

Fig. 4. Basic game flow diagram

4 Discussions and Future Work

The proposed game is not a complete MicroDYN test as it only implements one micro-world. Nevertheless, it provides possibilities to fully explore the potential of gaming approaches towards manifesting motivation in MicroDYN procedures. We believe that the compromise between MicroDYN and game design can be further explored to maintain motivation of the users. At the time of publication of this article a first empirical study was conducted to gather first experiences with this games-based approach for assessing collaborative CPS. The data analysis is still ongoing.

Collaborative CPS with innovative interactive technologies is a new research topic and requires dedicated further exploration. Furthermore, the collaborative gaming approach has not been sufficiently explored and lacks guidelines and case studies to strength the gaming concept and approach [18–20]. After analysing the feedback collected from experts during the design process and feedback from end users, we aim to document and substantiate the approach. Documentation will include guidelines to inform and assist such future design projects. Ras et al. [6] stated that current approaches for assessing collaborative CPS are limited because the agent-based approaches only simulate a collaborative interaction with other peers, instead of providing an authentic setting where peers are co-located physically to solve a problem.

References

1. Greiff, S., Wüstenberg, S., Funke, J.: Dynamic problem solving: a new measurement perspective. Appl. Psychol. Meas. **36**(3), 189–213 (2012)
2. Funke, J.: Dynamic systems as tools for analysing human judgement. Think. Reason. **7**, 69–89 (2001)
3. Papert, S.: Computer-based microworlds as incubators for powerful ideas. In: Taylor, R. (ed.) The Computer in the School: Tutor, Tool, Tutee, pp. 203–210. Teachers College Press, New York (1981)
4. Kröner, S., Plass, J.L., Leutner, D.: Intelligence assessment with computer simulations. Intelligence **33**(4), 347–368 (2005)
5. Knauff, M., Wolf, A.G.: Complex cognition: the science of human reasoning, problem-solving, and decision-making. Cogn. Process. **11**(2), 99–102 (2010)
6. Ras, E., Krkovic, K., Greiff, S., Tobias, E., Maquil, V.: Moving towards the assessment of collaborative problem solving skills with a tangible user interface. Turk. Online J. Educ. Technol. **3**(4), 95–104 (2014)
7. Ishii, H., Ullmer, B.: Tangible bits: towards seamless interfaces between people, bits and atoms. In: Proceedings of the ACM SIGCHI Conference on Human Factors in Computing Systems, pp. 234–241. ACM (1997)
8. Do-Lenh, S., Kaplan, F., Dillenbourg, P.: Paper-based concept map: the effects of tabletop on an expressive collaborative learning task. In: Proceedings of HCI 2009, pp. 149–158. ACM (2009)
9. Rogers, Y., Lim, Y.K., Hazlewood, W.R., Marshall, P.: Equal opportunities: do shareable interfaces promote more group participation than single user displays? Hum.-Comput. Interact. **24**(1–2), 79–116 (2009)
10. Dillenbourg, P., Evans, M.: Interactive tabletops in education. Int. J. Comput.-Support. Collab. Learn. **6**(4), 491–514 (2011)
11. Rick, J., Marshall, P., Yuill, N.: Beyond one-size-fits-all: how interactive tabletops support collaborative learning. In: Proceedings of IDC 2011, pp. 109–117. ACM (2011)
12. Scott, S.D., Carpendale, M.S.T., Inkpen, K.M.: Territoriality in collaborative tabletop workspaces. In: Proceedings of the 2004 ACM Conference on Computer Supported Cooperative Work, pp. 294–303. ACM (2004)
13. Zea, N.P., González Sánchez, J.L., Gutiérrez, F.L., Cabrera, M.J., Paderewski, P.: Design of educational multiplayer videogames: a vision from collaborative learning. Adv. Eng. Softw. **40**(12), 1251–1260 (2009)
14. Prensky, M.: Digital Game-Based Learning. McGraw-Hill, New York (2000)
15. Csikszentmihalyi, M.: Flow: The Psychology of Optimal Experience. Harper Perennial, New York (1990)
16. Malone, T.: Toward a theory of intrinsically motivating instruction. Cogn. Sci.: Multi. J. **54**, 333–369 (1981)

17. Tobias, E., Maquil, V., Latour, T.: TULIP: a widget-based software framework for tangible tabletop interfaces. In: Proceedings of the 2015 ACM SIGCHI Symposium on EICS, pp. 216–221. ACM, New York, NY, USA (2015)
18. Janssen, J., van der Meijden, H., Winkelmolen, M.: Collaborating in a 3D virtual world for culture and the arts. Metacognitive regulation in a 3D CSCL environment. Paper Presented at the 10th European Conference for Research in Learning and Instruction, Padova, Italy, pp. 26–30 (August 2003)
19. Klopfer, E., Perry, J., Scuire, K., Jan, M.-F., Steinkuehler, C.: Mystery at the museum—a collaborative game for museum education. In: Computer Support for Collaborative Learning: Learning 2005: The Next 10 Years! International Society of the Learning Sciences, pp. 316–320 (2005)
20. Hämäläinen, R.: Learning to collaborate: designing collaboration in a 3-D game environment. Internet Higher Educ. **9**, 47–61 (2006)

Comparative Judgment Within Online Assessment: Exploring Students Feedback Reactions

Anneleen V. Mortier[1(✉)], Marije Lesterhuis[2], Peter Vlerick[1], and Sven De Maeyer[2]

[1] Department of Personnel Management, Work and Organizational Psychology, Ghent University, Henri Dunantlaan 2, 9000 Ghent, Belgium
Anneleen.Mortier@UGent.be
[2] EduBROn, University of Antwerp, Venusstraat 35, 2000 Antwerp, Belgium

Abstract. Nowadays, comparative judgment (CJ) emerged as an alternative method for assessing competences and performances (e.g. Pollitt, 2012). In this method, various assessors compare independently several representations of different students and decide each time which of them demonstrate the best performance of the given competence. This study investigated students' attitudes (honesty, relevancy and trustworthiness) towards feedback that is based upon this method. Additionally, it studied the importance of specific tips in CJ-based feedback.

1 Introduction

Feedback on students competences is a valuable resource since it aims to facilitate learning and enhances their performance. In the educational practice, students often receive marks on their school tasks based on several predefined criteria. This implies that they were evaluated using absolute standards. Using this method, this might restrict feedback, since students mostly receive a generic mark. Additionally, personal influences such as personal beliefs or standards of the assessor can affect these assessments (Bejar 2012). Given these drawbacks, some authors argue in favor for an alternative assessment method, such as comparative judgment (CJ) (e.g. Pollitt 2012). In this method, various assessors compare independently several representations of different students and decide each time which of them demonstrate the best performance of the given competence. One of the strengths of this holistic approach is that it rules out the personal standards, leading to a higher consistency in judgments over different assessors (Bramley 2007; Pollitt 2012). Up until now, no research has been conducted on CJ-based feedback. Additionally, no research has investigated this type of feedback provided by an online tool. Since honest, relevant, and trustworthy feedback is vital for learning, the question arises how students will perceive CJ-based feedback. Additionally, we studied whether personalized tips are necessary for feedback acceptance and to facilitate learning.

E. Ras and D. Joosten-ten Brinke (Eds.): CAA 2015, CCIS 571, pp. 69–79, 2015.
DOI: 10.1007/978-3-319-27704-2_8

2 Theoretical Framework

Most of the times, performance is assessed using an analytical method, namely scoring rubrics. Those rubrics are a list consisting out of several criteria, which should map the assessing competence. Using the enlisted criteria, assessors are able to score students performance independently from each other and independently from previously assessed students. Afterwards, the scores on the criteria are combined, and the student receives a meta-score that should resemble his/her score for that performance on the assessed competence. However, this method has several issues (Pollitt 2012). Firstly, the competence is artificially divided into dimensions, assuming those dimensions to have strict boundaries, which is not the case. On the contrary, those dimensions often feel as overlapping, indicating that these boundaries are not so strict. Also, the whole competence is greater than the simple sum of its dimensions (Sadler 2009). Therefore, splitting the competence in different dimensions reduces information and the richness of that competence. Secondly, assessors report that they take other non-related aspects into account during their assessment. This is still the case even when they are trained or have more experience with the method (Crisp 2007). Lastly, it is argued that scoring also relies on making comparisons and thus, absolute judgment is not possible (Laming 2004).

Give these issues, (Pollitt 2004) argues to assess performance by making comparisons. Those comparisons should be made directly, since it is easier than giving a rating (Thurstone 1927). Using Comparative Judgment (CJ), several judges compare the competence representations (e.g. task or essay) of two students and decide overall which of them is the better. These comparisons are being repeated many times over many representations. Next, using the Bradley-Terry-Luce Model (Bradley and Terry 1952; Luce 1959), these comparisons are statistically translated into the odds of winning from one another (Pollitt 2012). Finally, these odds represent a measurement scale in which students representations are presented relatively to each other from worst to best performance (Bramley 2007).

One of the strengths of CJ is that it results in a high level of reliability because it depends on direct comparisons (Kimbell et al. 2009; Pollitt 2012). This addresses the need for more reliable measures, since the reliability of scoring seems to be problematic (van der Schaaf, Stokking and Verloop 2005). Another advantage of CJ is that it rules out assessors personal standards, because the final measurement scale is dependent on all judgments made by all judges. Thus, this scale represents the shared consensus of all the judges for the competence. Additionally, CJ seems to be a more favorable way to judge (Pollitt 2012), because comparing feels more natural (Laming 2004).

So far, previous scientific research mainly focused on the psychometric qualities of the CJ-method itself and on judges perception of this method. However, what is still lacking is how CJ-based results should be reported to students and how they perceive this feedback. Additionally, no research has been conducted on how students perceive this method itself. Indeed, if they find this method not trustworthy or honest, they will fail to accept CJ-based feedback and because of this, they will learn less (Anseel and Lievens 2009). Based upon this hiatus in the literature, we propose the following research questions:

Research question 1: Is feedback provided by an online tool using CJ perceived as honest?

Research question 2: Is feedback provided by an online tool using CJ perceived as relevant?

Research question 3: Is feedback provided by an online tool using CJ perceived as trustworthy?

Additionally, since the primary task of feedback is for individuals to learn, we also provided personalized tips to students based on their representations. However, pilot testing revealed that instructing judges to give additional arguments such as what is good about this paper, and what needs to be improved, increased the time for each judgment. This indicates that asking judges to provide extra details towards students, restricts the efficiency of the procedure. However, if these personalized tips seem necessary for feedback, this should be implemented in the judgment. Notwithstanding, this has not been investigated yet. Therefore, our last research question is:

Research question 4: Are personalized tips necessary when providing feedback based on CJ?

3 Research Methods

3.1 Setting up CJ

Participants and Essays. Hundred and thirty five students from 10 different secondary schools ranging all over Flanders (Belgium) were instructed to write three argumentative essays on different topics of equal difficulty. The order in which they had to write those tasks were randomized. Participants were all 5th year students with as main courses Economy and Languages. They had 25 min time to complete every task. Tasks were completed during school time and in the classroom. We provided feedback on only one task. All essays were digitalized by the research so that they could be electronically judged.

Judges. Sixty-five judges made the comparisons using an online tool (D-PAC). The sample of the judges consisted out of students teachers (n = 20), employed teachers tutoring language courses (n = 22), teacher trainers (n = 8), governmental officials from the Agency for Qualitative Assurance in Education and Training (n = 10), and some non-teaching professionals (n = 5). All judges were informed about the procedure and received information on the competence "argumentative writing", which they had to judge. This information was restricted to a 20 min session.

Procedure of Judging. Judges were invited to make the assessments at a PC-room at the University of Antwerp. This was done to give assistance if necessary, since our platform is newly developed and the usability of the system could be studied. The judges made comparisons for twice 3 h. During their assessment, they could make use of the instructions that were given to the students. Additionally, they possessed a description of what the student should master at the end of the last grade for the competence "argumentative writing". We chose to assess the representations at the level of the last grade, since this is the competence level students should possess to graduate, which is easier to judge.

Judgments were conducted as follows: two randomly chosen essays from two different students were presented side by side on a computer screen. These were always essays on the same topic. Judges were instructed to read them thoroughly. Next, they had to judge which one of both is perceived as best fitting the competence. This was done by clicking a button representing either "left is best" or "right is best".

Results of the CJ. Our 65 judges made a total of 1225 comparisons. On average, task 1 has been judged 18 times. The average time to complete 1 judgment was 2 min, 46 s. The ranking revealed a separation coefficient of 1.792. The separation coefficient is the ratio of the average spread of the quality parameters of the essays to the average amount of uncertainty in the position in the rank. A larger separation coefficient indicates that measurement error is a small proportion of the quality parameter. The alpha (analogous to Cronbach alpha) of the ranking was 0.783. This shows that the judges were rather consistent with each other in terms of standard and rank order.

Determining the Benchmark. Determining a benchmark on the ranking is vital for students to interpret the ranking. However, up until now, it is not clear how to build this in the CJ algorithm yet. Therefore, we decided to determine the benchmark after all the comparisons were completed. A group of experts was formed to determine the benchmark in the ranking. This group of experts consisted out of employed teachers, governmental officials from the Agency of Qualitative Assurance in Education and Training, teacher trainers, educational supervisors, and people that determine the competences of the final year. The benchmark was determined by what students should master at the end of the final 6th year of their secondary education. As all our study participants were 5th year students, most students failed to reach the benchmark.

Determining the Personalized Tips. When all comparisons were completed, a subset of judges were asked to read the papers that were selected for the interviews again and to formulate tips on what was good about the paper and what should be improved. We chose to not implement this during the comparative judgment itself, since it has not investigated yet how arguing affects judgments.

3.2 Setting up the Interviews

Sample. Of all the students that participated in writing the essays, a purposeful sample of 40 were chosen to participate in a semi-structured interview. Of this sample, 20 received the extra personalized tips. The other students did not receive this. Those 2 groups were matched in terms of school, place in the ranking, and the order they wrote the task. Based on this, the following subgroups were created: 12 students scoring low, 14 students scoring average, and 14 students scoring high. These subgroups were split in two that half of them received the extra personalized tips, whether the other half did not receive this.

Feedback Report. Students feedback report on the competence "argumentative writing" was constructed as follows: a short introduction to describe the setting and assure confidentiality. Next, a short description of the procedure of assessment, the assessed competence, and the accomplished task was given. Then, we provided descriptive information about the entire sample and who the judges were. Then, the results showed the ranking of all students. In this ranking, their representation of their essay was highlighted using a different color and shape (see Fig. 1). Additionally, the student's classmates were also represented in a different color. All the others that participated were light grayed, so that they appeared to be less relevant. The statistical derived reliability intervals were also light-grayed for the same reason. On this ranking, the benchmark was also represented, so that students could determine their pass or fail. It was made very clear that this benchmark reflected the required competence level to pass at the end of the final 6th year of their secondary education, as determined by subject matter experts.

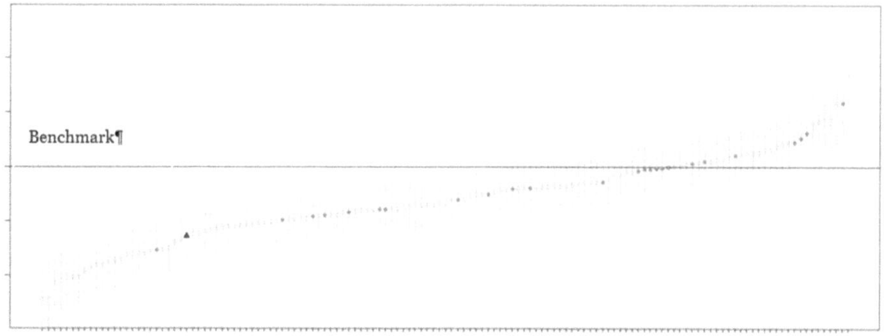

Fig. 1. Example ranking which was provided in the feedback report. The blue triangle represents the student, the orange dots represent the students' class mates, the grayed out dots represent all other students. Light gray vertical lines are confidence intervals. The black horizontal line represents the benchmark (Color figure online).

Next, for the students who received personalized tips, this enlisted into two categories: "positive aspects" and "aspects you still need to work on". All of the arguments that were given by the assessors were enlisted here. It was explained that it could be the case that certain aspects were a repetition because several judges stated this. Additionally, we also included their own task as a reminder of what they wrote. As last, we enclosed the paper that was revealed as the best paper from the comparisons on that particular topic. This allowed students to compare their task performance with the best performance, and should facilitate learning. Since the developed tool we used did not provide an electronic and automatic generated feedback report yet, each feedback report was constructed by the researchers and was presented on paper.

Conducting the Interviews. Feedback reports were handed over to each individual student during school hours and students went through this report independently. Next, a semi-structured interview was conducted to investigate the research questions mentioned above. Additionally, the duration that students needed to consult their report was recorded to assess feedback acceptance.

Coding the Interviews. Interviews were transcribed and coded following a thematic approach (Braun and Clarke 2006) using Nvivo 10 software. Codes were based upon the research questions they were related to (e.g. honest, trustworthy, and reliable). Subcodes were created based on the answers students provided. All subcodes informed us on why students perceived the reports honest, relevant, or trustworthy (or not). Analyses were conducted looking for differences and similarities among all students and between low-, middle- and high-scorers. For the last research question, the difference between students who received additional personalized tips and those students who did not were analyzed.

4 Results and Main Conclusions

Below, results and their interpretation are discussed in light of every research question. Allow us to explain the identification codes of students provided by citations with an example: studentLG0401. The first capital letter represents the position in the ranking (L = low, M = mean, H = high), the second capital letter represents whether the student received specific tips (G = only general feedback, S = specific tips). Then, the first two numbers (04) represent the school, the last two numbers (01) represent the student.

Research question 1: Is feedback provided by an online tool using CJ perceived as honest?

We asked students whether they found the CJ as an honest way to be assessed. This is important, because if they do not accept the method as being honest, they will not accept the feedback that is derived from that result. In general, they perceived this method as honest: 53 arguments were given pro, 17 arguments were given contra. The argument that was used the most was: "One is simply better than the other. I think it is also easier in order to make a ranking by ordering the worst to the best" (studentHS0913). Also, students indicated that the assessment was the same for everyone: "Everyone is assessed in the same manner. So, if everyone is evaluated using the same method, this is always fair" (studentMS0406). Another argument that was used for perceived fairness was the judges: "because a lot of people judged it" (studentHS0916), "they will say the same thing for everyone, if something is wrong, they will say so" (studentMG0415), and: "judges are honest about their judgments" (studentHS0410). Lastly, they argued that: "It was done anonymously. Judges could not judge other students differently, because they do not know who we are" (studentMS0413).

When breaking the ranking up, we see that students that are performing low gave more arguments against the honesty of the procedure. They argued that: "my score is depended on my class" (studentLG0501). Also, someone argued that: "teachers know what you are capable of, they also take your previous performance into account" (studentLG0501). This indicates that anonymity is perceived as both a positive asset of the procedure, since the judges will judge everyone the same. However, since judges do not know who is who, the learning curve of that student cannot be taken into account when making the assessment, and this is perceived negatively by students who have a large learning potential available.

Students that have a high score, gave only 2 arguments why the assessment was not fair: "all those judges cannot have the same vision; all of them thinking the same thing, that is not realistic" (studentHS0417). This statement reflects a misunderstanding of the procedure. Therefore, we consider to explain the procedure even in more detail in future assessments. Another argument was: "with this method, you either pass or fail. Using scores can show you that you are doing ok, but maybe less than the top performer. But here it is really: you are the best or you are the worst. So it is not so fair for people who perform weakly" (studentHG0404). This statement indicates that people, especially secondary school pupils, are used to thinking in terms of scores. However, this remark also expresses the need for a better defined ranking: now, students' ranking only presented a benchmark as performance indicator: you are either passed or you are failed. There is no other indication of either "acing" the test, dramatically failing the test, or anything in between that. Further research should investigate how this request for more differentiated feedback is reconcilable with the CJ-assessment method and how this can be communicated to assessees.

Research question 2: Is feedback provided by an online tool using CJ perceived as relevant?

To investigate this research question, we asked students whether they thought that the information they received was relevant. Overall, 9 specific arguments were given on parts of the feedback report that were perceived as irrelevant, whether 42 specific arguments were given for parts of the feedback report that were relevant. The part that was mostly perceived as irrelevant was the general information: the procedure, judges sample and assessee sample. Two students indicated that when they read this information in the beginning of the feedback report, they did not know what this information meant, since they expected feedback ("when reading it at the start, I was confused, because it did not really look like feedback" - studentLS0517). One student explained that (s)he did not like the statistics in the feedback report. Lastly, one student claimed that (s)he found the example best essay redundant. This student was one of the high performers. All stated that the graph and benchmark were relevant. Sixteen students argued that the procedure was relevant to read: "I found it very interesting to know how the assessment took place" (studentMS0804).

Then, when inspecting the arguments for lower performing students, the only specific argument that was given was: "it is good that we can compare our results with others" (studentLG0512). There were 6 specific argument on non-relevant parts of the feedback report, which were mainly the same as previously mentioned.

Concerning the general information, there are some mixed feelings: some students indicated that this was very boring to read and irrelevant. Others found it very interesting to read and to know how their essays were judged. This did not depend on their position in the ranking: low performances gave 2 arguments pro and 4 contra, high performers gave 3 arguments pro and 1 contra. Thus, we can conclude that in future feedback reports, assessees should receive the option to read extra information on the whole procedure.

Research question 3: Is feedback provided by an online tool using CJ perceived as trustworthy?

To determine whether students found the feedback trustworthy, we also asked whether they found the procedure trustworthy. Their views on the procedure are linked with their feedback, since this is an immediate result of the procedure. In general, students perceived CJ as a reliable method: 63 arguments were given why it is reliable, and 16 arguments were given why it was not reliable. Main arguments that were given to support trustworthiness were: comparison ("When comparing tasks, it is easier to spot the differences between what is correct and what is wrong I think." - studentHS0913), the amount and the schooling of the assessors ("I think it is more reliable because several people are judging this, instead of only 1" - studentMS0413; "The judges were people who know something about that topic" - studentHG0410), and that it was conducted anonymously ("We were judged by people who do not know us. So you will not be judged based on personal characteristics" - studentHS0416).

The main arguments for perceiving the method as unreliable were: it was not representative ("The top of our class is still beneath the threshold, so.. If we are supposed to reach the threshold by the end of the next year. It is impossible, we are nearly at the end of the term." - studentLG0512), and uncertainty of how the judges assessed their competences: "it depends on how they judged our essay" (studentMS0409), "It depends if someone read my essay fast and then just clicked away fast" (studentMG0911). These arguments are originated in a certain fear of not meeting the benchmark at the end of the final year, and in the unknowing of how the judges assessed their essays.

All of these arguments support the notion that students should be guided when receiving such a feedback report. It could be the case that they have a wrong interpretation of the procedure, thus leading to false beliefs which might affect the interpretation of the feedback report. If the feedback report is perceived negatively based on those false beliefs, this could even diminish the learning potential of the feedback report. Therefore, we advocate to guide students through such a report, so that they have a correct interpretation. Additionally, it would also help students if they could contact people to help and interpret the feedback report, to get more feedback, or even to ask certain things to judges, as one student indicated: "If I disagree with my teacher, I always ask him for more information, and have a dialogue with him. But now, this is very hard, I cannot summon all judges to ask them something" (studentGS0409).

Research question 4: Are personalized tips necessary when providing feedback based on CJ?

For our last research question, we inspected the answers of the two groups (personalized tips versus only general information). The largest difference between those groups is that people who received personalized tips, used this as an argument why the feedback is reliable and honest ("There were arguments showing why it was good and why it was not good. This makes it more convincing" - studentHS0402). Also, almost all students that received the personalized tips found this very relevant: "Definitely the arguments where they said what was good and what was not that good were good. This is also useful for future essays" (studentMS0413).

We also asked whether the students felt like they have learned something from their feedback report. When students received specific feedback, they argued more that they have learned from this than the students that only received the general part. This is striking, since both groups received an example paper (= the paper of the best student in the ranking), for learning purposes. However, students argued that this paper will not contribute to their learning, because "writing is something personal" (studentHS0917), "this is too long to read" (studentHG0403), "every essay is different" (studentGS0918), "I cannot really see what I did wrong from this text"(studentMG0415).

Another important thing to note is that, students had a one-on-one interview. This means that students that already had done the interview, and received their feedback report almost always shared this with their peers to compare. Therefore, almost all of them knew that some of them received personalized tips. Students who were in the general condition and then received their feedback report, almost always asked for their personalized tips: "Everything is interesting and useful, especially those tips, but I did not receive them?" (studentHG0404) Also, one student claimed that "I did not receive my feedback report" (studentHG0403).

Given all this, our results show that these personalized tips are indeed necessary in a feedback report. Not only to facilitate learning, but also to interpret the feedback and to perceive the procedure as reliable and honest.

5 Implications to Research and Practice

Our study aimed to give insight on how students perceive feedback based upon the CJ-method. The study results and study limitations allow us to formulate important implications for practice.

Firstly, it is shown that, overall, students consider CJ-based feedback as reliable, relevant, and honest. These are important findings and suggest the relevance and potential of this assessment method and for generating feedback in practice. When doing so, one should make sure that assessees are familiarized with the procedure and should be guided through the feedback report. This should avoid misunderstandings that might influence feedback perceptions and prevent learning.

Secondly, our results showed that personalized tips on how to improve performance are greatly needed and should thus be incorporated in feedback reports. Since the study participants recognized themselves in these tips and considered them as relevant, we expect that CJ-based feedback might enhance learning in practice.

Thirdly, the results also indicate and reconfirm humans' need for a quantitative score. So far, CJ only generated results that are based on comparisons. Assessees can interpret from the ranking if they are better than a certain amount of other assessees, yet they do not know what this actually means. As seen in the results, a summative part is vital to comprehend how they have performed. Therefore, CJ should find a way to incorporate this into this procedure, since it does not have anything like this at this point. Even the benchmark, which we have defined after completing the CJ, should already be a challenge to incorporate in the algorithm. Additionally, it should also be investigated what the impact is of implementing this for assessors: will this decrease the efficiency of judgments and perhaps have an impact on hollistic judging?

Our study also has implications for further research.

Firstly, although we demonstrated that students felt that they have learned something from their feedback report, further follow-up measurement of their feedback reactions and learning behavior is desirable. To what extent do their reported intentions and feedback perceptions result in actual behavioral change in task or school performance? Answering these type of research questions might demonstrate, among others, the predictive validity of the use of personalized tips in feedback reports.

A second interesting strand of further research consists of studying the generalizability of CJ-based feedback reactions and perceptions regarding the CJ-method in other samples than secondary school students. For instance, do adults, higher education students, and students that differ from the norm (e.g. children with dyslexia) hold different perceptions on CJ?

Summarizing, the study described above has illustrated that CJ-method can be embedded in online assessment of students competences such as their argumentative writing. Moreover, we showed that CJ-based feedback is a potential fruitful way to ameliorate students learning. We hope this study might encourage further research on limitations, strengths, and the practical implication of the CJ-method within the online assessment of human competences.

References

Anseel, F., Lievens, F.: The mediating role of feedback acceptance in the relationship between feedback and attitudinal and performance outcomes. Int. J. Sel. Assess. **17**(4), 362–376 (2009). doi:10.1111/j.1468-2389.2009.00479.x

Bejar, I.I.: Rater cognition: implications for validity. Educ. Meas. Issues Pract. **31**(3), 2–9 (2012). doi:10.1111/j.1745-3992.2012.00238.x

Bradley, R.A., Terry, M.E.: Rank analysis of incomplete block designs, 1. the method of paired comparisons. Biometrika **39**, 324–345 (1952). doi:10.2307/2334029

Bramley, T.: Paired comparisons methods. In: Newton, P., Baird, J.-A., Goldstein, H., Patrick, H., Tymms, P. (eds.) Techniques for Monitoring the Comparability of Examination Standards, pp. 246–294. Qualification and authority, London (2007)

Braun, V., Clarke, V.: Using thematic analysis in psychology. Qual. Res. Psychol. **3**(2), 77–102 (2006). doi:10.1191/1478088706qp063oa

Crisp, V.: Do assessors pay attention to appropriate features of student work when making assessment judgments? Paper presented at the International Association for Educational Assessment, Annual Conference, Baku, Azerbaijan (2007)

Kimbell, R., Wheeler, T., Stables, K., Shepard, T., Davies, D., Martin, F., Pollitt, A., Whitehouse, G.: E-scape portfolio assessment: phase 3 report. University of London, Goldsmiths College(2009)

Laming, D.: Human Judgment: The Eye of the Beholder. Thomson Learning, London (2004)

Luce, R.D.: Individual Choice Behaviors: A Theoretical Analysis. Wiley, New York (1959)

Pollitt, A.: Lets stop marking exams. Paper presented at the International Association for Educational Assessment, Annual Conference, Philadelphia, United States of America (2004)

Pollitt, A.: The method of adaptive comparative judgment. Assess. Educ. Principles Policy Pract. **19**(3), 1–20 (2012). doi:10.1080/0969594X.2012.665354

Sadler, D.R.: Transforming holistic assessment and grading into a vehicle for complex learning. In: Joughin, G. (ed.) Assessment, Learning, and Judgment in Higher Education, pp. 1–19. Springer, Netherlands (2009)

Thurstone, L.L.: The law of comparative judgment. Psychol. Rev. **34**(4), 273–286 (1927). doi:10.1037/h0070288

van der Schaaf, M.F., Stokking, K.M., Verloop, N.: Cognitive representations in raters assessment of teacher portfolios. Stud. Educ. Eval. **31**, 27–55 (2005). doi:10.1016/j.stueduc.2005.02.005

Automatically Generated Metrics for Multilingual Inline Choice Questions on Reading Comprehension

Alain Pfeiffer, Anna Kuraeva, Muriel Foulonneau, Younès Djaghloul, Eric Tobias, and Eric Ras(✉)

Luxembourg Institute of Science and Technology, IT for Innovative Services, 5, Avenue des Hauts-Fourneaux, 4362 Esch-sur-Alzette, Luxembourg
{alain.pfeiffer, anna.kuraeva, muriel.foulonneau, younes.djaghloul, eric.ras}@list.lu

Abstract. Assessment Item Generation (AIG) aims at creating semi-automatically many items from a template. This type of approaches has been used in various domains, including language learning and mathematics to support adaptation of tests to learners or allow the item authoring process to scale through decreasing the cost of items. We illustrate in this paper the automatic creation of inline choice items for reading comprehension skills using state-of-the-art approaches. However we show how the AIG process can be implemented to support the creation of items in multiple languages (English, French, and German) and how it can be complemented by the creation of item quality metrics to improve the selection of the generated items.

Keywords: Assessment item generation · Inline choice items · Cloze questions · Reading comprehension · Distractors · Text readability · Item quality

1 Introduction

Reading comprehension is a core skill that is to be evaluated in school systems for native and foreign language learning. It is part of the skills assessed in the context of PISA[1] and is, as a component of information literacy, part of the 21st Century Skills. It can be measured through various types of items, including choice questions on a text and cloze questions which alter the text itself. In the European FP7 project EAGLE[2] we work on the development of test items for information literacy skills following the ACRL framework [1]. In the Interlingua[3] project we develop test items to support cross-language learning through vocabulary and reading comprehension questions. In both contexts we focus on vocabulary and reading comprehension questions. In order to adapt to the reading context of users, we are developing a multilingual assessment item generation (AIG) module which supports the generation of inline choice items in

[1] http://www.oecd.org/pisa/.
[2] http://www.eagle-learning.eu/.
[3] http://www.interlingua-project.eu/.

E. Ras and D. Joosten-ten Brinke (Eds.): CAA 2015, CCIS 571, pp. 80–95, 2015.
DOI: 10.1007/978-3-319-27704-2_9

English, French, and German. It aims to generate inline choice questions for measuring reading comprehension from any type of texts.

Cloze questions have been used extensively for measuring for instance vocabulary skills [2], grammatical knowledge [3], as well as reading comprehension [4]. We focus on inline choice questions, which include distractors. The main challenges which have to be tackled to generate such items are related to (1) the choice of critical sentences in the text to identify sense-making parts from which to create the gaps, (2) gap selection in the selected sentences, and (3) the generation of distractors.

AIG processes have mainly been implemented for choice questions (e.g., [5]) and cloze questions (e.g., [2]). However, in most cases the AIG process does not follow a pedagogic approach [6]. Moreover, item creation is perceived as an art rather than a science [6]. By implementing an assessment item generation process, we also need to define clear requirements and measurable components that make a good item. While Haladyna et al. [7] provide guidelines for choice questions, we need to select specific rules that can be computed and then measured. A major limitation of the assessment generation process is the relatively low percentage of directly usable items produced in most cases (e.g., 3.5 % in [8]). However, engineering the item generation process can provide metrics related to the various components of the item. We, therefore, aim to provide a set of additional metrics. Our hypothesis is that (1) metrics can support the item authors in following best practices defined for the authoring of items, (2) they can help analyse item authoring practices, and (3) they can help predict the quality of the provided item and the educational context in which items are best suited. Those metrics can be applied to both automatically and manually generated items.

We have defined a set of requirements for the creation of inline choice questions for reading comprehension. We have then tested various approaches to implement the best possible system for the generation of these items (i.e., fill in blanks with options for each gap). We then present an evaluation of the various components of the system and metrics that can be attached to this type of items.

2 Related Research

The generation of inline choice items requires the following stages: (1) identifying relevant sentences from which creating gaps: those need to be important for the reading comprehension since the construct is reading comprehension, (2) the identification of a relevant part of the sentence to create a gap, (3) the creation of relevant distractors. We then need to assess the value of the item for a particular type of candidates. We, therefore, attempt to quantify relevant parameters that impact item difficulty in the context of reading comprehension (Fig. 1).

2.1 The Identification of Gaps in the Text

The first step consists in identifying the parts of the text that affect understanding at most or represent at best the meaning of the text. Shah [9] and Becker et al. [10] propose to first summarise the input to identify key sentences with automatic summarisation algorithms.

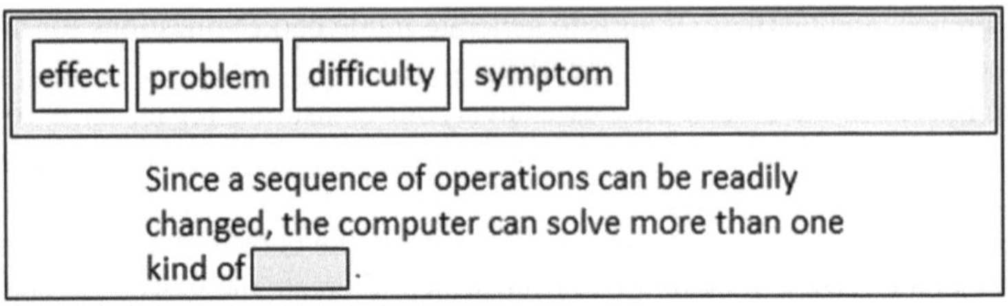

Fig. 1. Example inline choice item from the TAO interface (http://www.taotesting.com/get-tao/live-demos/).

The second step consists in the identification of relevant gaps in those sentences. Between 2011 and 2012 Mostow et al. [4], Heilman [11], and Iwata et al. [12] focused on generating questions out of any text for the purpose of text comprehension using NLP and machine learning techniques. Agarwal et al. [13], Agarwal [14] analysed the usefulness of discourse connectives for question generation of text inputs. Wu et al. [15] implemented an automatic grammar checker using N-grams to correct preposition-verb errors at run-time for English learning purposes in 2013.

We use summarization mechanisms and Part-of-Speech identification to identify relevant gaps for reading comprehension items.

2.2 Distractor Generation

In choice items and cloze questions including options, such as inline choice items, a core difficulty is represented by the generation of distractors, i.e., incorrect option which should be credible alternatives to the correct answer option [16]. The random selection of siblings in the semantic graph can provide relevant distractors [17, 18]. In domain model based approaches, Foulonneau and Grouès [19] apply semantic similarity metrics for improving the generation of distractors based on the graph structure of the domain model, while Mitkov et al. [8] compare approaches based on semantic (WordNet-based) and distributional similarity (i.e., occurrence in similar contexts in a corpus). In text-based item generation, Brown et al. [2] select single word term distractors from word frequency analysis, while Mitkov et al. [20] and Gütl et al. [21] identify semantic relations from the WordNet lexical dataset. For grammatical distractors, Chen et al. [3] define rules to modify the form and tense of a word. In order to select multi-word distractors, Mitkov et al. [20] select noun-phrases with the same head as the answer, while Gütl et al. [21] split the phrase into n-grams and randomly select the longest related n-grams in a phrase using WordNet. Finally, Aldabe and Maritxalar [22] propose using Latent Semantic Analysis (LSA), while Moser et al. [23] propose extending this approach in particular with an analysis of Stylometry [24].

Existing approaches usually allow for a preselection of candidate distractors. However, semantically similar distractors to the correct response for instance can be so close that they are also valid answers. It is also important that the distractors are not valid. Therefore, the distractors need to be credible alternatives but cannot be correct replacements for the gap key. Huang et al. [25] for instance discard synonyms and hypernyms using WordNet. Other approaches are based on the occurrence of the distractor in context in a particular corpus [26]. Smith et al., [27] demonstrated a tool called TEDDCloG[4] (Testing English with Data-Driven CLOze Generation), which finds distractors in a distributional thesaurus (UKWaC corpus, including 1,5 billion-words) and identifies a sentence including the key but for which no occurrence is found in the thesaurus when replacing the key with the distractors. Finally Zesch and Melamud [28] initially search for distractors with the same POS tag [29]. First they use context-insensitive rules, to create a distractor candidate set. They then use context-sensitive rules to generate a distractor black list taking into consideration the carrier sentence.

We use distributional similarity as a mechanism to optimise the generation of distractors because it provides a mechanism to support names and proper nouns in multiple languages. In addition, we apply rules related to item difficulty, dispersity, and specific matching rules in order to improve the distractor quality.

2.3 Features of Assessment Items that Impact Item Difficulty

Item quality is a critical issue for generated items. Most AIG creators assess the effectiveness of their system through a manual evaluation of "directly usable" items, i.e. one or more persons are asked to assess how many items could be used without edit or with minor edit [8]. However, usable items need to be assigned to particular educational contexts, i.e. difficulty and usefulness of the assessment of a particular construct for a particular population.

Gierl and Lai [6] propose to use item generation process engineering mechanisms to support the identification of psychometric properties at the template authoring stage for choice items. They distinguish between isomorphic items and non-isomorphic items. Isomorphic items are produced by a template that has variables which are only incidental to the construct. Items created from such templates have similar psychometric properties which can then be indicative for all items created from the same template if one item has been calibrated. Nevertheless, for non-isomorphic items calibration is so far necessary for all items. Gierl and Lai [30] suggest that when a cognitive model exists for the tasks that underlie the item template then it is possible to predict psychometric properties. However, such models seldom exist.

Another approach consists in analysing the parameters that affect item difficulty. This depends on the type of construct and the type of item under consideration.

Little research has been dedicated to identifying the core elements in an item that can explain its difficulty and, therefore, its suitable educational context, i.e. the expected audience. Sonnleitner [31] proposes the LLTM model (*Linearen Logistischen Test-Modells*) to identify partially the elements that contribute to the difficulty of items based on the LLTM model. However, the measure of the identified parameters has not been automated. Pho et al. [32] have applied text difficulty metrics to assessment items. This is particularly relevant to reading comprehension items. Foulonneau and Groués

[4] http://www3.nccu.edu.tw/~smithsgj/teddclog.html.

[19] propose using the semantic similarity of distractors to predict the difficulty of test items. They, however, only apply those metrics distractor similarity metrics to choice items. In this paper we propose using metrics to describe inline choice questions for measuring reading comprehension skills.

3 Inline Choice Item Generation

We have built a system to generate inline choice questions for reading comprehension in English, French, and German and a mechanism to assign metrics that can help item authors determine or predict item usability and difficulty. In this section we describe the assessment item generation system.

3.1 Gap Identification in the Text

To identify important sentences that impact reading comprehension, a summariser API is used. Three freely available multi-language summarisation systems, namely OpenTextSummarizer (OTS)[5], AutoSummarizer (AS)[6], and Classifier4J (C4J)[7] have been compared. With the AS summariser, which uses extraction-based summarisation, still in a beta phase and Rasheed[8] and Sujit[9] stating that both OTS and C4J are similar in summary quality using English entries, we decided to use C4J as summary library because it is available in a stable version for JAVA, contrary to OTS.

Gaps and their keys are selected from the sentences in the summary. Depending on the language of the text, three different part of speech taggers from the Stanford POS tagger API[10] are used to extract nouns or verbs. The language models for the POS tagger are included in the download package. Candidate gaps are then identified in the important sentences, as defined by the summariser.

3.2 Distractor Creation

We use the DISCO API (extracting DIStributionally related words using CO-occurrences)[11] to retrieve candidate distractors. It relies on distributional similarity algorithms as described in [33]. We first exclude distractors with a bad distributional similarity to the key. The distributional similarity is different from the semantic similarity. Semantic similarity is based on lexical resources such as WordNet. Distributional similarity is based on the assumption that words with similar meaning occur in similar contexts.

---

[5] http://libots.sourceforge.net/.

[6] http://autosummarizer.com/.

[7] http://classifier4j.sourceforge.net/index.html.

[8] http://www.researchgate.net/publication/262375542_Automatic_Text_Summarizer.

[9] http://sujitpal.blogspot.com/2009/02/summarization-with-lucene.html.

[10] http://nlp.stanford.edu/software/tagger.shtml.

[11] http://www.linguatools.de/disco/disco.html.

We then exclude distractors which are on the one hand the singular or plural of a key (e.g. house/houses) and discard distractors which contain the key (e.g. house/housewife) with a stemming algorithm. A Soundex algorithm removes phonetic similar words (e.g. sun/son). Then, we discard distractors which, grammatically, do not fit in the gap. We have to place each remaining distractor in the gap and check if they match. To verify grammatical fit, we use the Stanford Dependency API (Group, Stanfrod Dependencies, 2014). At this stage, candidate distractors are related to the key and have the same grammatical structure as the key. Still, a distractor can have the same grammatical structure as a key but the article of the key may not match the one of the distractor. This is important in both French and German. Particularly in German, articles change with grammatical cases, e.g.:

- Article: das
- Key: Haus
- Distractors: Hütte, Unterkunft, Gebäude

The following distractors (Hütte, Unterkunft, Gebäude) for the German key "Haus" are semantically related to the key but on a closer examination the article "das" does not fit grammatically with the words "Hütte" and "Unterkunft". To correct such errors, we use Google n-grams[12], more specifically, we query their web interface automatically, to increase the accuracy of distractors (similar to Becker et al. [10] for prepositions). The Google N-gram Viewer page offers a feature that outputs articles for an entered word (as presented for the German word "Haus" in Fig. 2). Due to the fact that we are restricted on a maximum of 80 queries by the interface, we can correct 80 distractors by simply checking if the article in the text is included in the list of articles the Google Ngram Viewer delivers.

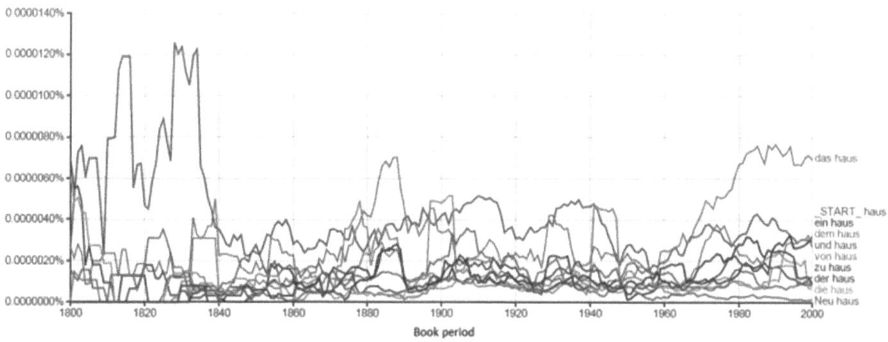

Fig. 2. Google N-grams viewer interface: n-gram articles for the German word \Haus" by entering *Haus" on the Google Ngram Viewer page

Nevertheless, the Kneser-Ney N-Gram language model would increase the distractor quality dramatically, because we would no longer be limited to 80 requests on

[12] https://books.google.com/ngrams.

the Google N-gram Viewer. Another approach would be to look up the words' article in a dictionary. However, the time needed to generate distractors would then partly depend on the Internet bandwidth. Another possibility would be to use a local dictionary. Due to the DISCO and Stanford models in use, a local dictionary would further increase the memory requirements. In contrary to n-grams which could be used for article correction, formative feedback and preposition correction, the dictionary would only be used for article correction, hence, would not be an optimal solution either.

4 Attaching Metrics to the Inline Choice Items

Inline choice questions are based on texts. The construct on reading comprehension suggests that text difficulty metrics are relevant as a factor of item difficulty. Like choice items, the structure of each gap and the relation between the distractors and the correct answers can impact item difficulty. We, therefore, focus on both types of metrics, i.e., distractor analysis and text difficulty.

4.1 Text Difficulty Metrics

The difficulty of texts, or text readability expresses how accessible a text is for the target population. As of today, there exists a wide range of matrices on how to measure text's difficulty in various languages. François highlights three periods in texts difficulty assessment: classic studies, the structurocognitivist paradigm, and the AI readability [34].

The best-known readability formulas (all for English) are Washburne and Vogel [35], Dale and Chall [36], and Flesch Reading Ease [37]. The latter, with its Flesch-Kincaid variation (the result of the formula is the school grade corresponding to the text's difficulty level), are still in wide use.

Flesch Reading Ease (FRE) score ranges from 0 to 100, where 0 is very difficult and 100 is very easy. The Flesch formula was adapted to several languages, notably as Kandel and Moles [38] formula for French and Amstad Readability Index [39] for German.

Modern readability formulas, independent of the language they are designed for, usually include an analysis of the text from either the lexical, the syntactic, or the semantic level.

The lexical level includes predictors as word frequency, word length and lexical diversity (often measured with type-token ratio (TTR) and frequency lists). The syntactic level, or grammatical complexity, usually includes sentence length and verbal forms with some verbal forms e.g. tenses, participles, or gerundives being more difficult to grasp than the others. The semantic level may include the level of personalisation (some studies proved that texts that address the reader with the second person singular is easier to understand) and the coherence and cohesion of the text. Certain studies (Dale and Tyler [40]) showed that texts written in informal style (increased use of second person singular) are easier to read. As for the metrics of coherence and cohesion, studies suggest that interphrasic coherence as well as the text's cohesion makes it easier to read [41, 42].

For inline choice items we propose metrics for all three levels, lexical, syntactic, and semantic. We have implemented metrics for each language. In Table 1 the arrows indicate the correlation of the predictor (direct ↑ or inverse ↓) to difficulty.

Table 1. Difficulty predictors for various languages

	French	English	German
	Kandel&Moles formula ↓	Flesch Reading Ease ↓	Amstad Readability index ↓
Lexical level	PA_Alteregola % ↑	PA_Alteregola % ↑	PA_Alteregola % ↑
	PA_Gougenheim_2000 % ↑	PA_COCA_2000 %↑	PA_uni-leipzig. de_2000 % ↑
	TTR_lemmas % ↓	TTR_without_lemmas % ↓	TTR_without_lemmas % ↓
Semantic level	Reference % ↓	Reference % ↓	Reference % ↓
	Conjunction % ↓	Conjunction % ↓	Conjunction % ↓
	Identification % ↓	Identification % ↓	Identification % ↓
Syntactic level	Number of Sentences longer than 30 ↑	Number of Sentences longer than 30 ↑	Number of Sentences longer than 30 ↑

For items in French, we propose the following metrics: *PA_Alteregola, PA_Gougenheim_2000, TTR based on lemmas, Number of Sentences longer than 30,* that we supplemented with the predictors of text cohesion: *Reference, Conjunction* and *Identification* as described in [42] as well as with *Kandel and Moles*' formula.

PA_Alteregola is a percentage of absence from the list of words given at the end of Alter Ego 1a textbook. In the experiment of François this predictor, correlated in direct proportion to difficulty, was proved to show the best correlation in regard to difficulty [43].

PA_Gougenheim_2000 is a frequency list-based predictor. Following the approach of François, we took the first 2000 words out of 8774 that the list originally contains. In the 1950s Georges Gougenheim created the list of most frequent words in French language. At first it contained 1475 words, where 1222 were lexical and 253 grammatical. Afterwards the list was complemented [44]. The original corpus was created out of oral interviews recordings with 275 people. It includes 163 texts, 312135 words and 7995 different lemmas. To count the absences from this list we lemmatised the words. We deliberately did not get rid of repetitions. We count each word's repetition as the new word's absence.

TTR based on lemmas. This is a classic indicator used to determine lexical diversity of the text. It is counted as

$$TTM = \left(\frac{number\ of\ types}{number\ of\ tokens}\right) * 100$$

where tokens are total of text's words of the text and types are unique words without repetitions.

LSDaoust. Percentage of sentences longer than 30 words. The length of sentence is another classic predictor that reflects difficulty: it was proven that longer sentences make a text more difficult. We selected '30' as a threshold following the results obtained by François [43, 45].

Kandel and Moles formula is a simple adaptation of Flesch Reading Ease formula for the French language.

The predictors of cohesion, such as *Reference, Conjunction* and *Identification* are described in Zeid et al. [42]. The influence of text cohesion on its difficulty is revealed in numerous studies, notably by Halliday and Hasan in [41]. Halliday and Hasan distinguish between lexical and grammatical cohesion. *Reference, Conjunction* and *Identification* belong to grammatical cohesion and are implemented based on lists of terms. *Reference* represents the 3rd person pronouns and the demonstrative pronouns [42]. They can be ana- and cataphoric. To calculate references, Zeid et al. count the mentioned pronouns and reports them to the total number of words in the text. *Conjunctions* are another dimension of text cohesion. The proportion of conjunctions is counted by reporting their number to the total number of words. Our list of French conjunctions was taken from M. Grevisse et A. Goosse, Le Bon Usage: grammaire française [46].

Identifications are recognized with the help of indefinite articles and determinants that indicate the noun mentioned previously (ex.: *I read a book. This book was written by a famous author).* By comparing the number of nouns that follow indefinite articles and reporting it to the number of nouns that follow the determinants, it is possible to count the number identifications. The proportion is counted by reporting this result to the total number of words.

4.2 Gap Disparity

The automatically generated distractors, are related to the key, i.e., the correct answer, as in the following example: Key: *computer*; Distractors: *hardware, software, and workstation*. The distractors hardware, software, and workstation have the following distributional similarities to the key computer:

- computer – hardware (0.711)
- computer – software (0.593)
- computer – workstation (0.579)

In addition to the listed similarities to the key above, we measure how related the distractors are to each other [18]. We compute a so-called dispersity value. It represents the distributional similarity or heterogeneity between options. The resulting value is an average distance and lies between 0 and 1.

The dispersity of a gap *D(G)* is computed as the average distances between options:

$$D(G) = \frac{\sum d(Option,\ Option)}{Count(Option)}$$

5 Experimentation with the System

In order to assess these metrics proposed for inline choice items we conducted an experiment with both automatically generated and manually created items. We selected texts in our three target languages: English, French, and German and generated inline choice items and related metrics: text difficulty metrics for the original texts, without gaps, and a specific text difficulty metric, word scarcity, for individual distractors and gap disparity metrics. We then asked three people to create distractors manually for English and French and two people for the German distractors. We compared the metrics obtained along two dimensions: their difference across language and in manually created vs. automatically generated items.

5.1 The Text Corpus for the Creation of Test Items

The corpus consists of 9 texts divided into 3 text sets in 3 languages. The first text set is short (around 1 page) texts in English, French, and German taken from parallel Wikipedia articles called *PC*[13]. The length of the texts is 17 sentences for French, 26 sentences for English and 17 sentences for German. The second set is composed of long texts (from 4 to 6 pages) taken from parallel Wikipedia articles called *Roman Empire*[14] in English, French, and German. The length of the texts is 123 sentences for French, 126 sentences for English, and 128 sentences for German. The third set consists in administrative texts, in all 3 languages, taken from the Labour Code[15]. The length of texts is 60 sentences in French, 67 sentences in English, and 53 sentences in German.

5.2 Manual and Automatic Creation of Gaps and Distractors

The following indication was given to the creators of the distractors: "Our objective is to create gap match items automatically from a text to measure reading comprehension. We are not measuring factual knowledge. We are not measuring language skills (e.g., grammar). We expect you to provide a set of 3 good distractors per gap. The items are cloze questions (fill in gaps) with 3 distractors (incorrect answer options) for each gap."

---

[13] Computer. http://en.wikipedia.org/wiki/Computer.
Computer. http://de.wikipedia.org/wiki/Computer.
Ordinateur. http://fr.wikipedia.org/wiki/Ordinateur. Accessed: 27 Feb. 2015.

[14] Roman Empire. http://en.wikipedia.org/wiki/Roman_Empire.
Römische Kaiserzeit. http://de.wikipedia.org/wiki/R%C3%B6mische_Kaiserzeit.
Empire romain. http://fr.wikipedia.org/wiki/Empire_romain. Accessed: 27 Feb. 2015.

[15] http://www.guichet.public.lu/entreprises/en/ressources-humaines/fin-relation-travail/licenciement-resiliation/licencier-preavis/.
http://www.guichet.public.lu/entreprises/de/ressources-humaines/fin-relation-travail/licenciement-resiliation/licencier-preavis/.
http://www.guichet.public.lu/entreprises/fr/ressources-humaines/fin-relation-travail/licenciement-resiliation/licencier-preavis/.

A good distractor is defined in the same way as for multiple choice questions by Haladyna and Downing [47]: a good distractor is plausible, incorporates expected errors, and is incorrect. Item authors all have qualification in the learning field, either as students, or as teachers/instructors. Three item authors have created distractors, three for the French and English texts, and two for the French texts. They received a cloze text, where only the gaps plus the extracted key were given to them. On the basis of the text, they were asked to handcraft distractors for each key.

5.3 Text and Term Difficulty

We analysed the texts from the text corpus with the various metrics (Table 1). Results for each language are presented in Tables 2, 3 and 4.

Table 2. Difficulty model for French

	Labour code	Roman empire	PC
Kandel & Moles formula ↓	52.44	73.37	52,86
PA_Alterego1a % ↑	87.26	84.69	81,97
PA_Gougenheim_2000 % ↑	42.57	41.32	36,43
Reference % ↓	10.53	13.95	10,41
Conjunction % ↓	5.64	6.11	5,95
Identification % ↓	0.71	1.82	0,93
TTR_lemmes % ↓	25.23	32.77	52,97
Daoust ↑	29	32	7
Number of words	2410	2960	538
Number of syllables	4072	4552	905
Number of sentences	81	147	18
Number of sentences longer than 30	29	32	7

Table 3. Difficulty model for English

	Labour code	Roman empire	PC
Flesch Reading Ease ↓	26.88	23.32	32.49
Reference % ↓	1.82	1.82	1.53
Conjunction % ↓	7.48	8.42	8.04
Identification % ↓	2.85	0.54	0.38
TTR_without_lemmas % ↓	23.70	33.80	53.43
LSDaoust ↑	29	39	2
Number of words	2139	3299	522
Number of syllables	3846	6274	959
Number of sentences	78	148	28
Number of sentences longer than 30	29	39	2

Table 4. Difficulty model for German

	Labour code	Roman empire	PC
Amstad index ↓	27.08	45.90	40.72
PA_uni.leipzig 2000 ↑	48.72	51.07	45.88
Reference %↓	16.16	15.90	13.21
Conjunction %↓	8.08	6.41	7.48
Identification % ↓	0.83	0.24	0
TTR _without_lemmas % ↓	35.87	44.69	63.84
LSDaoust %↑	31.48	20.35	21.05
Number of words	1324	3276	401
Number of syllables	2906	6443	810
Number of sentences	54	172	19
Number of sentences longer than 30	17	35	4

Some of the results we obtained for the original texts are unexpected. In the French version of the text *Roman Empire* shows 73.4 whereas this text is expected to be more difficult than *PC* that shows 52.8. The indices *PA_Alterego*, *PA_Gougenheim_2000* and *TTR_lemmes*, however, better represent the estimated text difficulty. It is also important to note the variation of indices for equivalent texts according to the language.

We can also note the discrepancies between indicators of the various categories across languages. Such metrics are typically implemented for a single language. Cross-language evaluation of text difficulty metrics represents a challenge for comparability. The simple Flesh Kincaid for instance shows that the text on the *Roman Empire* has the lowest score in English. However, in both French and German the text has a higher score for the equivalent metrics.

5.4 Gap Dispersity

This section provides the distractor evaluation process by means of three example texts in English, German, and French. It should be noted that experts are not always the same person across languages. Expert 1 for instance does not represent the same expert across languages, only for texts in the same language. The summaries are tagged and for every potential key, distractors are retrieved. We computed the gap distributional disparity value for both automatically created (AIG tool) and manually created options (Table 5). We then verified whether the options proposed by experts had been retrieved, even if discarded by DISCO (Table 6).

The AIG system provides a gap dispersity consistently significantly lower than human experts, which is expected since the AIG system was optimised according to DISCO distributional similarity. However, the experiment also shows that experts create manually very similar distributional similarity and it remains consistent across texts and gaps for every expert.

Table 6 shows that a significant number of distractors have been identified by the AIG system, even though not ranked highest. It should be noted that identifying exactly 3 distractors for each gap has sometimes appeared a challenging tasks for item authors.

Table 5. Average dispersity of gaps (German texts G1,G2, G3; French texts F1, F2, F3; and English texts E1, E2, E3)

	G1	G2	G3	F1	F2	F3	E1	E2	E3
AIG system	0.53	0.53	0.53	0.52	0.52	0.49	0.55	0.55	0.47
Expert 1	0.79	0.84	0.79	0.89	0.77	0.79	0.86	0.83	0.87
Expert 2	0.68	0.91	0.89				0.8	0.82	0.86
Expert 3	0.86	0.75	0.86						
Expert 4				0.91	0.84	0.81			

Table 6. Average proportion of expert distractors found by the AIG system

	German text 1	German Text 2	German text 3	French text 1	French text 2	French text 3	English text 1	English text 2	English text 3
Expert 1	0.56	0.63	0.41	0.61	0.50	0.48	0.46	0.44	0.50
Expert 2	0.63	0.39	0.32				0.58	0.53	0.57
Expert 3	0.33	0.31	0.32						
Expert 4				0.44	0.31	0.38			

2 experts have created non-existing German words as distractors (e.g. Verkürzung – Ferkürzung) for German texts, which impacts the ratio of distractors retrieved from DISCO. Due to the fact that DISCO only contains correct and existing German words, the resulting dispersity value is 1 for those gaps.

6 Conclusion

In this article we show an assessment item generation system that implements an inline choice generation algorithm for reading comprehension skills in French, English, and German as well as complementary quality metrics. Indeed one of the main challenges of assessment item generation is related to the usability of the generated items. AIG systems can generate numerous items, but they are not all directly usable, i.e., usable without manual edits and they do not have an even educational value. Since it is not possible to calibrate all generated items because of cost and scalability issues, we illustrate the implementation of an additional component that provides metrics to support a pre-selection process among the generated items. One of the main challenges tackled by our system is the generation of items in multiple languages. Thus, we take advantage of multilingual tools with uneven performance across languages. We are indeed facing performance issues of current NLP tools and different linguistic structures as illustrated by our findings, with the text difficulty metrics.

In future work, we will compare the various text difficulty and dispersity metrics to item difficulty. We will improve the inline choice question generation through a refinement of the gap identification methodology. Finally, we will adapt our process to other types of items and other types of constructs.

Acknowledgements. The research leading to these results was funded by the INTERREG IV A *"Grande Région"* 2007–2013 under grant agreement No. 138 GR DELUX 2 3 274.

References

1. ACRL: Framework for Information Literacy for Higher Education (2015)
2. Brown, J.C., Frishkoff, G.A., Eskenazi, M.: Automatic question generation for vocabulary assessment. In: Human Language Technology Conference and Conference on Empirical Methods in Natural Language Processing (HLT/EMNLP). pp. 819–826. Association for Computational Linguistics, Vancouver, Canada (2005)
3. Chen, C.Y., Liou, H.C., Chang, J.S.: Fast: an automatic generation system for grammar tests. In: COLING/ACL on Interactive Presentation Sessions, pp. 1–4. Association for Computational Linguistics, Morristown, NJ, USA (2006)
4. Mostow, J., et al.: Using automated questions to assess reading comprehension, vocabulary, and effects of tutorial interventions. Technol. Instr. Cogn. Learn. **2**, 97–134 (2004)
5. Papasalouros, A., Kanaris, K., Kotis, K.: Automatic generation of multiple choice questions from domain ontologies. In: e-Learning, Citeseer (2008)
6. Gierl, M.J., Lai, H.: Using weak and strong theory to create item models for automatic item generation. Autom. Item Gener.: Theor. Pract., 26 (2012)
7. Haladyna, T.M., Downing, S.M., Rodriguez, M.C.: A review of multiple-choice item-writing guidelines for classroom assessment. Appl. Measur. Educ. **15**(3), 309–333 (2002)
8. Mitkov, R., Ha, L.A., Karamanis, N.: A computer-aided environment for generating multiple-choice test items. Nat. Lang. Eng. **12**(2), 177–194 (2006)
9. Shah, R.: Automatic question generation using discourse cues and distractor selection for cloze questions. In: Language Technology and Research Center (LTRC), International Institute of Information Technology, Hyderabad (2012)
10. Becker, L., Basu, S., Vanderwende, L.: Mind the gap: learning to choose gaps for question generation. In: Proceedings of the 2012 Conference of the North American Chapter of the Association for Computational Linguistics: Human Language Technologies, Association for Computational Linguistics (2012)
11. Heilman, M.: Automatic Factual Question Generation from Text. Carnegie Mellon University, Pittsburgh (2011)
12. Iwata, T., et al.: Automatic Generation of English Cloze Questions Based on Machine Learning. NTT Communication Science Laboratories, Kyoto (2011)
13. Agarwal, M., Shah, R., Mannem, P.: Automatic question generation using discourse cues. In: Proceedings of the 6th Workshop on Innovative use of NLP for Building Educational Applications, Association for Computational Linguistics (2011)
14. Agarwal, M.: Cloze and Open Cloze Question Generation Systems and their Evaluation Guidelines. International Institute of Information Technology, Hyderabad (2012)
15. Wu, J.-C., Chang, J., Chang, J.S.: Correcting serial grammatical errors based on N-grams and syntax. 中文計算語言學期刊 **18**(4): 31–44 (2013)
16. Haladyna, T.M.: Automatic item generation - a hitorical perspective. In: Gierl, M.J., Haladyna, T.M. (eds.) Automatic Item Generation. Routledge, New York (2013)
17. Linnebank, F., Liem, J., Bredeweg, B.: Question generation and answering. DynaLearn, Deliverable D3.3, EC FP7 STREP Project 231526 (2010)

18. Foulonneau, M.: Generating educational assessment items from linked open data: the case of DBpedia. In: García-Castro, R., Fensel, D., Antoniou, G. (eds.) ESWC 2011. LNCS, vol. 7117, pp. 16–27. Springer, Heidelberg (2012)
19. Foulonneau, M., Grouès, G.: Common vs. expert knowledge: making the semantic web an educational model. In: 2nd International Workshop on Learning and Education with the Web of Data (LiLe–2012 at WWW-2012 conference), Lyon, France (2012)
20. Mitkov, R., et al.: Semantic similarity of distractors in multiple-choice tests: extrinsic evaluation. In: Workshop on Geometrical Models of Natural Language Semantics (GEMS 2009), pp. 49–56. Association for Computational Linguistics, Morristown, NJ, USA (2009)
21. Gütl, C., Lankmayr, K., Weinhofer, J.: Enhanced approach of automatic creation of test items to foster modern learning setting. In: 9th European Conference on e-Learning (ECEL 2010), Porto, Portugal, pp. 225–234. (2010)
22. Aldabe, I., Maritxalar, M.: Automatic distractor generation for domain specific texts. In: Loftsson, H., Rögnvaldsson, E., Helgadóttir, S. (eds.) IceTAL 2010. LNCS, vol. 6233, pp. 27–38. Springer, Heidelberg (2010)
23. Moser, J.R., Gütl, C., Liu, W.: Refined distractor generation with LSA and stylometry for automated multiple choice question generation. In: Thielscher, M., Zhang, D. (eds.) AI 2012. LNCS, vol. 7691, pp. 95–106. Springer, Heidelberg (2012)
24. Holmes, D.: The evolution of stylometry in humanities scholarship. Literary Linguist. Comput. **13**(3), 111–117 (1998)
25. Huang, Y.-T., et al.: TEDQuiz: automatic quiz generation for TED talks video clips to assess listening comprehension. In: 2014 IEEE 14th International Conference on Advanced Learning Technologies (ICALT), IEEE (2014)
26. Deane, P., et al.: Creating vocabulary item types that measure students' depth of semantic knowledge. In: ETS Research Report Series, pp. 1–19 (2014)
27. Smith, S., Avinesh, P., Kilgarriff, A.: Gap-fill tests for language learners: corpus-driven item generation. In: International Conference on Natural Language Processing, Macmillan Publishers, India (2010)
28. Zesch, T., Melamud, O.: Automatic generation of challenging distractors using context-sensitive inference rules. In: Proceedings of the Ninth Workshop on Innovative Use of NLP for Building Educational Applications (2014)
29. Hoshino, A., Nakagawa, H.: Assisting cloze test making with a web application. In: Society for Information Technology and Teacher Education International Conference (2007)
30. Gierl, M.J., Lai, H.: Using weak and strong theory to create item models for automatic item generation. In: Gierl M.J., Haladyna T.M. (eds.) Automatic Item Generation. Routledge, New York (2013)
31. Sonnleitner, P.: Using the LLTM to evaluate an item-generating system for reading comprehension. Psychol. Sci. **50**(3), 345 (2008)
32. Pho, V.-M., et al.: Multiple choice question corpus analysis for distractor characterization. In: 9th International Conference on Language Resources and Evaluation (LREC 2014) (2014)
33. Kolb, P.: Disco: a multilingual database of distributionally similar words. In: Proceedings of KONVENS-2008, Berlin (2008)
34. François, T., Miltsakaki, E.: Do NLP and machine learning improve traditional readability formulas? In: Proceedings of the First Workshop on Predicting and Improving Text Readability for Target Reader Populations, Association for Computational Linguistics (2012)
35. Washburne, C., Vogel, M.: Are any number combinations inherently difficult? J. Educ. Res. **17**(4), 235–254 (1928)

36. Dale, E., Chall, J.S.: A formula for predicting readability: Instructions. Educ. Res. Bull. **27**, 37–54 (1948)
37. Flesch, R.: A new readability yardstick. J. Appl. Psychol. **32**(3), 221 (1948)
38. Kandel, L., Moles, A.: Application de l'indice de flesch à la langue française. J. Educ. Res. **21**, 283–287 (1958)
39. Amstad, T.: Wie verständlich sind unsere Zeitungen? Studenten-Schreib-Service (1978)
40. Dale, E., Tyler, R.W.: A study of the factors influencing the difficulty of reading materials for adults of limited reading ability. Libr. Q. **4**(3), 384–412 (1934)
41. Halliday, M.A.K., Hasan, R.: Cohesion in English. Routledge, New York (2014)
42. Zeid, E.A., Foulonneau, M., Atéchian, T.: Réutiliser des textes dans un contexte éducatif. Document Numérique **15**(3), 119–142 (2012)
43. François, T., Fairon, C.: An AI readability formula for French as a foreign language. In: Proceedings of the 2012 Joint Conference on Empirical Methods in Natural Language Processing and Computational Natural Language Learning, Association for Computational Linguistics (2012)
44. Mesnager, J.: Mots fréquents ou mots usuels. Communication et langages **84**(1), 33–46 (1990)
45. François, T., Fairon, C.: Les apports du TAL à la lisibilité du français langue étrangère (2013)
46. Goosse, A., Grevisse, M.: Le bon usage: grammaire française, Duculot (1993)
47. Haladyna, T.M., Downing, S.M.: A taxonomy of multiple-choice item-writing rules. Appl. Measur. Educ. **2**(1), 37–50 (1989)

A Perspective on Computer Assisted Assessment Techniques for Short Free-Text Answers

Shourya Roy[1(✉)], Y. Narahari[2], and Om D. Deshmukh[1]

[1] Xerox Research Centre India, Bangalore, India
{shourya.roy,om.deshmukh}@xerox.com
[2] Indian Institute of Science, Bangalore, India
hari@csa.iisc.ernet.in

Abstract. Computer Assisted Assessment (CAA) has been existing for several years now. While some forms of CAA do not require sophisticated text understanding (e.g., multiple choice questions), there are also student answers that consist of free text and require analysis of text in the answer. Research towards the latter till date has concentrated on two main sub-tasks: (i) grading of essays, which is done mainly by checking the style, correctness of grammar, and coherence of the essay and (ii) assessment of short free-text answers. In this paper, we present a structured view of relevant research in automated assessment techniques for short free-text answers. We review papers spanning the last 15 years of research with emphasis on recent papers. Our main objectives are two folds. First we present the survey in a structured way by segregating information on dataset, problem formulation, techniques, and evaluation measures. Second we present a discussion on some of the potential future directions in this domain which we hope would be helpful for researchers.

Keywords: Automatic scoring · Short answer grading · Assessment

1 Introduction

Assessing students' acquired knowledge is one of the key aspects of teachers' job. It is typically achieved by evaluating and scoring students' responses in classroom assessments such as quizzes, examinations, and worksheets. Assessments are important for teachers as these provide them insights on how effective their teaching has been. However, assessment is a monotonous, repetitive and time consuming job and often seen as an overhead and non-rewarding[1]. In addition, it seldom helps teachers to improve their knowledge of subject matters.

Computer Assisted Assessment(CAA) has been prevalent in schools and colleges for many years now albeit for questions with constrained answers such as multiple choice questions (MCQs). There have been several studies on MCQs

[1] https://www.experience.com/alumnus/article?channel_id=education\&source_page=editor_picks\&article_id=article_1133291019105 Assessment (or grading) takes of the order 20 % time for teachers.

E. Ras and D. Joosten-ten Brinke (Eds.): CAA 2015, CCIS 571, pp. 96–109, 2015.
DOI: 10.1007/978-3-319-27704-2_10

which brought out important aspects such as high degree of correlations with constructed response items [37]. While assessment of answers to MCQs are easier for computers, they have been reported to suffer from multiple shortcomings compared to questions requiring free-text answers. Firstly, they are less reliable owing to pure guessing paying some dividends. Techniques which do not account for influence of guessing strategies used by students do not lead to reliable assessment [42]. Secondly, presence of alternative responses provide inadvertent hints which may change nature of problem-solving and reasoning. Finally, in many cases MCQs are not appropriate to measure acquired knowledge such as hypothetical reasoning and self-explanation in Science courses [51]. Consequently, use of open-ended questions that seek students' constructed responses is more commonly found in educational institutions. They reveal students' ability to integrate, synthesize, design, and communicate their ideas in natural language. We call them *free-text* answers. In this paper we consider *short* free-text answers which are at least a sentence long but less than 100 words in length (broadening from the definition of up to 20-word answers from previous work [19]).

Assessment of free-text answers is more laborious and subjective for humans as well as much harder to automate. Research towards the same started multiple decades ago (with publications first appearing in 1960s [34]) and till date has concentrated on two main tasks: (i)grading of essays, which is done mainly by checking style, correctness of grammar, fluency etc. of essays and (ii) assessment of short free-text answers. While the former has seen a vast amount of research work, Jordan had observed that short-answer free-text e-assessment has remained an underused technology [20]. Multiple surveys have been written about automatic grading of essays [7,10,49]. In this paper, we present a structured survey of techniques developed for assessment of short free-text answers which to date is the first attempt to the best of our knowledge.

CAA[2] techniques for short free-text ingest student answers and assign scores usually by comparing to one or more correct answers. Developing a general solution to this is a hard problem owing to multiple reasons viz. linguistic variations in student answers (multiple ways of expressing the same answer), subjectivity of questions (multiple correct answers) and topical variations (Science vs Literature). At a broad level, two types of automatic approaches for scoring have been followed by researchers. Knowledge based approaches involve experts creating all possible model answers for a question and representing them in computer understandable manner. Computer systems then use these model answers to automatically score student responses. On the other hand, machine learning based approaches develop statistical *models* based on a collection of expert graded answers. Loosely speaking, these techniques attempt to learn characteristics (or features) of answers which make them correct. Knowledge-based approaches are useful if variations possible in student answers are limited and can be enumerated. However, considering reasons described above such as linguistic diversity and subjectivity of questions, it could be laborious and ineffective in many cases.

[2] We use the terms "computer assisted assessment(CAA)" and "automated assessment" interchangeably in this paper.

Table 1. Summarized view of data and tasks mentioned in relevant prior work

Ref.	Topic	Level	Nature of answers	Scoring scale
[35,45–47]	GCSE Biology Examinations	14–16 year old pupils	up to 5 lines (about 200 answers for 9 questions)	0–2
[23,48]	Reading comprehension and mathematics	7th and 8th Graders	Short answers up to 100 words	0–2
[28]	1999 Science National Test Paper A and B	11 year old pupils	Single word, single value; short explanatory sentence (120 answers; 4 questions)	0–2
[13,53]	Introductory course in computer literacy	100 College students	short answers with multiple (3–9) correct concepts associated (192 answers; 36 questions)	
[32,33]	Science	3rd to 6th Graders	moderately short verb phrases to several sentences (15,400 answers; 287 questions)	8-point scale
[27]	Assessment of summaries based on reading comprehension	75 undergraduate students	75–100 word long	
[9]	High school Physics	Undergraduate students	at most 1–2 sentences (8000 responses)	4-point scale
[41]	300 Middle school virtual environment scenarios	Middle school Science students	short answers of usually 50–60 words	0–4
[51]	Creative problem solving in Earth Sciences	226 High school students	short-text in Chinese	
[24]	Summary writing for reading comprehension	6th to 9th graders	summaries of about 4 sentences	0–4
[3]	United States Citizenship Exam	Crowd workers on AMT	Up to a couple of sentences (698 respondents; 20 questions)	Boolean Correct and incorrect
[22]	Critical thinking tasks GRE Analytical Writing Prompts	Students from 14 colleges and universities	short answers (5–10 open ended questions)	5-point scale
[11,29,30]	80 questions from Introductory Data Structure Course	Undergraduate students	Short answers of about 1–2 lines	0–5
[40]	87 questions on Object Oriented Programming	Undergraduate students	heterogeneous; about 1–2 lines maximum	
[1]	Essays on a variety of topics	10th grade students	50 words (17,000 responses)	

Oragnization of the paper: We start by presenting a structured view of prior research in automatic assessment of short free-text answers in an organized manner. Starting with types of data and domains researchers looked at, we follow up with technical problem formulations and solutions developed before leading to evaluation metrics used. In Sect. 5, we provide insights obtained from prior work leading to new research directions in this topic. We feel that such a structured view of research would be more useful to researchers than merely describing all prior work in some order. Finally, we do feel that this work is timely considering the recent trend of large scale democratization of education through Massive Online Open Courses(MOOCs). While content from leading colleges are being floated around to students all over the world, assessments in MOOCs have been quite primitive with usage of multiple choice and 1–2 word/number/formulae questions. Research in automatic assessment has to take leaps over the next few years, supported by advances in machine learning and natural language processing techniques, to enable MOOCs to have assessment of equivalent quality to traditional pedagogical ecosystem.

2 Nature of Data and Tasks

In this section, we provide a summarized view of the wide variety of tasks, subject matter, student population level and size as well as scoring scale used in prior work towards automated assessment of short free-text answers in Table 1(blank cells indicate information not found in respective papers). It is evident that a wide variety of data was used in prior research in computer aided assessment of short free-text answers with little standardization in scoring scheme. While such heterogeneity implies possible wide applicability of techniques, generalizability of developed techniques is not proven. One of the reasons being these datasets were seldom shared and hence tried out by subsequent research to move the state of the art forward. We will come back to these issues while discussing future research directions in Sect. 5.

3 Techniques

In this section, we review techniques which have been used for automatic assessment in prior art. Again, we observe that a wide variety of techniques have been used which we group under key themes and present in an organized manner.

3.1 Natural Language Processing (NLP)

Natural Language Processing (NLP) is a well-established field of research focusing on developing techniques for computers to understand and generate natural language text. Natural Language Understanding (NLU), a sub-field of NLP, is the process of disassembling, parsing and canonicalizing natural language text.

NLU techniques have been applied to extract syntactic and semantic structures from short free-text answers. These techniques typically require certain amount of data cleaning owing to the noisy nature of the free-text answers. Spelling and punctuation correction, lemmatization, etc. are commonly applied to clean surface form of the text. Stopword removal and stemming are two other commonly used NLU pre-processing steps towards eliminating non-indicative features and reducing variation of words. Researchers have also developed custom parsing methods to handle language errors in student responses to provide accurate assessments [15]. Parse trees obtained from parsers not only show shallow structure of free-text answers but also can be used to extract higher level features indicating clause structure, negation etc. [48]. Siddiqi et al. developed a system, IndusMarker, based on syntactic structure of student responses using freely available linguistic tools such JOrtho[3] and Stanford Parser[4] to compare extracted structures with examiner specified grammatical structures to arrive at a score [39,40]. They also developed a XML like Question Answer Markup Language (QAML) to capture structure extracted from text. Lexicons and dictionaries play important role in NLU techniques. Given high degree of domain specificity of different assessment tasks, it is quite common to develop domain specific lexicons to include relevant keywords and variations thereof [41]. Towards developing an assessment system for Biology domain, Sukkarieh et al. observed that many relevant terms were missing in the training data which they had to add manually to the lexicon [47]. In webLAS [2], regular expressions are created out of the model answers and given answers are evaluated against these regular expressions to get a grade. The WebLAS system, the system presented in [35] and a few other short answer assessments systems are compared and contrasted in [55]. Concepts from theoretical linguistics are also beginning to be used: for example, [17] uses under-specified semantic formalism *Lexical Resource Semantics (LRS)* to evaluate the meaning of the answers to content-based reading comprehension tasks.

ETS 'e-rater' is a rating engine to evaluate responses to short-answer questions [4]. They argue that domain specific NLP techniques need to be used for these evaluation tasks and motivate the use of *metonyms*: words or multiword terms that can be substituted for each other in a given domain. Authors in [22] compared how the hand-assigned scores compare with machine-assigned scores under a variety of circumstances (difficulty of task, nature of task, gender-bias, ethnicity-bias etc.) where the machine-assignment was done using the 'e-rater' system.

3.2 Information Extraction and Pattern Matching

Information extraction (IE) techniques pull out pertinent information from syntactically analysed pieces of text answers by applying a set of *patterns*. Patterns are defined either on surface text (words, phrases) or structural elements such as parts of speech (PoS) tags. In the case of short free-text answers, they are typically created by subject matter experts to indicate important concepts which should be present in answers.

OpenMark system from Open University in United Kingdom compared student responses with model answers using regular expressions based on algorithmic manipulation of keywords [5]. However, most prior work used patterns of higher complexity defined in terms of PoS tags and other structural elements obtained from NLU tools such as parser. Automated Text Marker system was developed on the principle of breaking down student answers as well

[3] http://jortho.sourceforge.net/.
[4] http://nlp.stanford.edu/software/lex-parser.shtml.

as model answers into smallest viable units of *concepts* with linguistic dependencies between concepts. [6]. To make the system adaptable they employed additional thesauri (for synonym, metonym) and other simplification rules such as removing articles and other "unnecessary" words. Similarly c-rater® matched the syntactical features of student responses (subject, object and verb) to those of model answers [23]. It used handcrafted rules to take care of different types of variations (syntactic and inflexional variation, synonyms) that existed in student responses. Dzikovska et al. used a syntactic parser and a set of hand-authored rules to extract semantic representations from student responses which were then matched against semantic representations of expected correct answers supplied by tutors [8]. Sukkarieh et al. used a Hidden Markov Model(HMM) based PoS tagger, and a Noun Phrase (NP) and Verb Group (VG) chunker for developing the Oxford-UCLES system. It bootstraped patterns by starting with a set of keywords and synonyms and searching through windows of text for new patterns [47]. Another popular system AutoMark employed templates to specify expert-written snippets of text which were looked for matches in student answers [28]. The templates were designed in a way that they could handle variations in the input text by listing possible words and phrases, lemmatisation of verbs and sentence structure. A very similar technique was applied in [18] with a differential ability to flag (for human validation) a student response which failed to match a model answer but is recognized being a close one.

The primary challenge with information extraction based techniques is to arrive at patterns to cover all possible variations in student answers. In addition, this needs to be done manually for every assessment exercise by subject matter experts which makes the entire exercise an expensive one. On the other hand, as these techniques work on the principle of identifying missing concepts, they have the advantage of crafting feedback for students easily based on knowledge of (un)matched patterns.

3.3 Machine Learning

Classification and regression are the two most popular supervised learning paradigms in machine learning literature. Both techniques attempt to learn unknown functions from which a set of labelled data has been generated and use the estimated functions to predict labels of future unlabeled data. For data in n-dimensional real valued feature space, classification techniques learn functions of type $\mathbb{R}^n \rightarrow \mathcal{A}$ where $\mathcal{A}$ is a set of discreet *class labels*. Regression techniques on the other hand learns real valued functions of type $\mathbb{R}^n \rightarrow \mathbb{R}$. In our context, the data points are answers, scores are labels (or continuous values in regression), scored answers are labelled data and new answers are unlabelled data for prediction. Sukkarieh et al. used statistical text classification techniques which do not require complete and accurate parsing (which is difficult owing to ungrammatical and incomplete sentences). They applied classification techniques such as k-Nearest Neighbor, Inductive Logic Programming, Decision Tree and Naïve Bayes to perform two sets of experiments viz. on raw text answers and annotated answers [35,45]. Annotation involved domain experts highlighting parts of answers that deserved a score. Machine learning wisdom says that performance of classification techniques depend heavily on the choice and synthesis of features which is evident in prior work for assessment tasks as well. Sukkarieh et al. developed Maximum Entropy classifier using features based on lexical constructs such as presence/absence of concepts, order in which concepts appear, role of a word in a sentence(e.g. active/passive) etc. to predict if a student response is entailed in at least one of the model answers [44]. Nielsen et al. used carefully crafted features using NLP preprocessing obtained from lexical and syntactic forms of text [31]. Dzikovska et al. used lexicial similarity scores (number of overlapping words, F1 score, Lesk score and cosine score) to train a Decision Tree classifier to categorize student responses into one of the 5 categories [9]. For summary assessment Madnani et al. used logistic regression classifier on a 5 point scale [24]. They used interesting features to commonalities between an original passage and a summary such as BLEU score (commonly used for evaluating Machine Translation systems), ROUGE (a recall based metric that measures the lexical and phrasal overlap between two pieces of text), overlap of words and phrases etc. Regression techniques were used for automated assessment to arrive at a real valued score which were later rounded off as per scoring scale. Here again we see use of interesting features with state of the art regression techniques. Sil et al. used Support Vector Machines with Radial Basis Function kernels (RBF-SVM) for learning non-linear regression models of grading with several higher order features derived from free-text answers [41]. Wang et al. applied regression technique for assessing creative answer assessment [51].

3.4 Document Similarity

Large number of techniques have been developed for measuring similarity between a pair of text. Variations exist with respect to representations used for text similarity computation. *Lexical similarity* techniques use surface form text but often give suboptimal results owing to not considering semantics (`automobile` and `car` are considered as distinct as `automobile` and `banana`) and context (`Apple computer` and `apple pie` are considered similar as they share a term). *Corpus based similarity* (or semantic similarity) techniques such as Latent Semantic Analysis (LSA) have shown to perform well by addressing these problems. LSA (and related techniques) project documents to a suitably chosen lower dimensional subspace, where cosine similarity has shown to be a reasonable estimate of semantic similarity. *Knowledge based measures* use background knowledge such as Wordnet[5] or domain specific ontologies to estimate how similar two documents are.

Mohler et al. compared performance of corpus based measures with a number of unsupervised knowledge based measures [30]. Their experiments on a 630 answer dataset did not bring out significant differences in performances of different measures. However, the authors opined that corpus based measures are

[5] http://wordnet.princeton.edu/.

more generalizable as their performance can be improved by improving corpora relevance and increasing corpora size. In a follow up paper, they proposed hybrid techniques using graph alignment on dependency graph (between students' answers and instructor's answer-key) and lexical semantic similarity measures [29]. On the same dataset, Gomaa and Fahmy compared several lexical and corpus based similarity algorithms (13 string based and 4 corpus) and their combinations for grading answers in 0–5 scale [11]. Combination of different string matching and overlap techniques were studied by Gutl on a small scale dataset [16]. Mintz et al. compared different measures such as Word Count, Information Content [36] and Coh-Metrix [26] to score summaries based on features such as *narrativity*, *syntactic simplicity* etc. [27].

LSA has been extensively used for assessment tasks as researchers observed that capturing semantic similarity is most important (student answer should *mean* the same and not necessarily *read* the same as model answers). One of the early tutoring systems AutoTutor [52] used LSA to compare students' answers to model answers by calculating distance between their corresponding vector projections [13]. If cosine similarity of a student response was greater than a threshold then the answer was considered correct. In addition to correct answers, they also had a list of anticipated bad answers – high similarity with those indicated incorrect student response. In a related work, they studied effect of size and specificity of corpora used for creating LSA space on accuracy of automatic assessment [53]. They reported that performance of automatic assessment improved with corpus size though the increase was not linear. They also reported that the performance improved with specificity and relevance of corpus to the task at hand which is a well accepted wisdom in the field now.

LSA based techniques did not always give good performance due to not considering linguistic characteristics such as negation, attachment, predication, modification etc. Researchers also tried adding higher level NLP features such as POS tags but they did not claim to produce significant improvement over vanilla LSA based techniques [21,54].

3.5 Clustering

Basu et al. used clustering techniques to group responses into a two level hierarchy of clusters based on content similarity [3]. They used human supervision as labeled examples to learn similarity metrics using features such as difference in length, fraction of words with matching base forms etc. They observed that TFIDF[6] was the best similarity metric for performing clustering. Obtained clusters could help teachers efficiently grade a group of responses together. They also provided early results on automatic labeling (correct/wrong) based on content similarity. Not for subjective questions, but a very similar idea for evaluating handwritten answer scripts were proposed by [25].

---
[6] http://en.wikipedia.org/wiki/Tf%E2%80%93idf.

4 Evaluation

An important aspect of CAA for short free-text answer assessment task is to use appropriate evaluation metrics for judging goodness of developed automated techniques. Typically, performance of automatic assessment techniques is measured in terms of agreement with human assigned scores (often average of multiple human scores). Various measures of correlation such as Pearson's Correlation Coefficient, Cohen's Kappa etc.[7] have been used to quantifiably measure extent of agreement.

Sil et al. used a χ^2 test with a threshold of $p < 0.05$ to determine statistical significance of Pearson's Correlation Coefficient [41]. Graesser et al. introduced the notion of *compatibility percentage* for grading answers which matched ideal answers only partially before applying correlation analysis [13]. Similarly, Kanejiya et al. asked human experts to evaluate answers on the basis of *compatibility score*(between 0 and 1) before applying correlation analysis [21]. Sukkarieh et al. used kappa statistics with respect to percentage agreement between two human annotators for evaluation [44,48]. Mohler et al. reported Root Mean Square Error (RMSE) for the full dataset as well as median RMSE across each individual questions [29]. In a prior work, Mohler also highlighted lack of proper analysis before using Pearson's Correlation Coefficient(e.g. normal distribution, interval measurement level, linear correlational model etc.) as well as abundance of possible measures(e.g. Kendall's tau, Goodman-Kruskal's Gamma).

Performance of supervised classification based techniques is represented as a two dimensional table known as *confusion matrix*[8]. Rows in confusion matrix represent human expert assigned grades and columns are computer assigned grades. A cell c_{ij} represents number of answers which are scored i by human and j by the automated technique. Principal diagonal elements represent number of answers where both have agreed. On the basis of confusion matrix, multiple measures such as *accuracy*, *precision* and *recall*, F_1, *specificity* and *sensitivity* etc. have been used to determine how well predicted scores matched with ground-truth scores [24,28]. Classifiers have parameters using which one can trade off precision for recall or vice versa. One known problem with these measures is that they can grossly misreport in case of uneven class distribution e.g. number of correct responses being much more than number of wrong ones. Dzikovska et al. reported both macro-averaged and micro-averaged measures with the latter taking class size into account (there by favoring techniques doing well on larger classes) [9].

5 Discussion

In this section we identify a few possible future research directions in automatic assessment of short free-text answers:

[7] http://en.wikipedia.org/wiki/Inter-rater_reliability.

[8] http://en.wikipedia.org/wiki/Confusion_matrix.

- We observe that there is a lot of variation in short free-text answers(Refer Table 1). Techniques developed for assessing answers to Science questions for middle school students are not expected to work well for assessing summaries written by undergraduate students. Variations with respect to factors such as subject matter, level of students, length and type of text need to be accounted for in the techniques. *A matchmaking framework providing guidance to choose the most appropriate technique for an assessment use-case would be valuable to practitioners.* On a related note there is a dire need of creating and sharing datasets across researchers as mentioned in Sect. 2. Benchmark datasets in machine learning and natural language processing have enabled researchers to come up with new techniques as well as report quantifiable progress over the years. Similar activity would enable assessment techniques to build on vast amount of existing prior work as reviewed in this paper.
- Almost all prior work have assumed existence of model answers for questions for automated assessment of student answers. *An interesting problem would be to develop techniques which can perform assessment without model answers* leveraging a large relevant knowledge base such as wikipedia[9] and babelnet[10]. Work in automatic question answering from the Web would be a starting point though most of those have focused on factual questions [50].
- Assessment is a long term exercise over months and years. Students undergo a number of quizzes and examinations through out their academic career. Most research described in this paper has considered each assessment independently – ignoring prior knowledge of student performance. If a student performed well in all prior examinations then it is probable that she will perform well in the current assessment as well. *Techniques considering a student model along with free-text answers can overcome limitations of techniques which work only based on answer content.* This is analogous to *prior* in Bayesian framework which is combined with observed data for inferencing.

6 Conclusion

Assessment is important for teachers to understand students' acquired knowledge but it takes up a significant amount of their time and is often seen as an overhead. CAA addressed this problem to some extent by enabling automatic assessment for certain types of questions and letting teachers spend more time in teaching. However the benefit and adoption of CAA in schools and colleges has been marginal owing to their relatively limited applicability. Towards expanding the reach of teachers' pedagogy, computers have been in use for content dissemination over the internet in the form of distance learning and e-learning. Massive Online Open Courses (MOOCs), over the last few years, have expanded the reach of high quality pedagogical materials by orders of magnitude. However, till date certifications and degrees from MOOCs are much less acknowledged and respected than the ones from traditional pedagogical ecosystem. We believe the

[9] http://www.wikipedia.org/.
[10] http://babelnet.org/.

difference in assessment methodologies is one of the key reasons for the same. While classroom-based education system primarily use subjective questions to holistically assess students acquired knowledge, MOOCs have been wanting with their MCQ based and peer assessment practices. Need of the hour is large scale assessment systems capable of handling all types of answers; at least short free-text answers. This is an overwhelming task and consolidated research effort will be needed to bridge the gap over the next few years.

References

1. The hewlett foundation: Short answer scoring. http://www.kaggle.com/c/asap-sas, Accessed on 6 March 2015
2. Bachman, L., Carr, N., Kamei, G., Kim, M., Pan, M., Salvador, C., Sawaki, Y.: A reliable approach to automatic assessment of short answer free responses. In: Proceedings of the 19th International Conference on Computational Linguistics, pp. 1–4 (2002)
3. Basu, S., Jacobs, C., Vanderwende, L.: Powergrading: a clustering approach to amplify human effort for short answer grading. Trans. Assoc. Comput. Linguist. **1**, 391–402 (2013)
4. Burstein, J., Wolff, S., Lu, C.: Using lexical semantic techniques to classify free responses. In: Viegas, E. (ed.) Breadth and Depth of Semantic Lexicons, vol. 10, pp. 227–244. Springer, The Netherlands (1999)
5. Butcher, P.G., Jordan, S.E.: A comparison of human and computer marking of short free-text student responses. Comput. Educ. **55**(2), 489–499 (2010)
6. Callear, D., Jerrams-Smith, J., Soh, V., Dr. Jerrams-smith, J., Ae. H.P.: CAA of short non-MCQ answers. In: Proceedings of the 5th International CAA Conference (2001)
7. Dikli, S.: An overview of automated scoring of essays. J. Technol. Learn. Assess. (JTLA) **5**(1), 36 (2006)
8. Dzikovska, M., Bell, P., Isard, A., Moore, J.D.: Evaluating language understanding accuracy with respect to objective outcomes in a dialogue system. In: EACL, pp. 471–481. The Association for Computer Linguistics (2012)
9. Dzikovska, M., Nielsen, R.D., Brew, C.: Towards effective tutorial feedback for explanation questions: a dataset and baselines. In: HLT-NAACL, pp. 200–210. The Association for Computational Linguistics (2012)
10. Gomaa, W.H., Fahmy, A.A.: Tapping into the power of automatic scoring. In: The Eleventh International Conference on Language Engineering, Egyptian Society of Language Engineering (ESOLEC) (2011)
11. Fahmy, A.A., Gomaa, W.H.: Short answer grading using string similarity and corpus-based similarity. Int. J. Adv. Comput. Sci. Appl. (IJACSA) **3**(11), 210–214 (2012)
12. Graesser, A.C., Person, N.K.: Question asking during tutoring. Am. Edu. Res. J. **31**, 104–137 (1994)
13. Graesser, A.C., Wiemer-Hastings, P.M., Wiemer-Hastings, K., Harter, D., Person, N.K.: Using latent semantic analysis to evaluate the contributions of students in autotutor. Interact. Learn. Environ. **8**(2), 129–147 (2000)
14. Grundspenkis, J.: Development of concept map based adaptive knowledge assessment system. In: IADIS International Conference e-Learning, pp. 395–402 (2008)

15. Guest, E., Brown, S.: A new method for parsing student text to support computer-assisted assessment of free text answers. In: 11th CAA International Computer Assisted Assessment Conference, pp. 223–236. Loughborough University, Loughborough, UK, July 2007
16. Gütl, C.: Moving towards a fully automatic knowledge assessment tool. Int. J. Emerg. Technol. Learn. (iJET), 3(1) (2008)
17. Hahn, M., Meurers, D.: Evaluating the meaning of answers to reading comprehension questions a semantics-based approach. In: The 7th Workshop on the Innovative Use of NLP for Building Educational Applications, ACL, pp. 326–336 (2012)
18. Jordan, S., Mitchell, T.: e-assessment for learning? the potential of short-answer free-text questions with tailored feedback. Br. J. Educ. Technol. **40**(2), 371–385 (2009)
19. Jordan, S.: Student engagement with assessment and feedback: some lessons from short-answer free-text e-assessment questions. Comput. Educ. **58**(2), 818–834 (2012)
20. Jordan, S.: Short-answer e-assessment questions: five years on (2012)
21. Kanejiya, D., Kumar, A., Prasad, S.: Automatic evaluation of students' answers using syntactically enhanced LSA. In: Proceedings of the HLT-NAACL Workshop on Building Educational Applications Using Natural Language Processing, vol. 2, pp. 53–60. Association for Computational Linguistics, Stroudsburg, PA, USA (2003)
22. Klein, SP., et al.: Characteristics of hand and machine-assigned scores to college students answers to open-ended tasks. In: Probability and Statistics: Essays in Honor of David A. Freedman, pp. 76–89. Institute of Mathematical Statistics (2008)
23. Leacock, C., Chodorow, M.: C-rater: automated scoring of short-answer questions. Comput. Humanit. **37**(4), 389–405 (2003)
24. Madnani, N., Burstein, J., Sabatini, J., OReilly, T.: Automated scoring of a summary writing task designed to measure reading comprehension. In: Proceedings of the 8th Workshop on Innovative use of NLP for Building Educational Applications, pp. 163–168. Citeseer (2013)
25. Manohar, P., Roy, S.: Crowd, the teaching assistant: educational assessment crowdsourcing. In: HCOMP, AAAI (2013)
26. McNamara, D.S., Graesser, A.C., McCarthy, P.M., Cai, Z.: Automated evaluation of text and discourse with Coh-Metrix. Cambridge University Press, Cambridge (2014)
27. Mintz, L., DMello, S., Stefanescu, D., Graesser, A.C., Feng, S.: Automatic assessment of student reading comprehension from short summaries. In: Educational Data Mining Conference (2014)
28. Mitchell, T., Russell, T., Broomhead, P., Aldridge, N.: Towards robust computerized marking of free-text responses. In: Proceedings of 6th International Computer Aided Assessment Conference (2002)
29. Mohler, M., Bunescu, R.C., Mihalcea, R.: Learning to grade short answer questions using semantic similarity measures and dependency graph alignments. In: The Association for Computer Linguistics, ACL, pp. 752–762 (2011)
30. Mohler, M., Mihalcea, R.: Text-to-text semantic similarity for automatic short answer grading. In: Proceedings of the 12th Conference of the European Chapter of the Association for Computational Linguistics, pp. 567–575. Association for Computational Linguistics (2009)
31. Nielsen, R.D., Buckingham, J., Knoll, G., Marsh, B., Palen, L.: A taxonomy of questions for question generation. In: Proceedings of the Workshop on the Question Generation Shared Task and Evaluation Challenge (2008)

32. Nielsen, R.D., Ward, W., Martin, J.H.: Recognizing entailment in intelligent tutoring systems. Nat. Lang. Eng. **15**(4), 479–501 (2009)
33. Nielsen, R.D., Ward, W., Martin, J.H., Palmer, M.: Annotating students' understanding of science concepts. In: LREC, European Language Resources Association (2008)
34. Page, E.B.: The imminence of grading essays by computer. Phi Delta Kappan, vol. 48, pp. 238–243 (1966)
35. Pulman, S.G., Sukkarieh, J.Z.: Automatic short answer marking. In: Proceedings of the Second Workshop on Building Educational Applications Using NLP, EdAppsNLP 05, pp. 9–16. Association for Computational Linguistics, Stroudsburg, PA, USA (2005)
36. Resnik, P.: Using information content to evaluate semantic similarity in a taxonomy. In: Proceedings of the 14th International Joint Conference on Artificial Intelligence, vol. 1, pp. 448–453 (1995)
37. Rodriguez, M.C.: Construct equivalence of multiple-choice and constructed-response items: a random effects synthesis of correlations. J. Educ. Meas. **40**(2), 163–184 (2003)
38. Shermis, M.D., Burstein, J., Higgins, D., Zechner, K.: Automated essay scoring: writing assessment and instruction. In: International Encyclopedia of Education, pp. 20–26 (2010)
39. Siddiqi, R., Harrison, C.: A systematic approach to the automated marking of short-answer questions. In: IEEE International Multitopic Conference, 2008, INMIC 2008, pp. 329–332 (2008)
40. Siddiqi, R., Harrison, C.J., Siddiqi, R.: Improving teaching and learning through automated short-answer marking. IEEE Trans. Learn. Technol. **3**(3), 237–249 (2010)
41. Sil, A., Ketelhut, D.J., Shelton, A., Yates, A.: Automatic grading of scientific inquiry. In: Proceedings of the Seventh Workshop on Building Educational Applications Using NLP, pp. 22–32. Association for Computational Linguistics (2012)
42. Singley, M.K., Taft, H.L.: Open-ended approaches to science assessment using computers. J. Sci. Educ. Technol. **4**(1), 7–20 (1995)
43. Sukkarieh, J.Z., Bolge, E.: Building a textual entailment suite for the evaluation of automatic content scoring technologies. In: LREC, European Language Resources Association (2010)
44. Sukkarieh, J.Z., Mohammad-Djafari, A., Bercher, J.-F., Bessie're, P.: Using a maxent classifier for the automatic content scoring of free-text responses. In: AIP Conference Proceedings-American Institute of Physics, vol. 1305, p. 41 (2011)
45. Sukkarieh, J.Z., Pulman, S.G.: Information extraction and machine learning: auto-marking short free text responses to science questions. In: Proceedings of the 2005 Conference on Artificial Intelligence in Education: Supporting Learning Through Intelligent and Socially Informed Technology, pp. 629–637. IOS Press (2005)
46. Sukkarieh, J.Z., Pulman, S.G., Raikes, N.: Auto-marking: using computational linguistics to score short, free text responses. In: International Association of Educational Assessment, Philadephia (2004)
47. Sukkarieh, J.Z., Pulman, S.G., Raikes, N.: Auto-marking 2: an update on the ucles-oxford university research into using computational linguistics to score short, free text responses. In: International Association of Educational Assessment, Philadephia (2004)
48. Sukkarieh, J.Z., Blackmore, J.: c-rater: Automatic content scoring for short constructed responses. In: FLAIRS Conference, AAAI Press (2009)

49. Valenti, S., Neri, F., Cucchiarelli, A.: An overview of current research on automated essay grading. J. Inf. Technol. Educ. Res. **2**, 319–330 (2003)
50. Voorhees, E.M., Tice, D.M.: Building a question answering test collection. In: Proceedings of the 23rd Annual International ACM SIGIR Conference on Research and Development in Information Retrieval, pp. 200–207 (2000)
51. Wang, H.-C., Chang, C.-Y., Li, T.-Y.: Assessing creative problem-solving with automated text grading. Comput. Educ. **51**(4), 1450–1466 (2008)
52. Wiemer-Hastings, P., Graesser, A.C., Harter, D.: The foundations and architecture of autotutor. In: Goettl, B.P., Halff, H.M., Redfield, C.L., Shute, V.J. (eds.) ITS 1998. LNCS, vol. 1452, pp. 334–343. Springer, Heidelberg (1998)
53. Wiemer-Hastings, P., Wiemer-Hastings, K., Graesser, A.: Improving an intelligent tutor's comprehension of students with latent semantic analysis. In: Artificial Intelligence in Education, vol. 99 (1999)
54. Wiemer-Hastings, P., Zipitria, I.: Rules for syntax, vectors for semantics. In: Proceedings of the 23rd Annual Conference of the Cognitive Science Society, NJ (2001)
55. Ziai, R., Ott, N., Meurers, D.: Short answer assessment: establishing links between research strands. In: The 7th Workshop on the Innovative Use of NLP for Building Educational Applications, ACL, pp. 190–200 (2012)

Detecting Cascading Errors in Mathematic Exercises

Edgar Seemann([✉])

Furtwangen University, Furtwangen im Schwarzwald, Germany
edgar.seemann@hs-furtwangen.de

Abstract. The adoption and acceptance of automatic assessment techniques for exercises and exams has increased considerably in recent years. While for some types of electronic tests, particularly memorizing tasks with closed-ended questions, this adoption is relatively straight forward, other types of tests are more challenging to assess without the need for human intervention. In computer science a technique called *unit testing* can help to automatically assess programming exercises. The idea is to write a small computer program, which can evaluate the answer for a specific programming exercise. In this paper, we will show, how the idea of unit testing may be applied in the field of engineering mathematics. The resulting automated assessment system can process and analyze a wide range of mathematical expressions (e.g. functions, number sets etc.), as well as deal with ambiguities in mathematical representations. More over, the system can detect and handle follow up and cascading errors by checking for intermediate results within a unit test, thus, assuring a fair grading result even in the presence of small oversight errors at the beginning of an exercise solution. Next to the evaluation of exercises, we will also discuss how to phrase mathematical questions in such an assessment framework. The developed technique may be used for large scale (online) courses or acceptance tests.

Keywords: Mathematics · Assessment · Unit testing · Grading · Teaching · Tutoring · Online courses

1 Introduction

Automated assessment of exercises and exams has become increasingly popular in recent years. In medical degree courses, automated multiple choice tests have been common for a long time. On the one hand this is due to the fact, that medical degrees have been very popular. Thus, resulting in large student numbers and consequently large numbers of exams, which needed to be assessed. On the other hand, exams in medical domains heavily rely on memorization and recognition tasks. Therefore, questions can typically be posed as closed-ended or multiple choice questions.

Student numbers in all domains have increased considerably in recent years, while university budgets typically lag (News 2014). In Germany e.g. the number

E. Ras and D. Joosten-ten Brinke (Eds.): CAA 2015, CCIS 571, pp. 110–119, 2015.
DOI: 10.1007/978-3-319-27704-2_11

of students rose by nearly 35 % from 2007 till 2013 (Statista 2014). These large student numbers and the rise of massive open online courses (MOOCs) have further increased the need for automatic testing tools.

More automated assessment could not only lower the teaching staff's increasing workload, but would also allow to test students more often. Thus, giving the students more frequent feedback on their learning success. In fact, most of the popular e-learning systems (e.g. (Moodle 2013) or (OLAT 2013)) incorporate a software module to create simple electronic tests. These simple electronic tests are used by many institutions from high schools to universities.

The adoption of automated tests can be relatively straight forward for some domains, e.g. medicine. For other domains, which traditionally use open-ended questions (e.g. the humanities) or have a focus on technical understanding, this is a more challenging task.

In technical domains as e.g. engineering or mathematics automated tests are not commonly used. While there are e-learning and e-teaching systems tailored towards technical and mathematical education and math tutoring (e.g. (Koedinger and Corbett 2006; Melis and Siekmann 2004; Cheung et al. 2003; Beal et al. 1998)), those are, to our knowledge, not used to a larger extent at universities. In fact, the development and active use of many of those systems seem to have halted. Despite promising results (e.g. (Livne et al. 2007)) the same holds true for many automatic grading systems, which have been developed specifically for the field of mathematics (e.g. (Sandene et al. 2005; Joglar et al. 2013)). Notable exceptions are the tools iMathAS (Platz et al. 2014) and WeBWorK (Baron 2010). To the best of our knowledge, none of these systems is able to deal with follow up or cascading errors in a systematic manner. Peer grading systems (e.g. (Caprotti et al. 2013)) also try to address automatic grading by delegating the process from teachers to peers. Their obvious drawbacks are in the areas of possibly unbalanced and non-immediate feedback.

In this paper we present a novel technique for the automatic assessment of technical and in particular mathematic exercises. In the field of mathematics, we encounter exercises at both ends of the spectrum. On the one hand, there are exercises with a single numerical answer. These exercises are easily assessed by an automatic computer system. On the other hand, there are more complex exercises requiring multiple solution steps or resulting in multiple numerical values, vectors, functions or other mathematical constructs. In order to be able to analyze more complex exercises we draw inspiration from the concept of unit testing, which is popular in the field of computer science (Kolawa and Huizinga 2007).

The idea is to think of a mathematical exercise as an algorithm. Students have to execute the algorithm by inserting given data e.g. numeric values to solve a particular exercise. These algorithms are typically multi-step processes with successive intermediate results. In order to assure a fair assessment result, all of these steps should be taken into account. This means, in particular, that not only the final result, e.g. the last computed number, should be considered when posing a question. On the computer side, we can implement the algorithm for the exercise solution as a small computer program or unit test. This program not only compares the final result, but computes all necessary intermediate steps. This way, the automatic assessment system is also able to detect follow up or cascading errors and handle them accordingly. Imagine e.g. a student makes a mistake in the first step of an exercise. The computer algorithm may continue its execution based on the student's result instead of the correct one. Thus, it can be verified whether subsequent steps are correct.

By applying this technique, we avoid an all-or-nothing style grading, where students only succeed, when all steps are correct. This kind of exercises can also be used interactively during the learning process not only for a final assessment in a course. In fact, in order to keep students motivated it is crucial to provide a more detailed feedback and reward students for partial results. Student engagement, particularly of the less talented students, drops dramatically, when all-or-nothing grading is applied in the learning process (Seemann 2014).

Obviously, this process requires teachers and professors to design exercises more carefully. When posing complex questions, we need to include meaningful intermediate steps. For each type of exercise, we have to provide not only the solution, but also a computer program of how to solve it and test for partial results or cascading errors. In the following sections we will detail how such exercises are implemented and how variations of the exercises can be generated.

2 Unit Testing

In computer science unit testing is a technique to validate the functionality of a software program. Software programs and complex algorithms are typically split into multiple distinct parts, which compute a subset of the overall functionality. This makes the source code more manageable and easier to understand. Therefore, in order to implement and validate the functionality of an algorithm, a programmer proceeds in the following steps:

1. Split the algorithm into meaningful parts
2. Define input/output parameters for the individual parts
3. Implement test cases for each part

Unit tests typically have a number of interesting properties. First, it should not matter how some functionality is implemented. And second, a unit test should consider edge and corner cases of an algorithm.

A program to pick an arbitrary number from a list of numbers could, e.g., be divided into two parts. One part, which computes a random position between 1 and the length of the list and a second part, which picks the number from this random position.

A so-called test case would then be used to verify the functionality of each of those parts. A test case is constructed in the following manner. First, an input value is chosen from all possible input data sets. Then the desired output data is either directly given or the properties of the output data are specified. That is, given appropriate input data and output data, which is known to be correct, we can check whether the provided algorithmic implementation is correct.

A sample test case for the second part of the above example could be implemented in JUnit, a unit testing framework for Java (JUnit 2014), as follows:

```
@Test
public void TestCase2() {
    // input data
    int[] list = {4,7,5,2,4};
    int pos = 3;
    // output data
    int correct = 2;
    // compare
    int result = pickFromList(list, 3);
    assertEquals(result, correct);
}
```

For the automatic assessment of math exercises, we treat the exercise problem as an algorithm. Similar to a computer program, we then divide the algorithm into multiple parts. An exercise to compute the distance of a point P to a given plane E could e.g. be divided into one part, which computes an orthogonal vector to E, another part which computes a connecting vector between the plane E and the point P and a third part, which executes the projection onto the orthogonal vector.

A test case would be constructed in a similar way by defining:

- Input data
- An algorithmic implementation
  (known to be correct)
- Output data

The output data of a test case always corresponds to a student's response. Unlike before, we cannot assume this output data to be valid. Instead we need to provide an algorithmic implementation which is known to be correct. Thus, instead of testing the algorithm, we are testing the output data. The input data for the first test case is given by the exercise problem itself. For the above example, the plane in 3D space. For successive test cases, we can precompute valid input values, e.g. the orthogonal vector.

In order to detect follow up or cascading errors, however, we need to modify this procedure. Imagine e.g. that a student makes a mistake in the computation of the orthogonal vector. Then, all subsequent test cases would fail as well, since the student's results depend on this first computed value. If a test case is dependent on the output of a previous test case, we therefore can use this output as an input value of the test case. That is, instead of using precomputed valid input values for each test case, we use the outputs of earlier test cases as input for subsequent test cases. Note that, we obtain a directed acyclic graph of test cases which needs to be evaluated.

We can implement the necessary algorithms for our test cases using mathematical programming languages e.g. Matlab or Maxima. Section 4 will detail some examples. For grading, we attribute points to each test case. A student's grade is then computed by summing the points of all test cases.

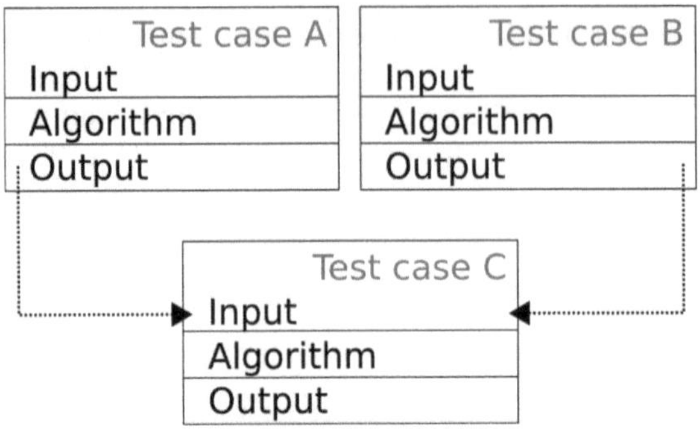

Fig. 1. Follow up error can be detected by using output data of previous test cases as input data for subsequent test cases in an acyclic direct graph.

3 Exercise Design

It is important to design exercise problems specifically for such an automatic grading system. This does not mean, that existing problems cannot be used, but exercise problems have typically to be adapted. In fact, the presented system allows teachers to represent a wide range of possible questions. Thus, giving them much more flexibility in the exercise design as it is the case with common systems for electronic tests (Fig. 1).

When phrasing a problem or question, teachers have to keep in mind that the students' responses need to be covered by a test case. In particular, this means that they need to clearly specify not only the input information given in the exercise, but also the required intermediate results a student needs to provide.

Let us look at an example exercise where students have to show that they master the principle of orthogonal projection by applying it to an application in the field of analytical geometry. The specific exercise is to compute the distance between a point P and a plane E in 3D space. In this example, a teacher would e.g. require students to enter both the final result and two intermediate values: the orthogonal vector and a difference vector, which connects an arbitrary point in the plane with P. Thus, resulting in three test cases in our unit testing framework.

The exercise problem could be specified in the following manner:

Compute the distance between the point $P = (3, 3, -2)$ and the plane E using an orthogonal projection. The plane E is given as

$$E : x = \begin{pmatrix}1\\1\\0\end{pmatrix} + s\begin{pmatrix}1\\0\\1\end{pmatrix} + t\begin{pmatrix}0\\1\\1\end{pmatrix}.$$

(a) Compute a vector n orthogonal to E
(b) Which vector v can you use for this projection?
(c) What is the absolute value d of the distance?

That is, the exercise problem is split into three steps. For each step the students have to provide an intermediate solution, which will be used as output or input data for the unit tests. Each subquestion (a), (b) and (c) correspond to one test case.

The division into the subquestions is not only useful for the assessment system, it can also support or guide students to find the correct solution approach. Additionally, students are required to execute the individual solution steps instead of just filling numbers into an existing formula, which they have learned by heart. In fact, in today's high school and even university education many students revert to filling numbers in formulas without a deeper understanding of the problems.

By using test cases, whose outputs and inputs depend on one another, we can allow rather complex exercise problems. In common multiple choice or fixed answer testing systems, it is not possible to pose this kind of problems. A single mistake at the beginning of the exercise would render all subsequent steps wrong. This all-or-nothing grading makes automatic assessment less fair and decreases student motivation.

3.1 Covering the Solution Space

Even though, the proposed technique allows for a much wider variety of math exercises to be used in electronic tests, there are, of course, still math problems which cannot be covered easily using such an automatic system. It is, e.g. extremely difficult to test mathematic proofs as the space of possible solution steps is, in most cases, too large. For these kinds of problems teachers have to resort to classic pen and paper tests.

In the field of engineering maths, however, proofs are rarely used as exam questions and students are mostly asked to solve more applied exercises. These questions often require them to follow a certain procedure or algorithm (e.g. computing the center of gravity, solving a differential equation). For these types of exercises, it is typically evident how to cover the complete solution space. In order to allow possible alternative solutions, teachers need to provide additional unit tests.

The general rule is: the more open the question, the more difficult it is to cover the solution space and follow-up errors using unit tests.

3.2 User Interface

In our system teachers can write exercises in a LaTeX syntax, which is automatically translated to HTML. As a user interface, a modern web form is used, where students can enter mathematic expressions in the familiar Matlab syntax. Note that, the target audience are university students, which are familiar with programming in Matlab. Below, you can find a screen shot of the user interface for our example question:

As can be seen, the individual subquestions are marked in green or red depending on whether the corresponding test case has succeeded or failed.

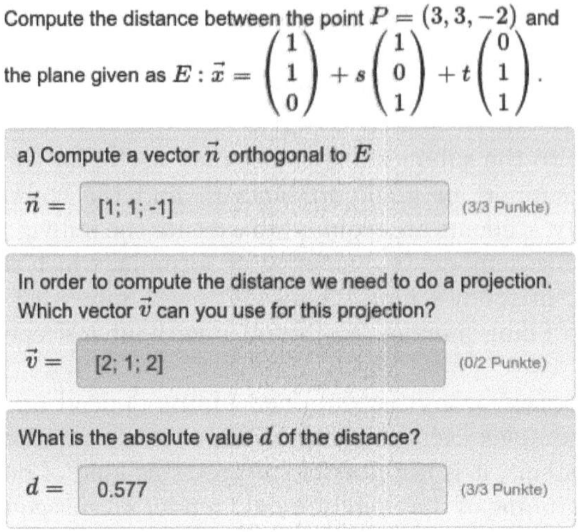

Fig. 2. User interface for the assessment system with validation results represented as background colors.

In the example displayed in Fig. 2 the student has made a mistake in subquestion (b), but based on this incorrect intermediate result, the test case for the final result succeeded.

4 Exercise Implementation

In order to validate the students' responses, all intermediate results are fed into a software validation program. This program executes all test cases defined for the exercise. A test case may be implemented in any programming language, but mathematic languages like Matlab or Maxima are the obvious choice due to their large libraries of mathematical functions and of course due to their convenient syntax. It is important to realize, that test cases may leverage the full power of the programming language and the implementations of test cases may range from a simple numeric comparison to complex algorithms.

For the sample question given in Sect. 3, there are three test cases. The first test case needs to verify that the vector n provided by the student is indeed orthogonal to the given plane. Therefore the input data needed is comprised of the two defining vectors $\begin{pmatrix}1\\0\\1\end{pmatrix}$ and $\begin{pmatrix}0\\1\\1\end{pmatrix}$. The output data is the vector n provided by the student. To complete our test case, we need to define an algorithmic implementation of the property, which we want to verify. This could e.g. be solved by the following program:

```
function isValid = testCase1()
    // input data
    r1 = [1; 0; 1];
```

```
    r2 = [0; 1; 1];
    // reference solution
    o = cross(r1,r2);
    // output data
    n = userField1();
    // result
    isValid = rank([n o])==1;
```

That is, once the input data is specified, the program computes a reference solution o, which is used to compare to the student response. Obviously, the subquestion has not one, but an infinite number of solutions. Any multiple of an orthogonal vector is again orthogonal. In order to check whether the vector n is a multiple of o we compute the rank of the matrix consisting of the two vectors. If the corresponding matrix has rank 1, the vectors are co-linear.

Note that, it is impossible to allow questions with an infinite number of possible solutions in multiple choice or fixed answer electronic tests. By using programmable test cases, however, teachers may use a much larger variety of exercise problems. In fact, once test cases are implemented, it is easy to create variations of the same exercise problem by changing the input values.

The third test case in our example, depends on the results of the first two steps. This could be implemented as follows:

```
function isValid = testCase3()
    // input data
    eps = 0.01;
    n = userField1();
    v = userField2();
    // reference solution
    p = v'*n/norm(n);
    // output data
    d = userField3();
    // result
    isValid = (p-d)<eps;
```

Note, that the test case uses the input provided by the student instead of correct reference values. This allows the system to handle follow up errors. That is, a student's solution is correct, if it is correct based on his/her previous intermediate results. Consequently a mistake early in the solution process does not necessarily result in mistakes for subsequent steps. Due to rounding errors and inexact number representations in the computer, we allow for a small ε-difference between the input and the reference solution when floating point numbers are involved.

A good implementation of a test case is often more complex. E.g. a test case may check whether an intermediate response simplifies the exercise problem. Imagine a problem, where a student has to compute the maxima and minima values of a function. If the student's derivative results in an overly simple function all subsequent steps are, actually, much easier. In those cases, subsequent test case implementations should check the provided intermediate results and add a penalty if appropriate. For polynomials, e.g. a test case could verify whether the degree of the derivative is above a certain value.

Most test cases, at some point, have to do a comparison between two mathematic expressions. In the above example, this comparison is rather trivial, since we compare two integer values or two floating point values. But there are, of course, more sophisticated problems, which need to be considered in test cases. We will quickly review the variety of mathematic expressions our system can handle in the subsequent section.

4.1 Comparing Mathematic Expressions

Due to equivalent mathematic representations, it is not always straight forward for mathematic tests to decide whether a provided input expression is correct. By using a mathematic programming languages to implement test cases, however, the developed system is able to handle a large variety of representations of mathematic expressions, e.g. numbers, vectors and matrices as well as sets, intervals and functions. In order to compare input vectors or matrices with a reference solution, we have to consider different number representations. The vector `[2/5; 2.718]` is e.g. equal to the vector `[0.4; exp(1)]`. This can be achieved by computing the minimal difference between the values of the vector's components. For matrices, we may similarly implement a comparison as `max(max(inputMatrix-solutionMatrix))<` `eps` with `eps` a small number which allows for rounding errors. For mathematic functions a comparison is more complex. The term $x(x+1)$ e.g. is equivalent to x^2+x. In order to simplify mathematic expressions, symbolic math packages may be used and techniques as described in (Fateman 1972) allow to match similar function representations. Again, this is not possible with other electronic tests.

Currently, we have implemented exercises for university level courses in engineering maths. Exercise topics range from function analysis to vector algebra. The system is used both for self-tests during the course of the semester, as well as for the final exam.

5 Conclusion

In this paper, we have described a novel grading system for the assessment of mathematic or engineering exercises. The idea is to use small but sophisticated computer programs to validate the correctness of a student response. These computer programs are inspired by the concept of unit tests, which are popular in software engineering.

Designing electronic tests based on the proposed system requires an additional effort. In common electronic tests, teachers have to design a question and provide an appropriate mathematic solution e.g. as a numeric value of multiple choice answer. Our systems requires teachers to implement an algorithmic test case for each exercise using a programming language. This additional effort, however, results in a new flexibility. Teachers may use a much larger variety of questions, since the system "understands" mathematical expressions and can compare different representations of numbers and functions. For the students the benefit lies in a fairer grading result. Follow up errors can be detected and handled appropriately. Thus, avoiding the all-or-nothing style grading of most other assessment systems. This is particularly important to keep students motivated and improve their learning success when the system is used throughout the course of a semester.

References

Baron, L.: Helping teachers generate better homework: MAA makes time for WeBWorK. MAA Focus Newsmagazine Math. Assoc. Am. **30**(5), 18–19 (2010)

Beal, C., Beck, J., Woolf, B: Impact of intelligent computer instruction on girls' math self concept and beliefs in the value of math. In: Annual meeting of the American Educational Research Association (1998)

Caprotti, O., Ojalainen, J., Pauna, M., Seppl, M.: Weps peer and automatic assessment in online math courses (2013)

Cheung, B., Hui, L., Zhang, J., Yiu, S.: Smarttutor: an intelligent tutoring system in web-based adult education. J. Syst. Softw. **68**, 11–25 (2003)

Fateman, R.J.: Essays in algebraic simplification. In: Ph.D. thesis at the Massachusetts Institute of Technology (1972)

Joglar, N., Risco, J.L., Snchez, R., Colmenar, J.M., Daz, A.: Testing in math courses a new tool for online exams automatically graded: a teaching and learning experience (2013)

JUnit: Unit testing framework (2014). http://junit.org

Koedinger, K., Corbett, A.: Cognitive tutors: technology bringing learning science to the classroom. In: Sawyer, K. (ed.) The Cambridge Handbook of the Learning Sciences, pp. 61–78. Cambridge University Press, Cambridge (2006)

Kolawa, A., Huizinga, D.: Automated Defect Prevention: Best Practices in Software Management. Wiley-IEEE Computer Society Press, New York (2007)

Livne, N., Livne, O., Wright, C.: Can automated scoring surpass hand grading of students' constructed responses and error patterns in mathematics (2007)

Melis, E., Siekmann, J.H.: ActiveMath: an intelligent tutoring system for mathematics. In: Rutkowski, L., Siekmann, J.H., Tadeusiewicz, R., Zadeh, L.A. (eds.) ICAISC 2004. LNCS (LNAI), vol. 3070, pp. 91–101. Springer, Heidelberg (2004)

Moodle: moodle learning management system (2013). http://moodle.org

News, U.W.: Student numbers soar by 35 %, university funding lags (2014)

OLAT: Online Learning and Training (2013). http://olat.org

Platz, M., Niehaus, E., Dahn, I., Dreyer, U.: IMathAS and automated assessment of mathematical proof (2014)

Sandene, B., Bennett, R., Braswell, J., Oranje, A.: Online assessment in mathematics (2005)

Seemann, E.: Teaching computer programming in online courses - how unit tests allow for automated feedback and grading. In: International Conference on Computer Supported Education (2014)

Statista: Statistik der Studierendenzahlen an deutschen Hochschulen (2014). http://de.statista.com/statistik/daten/studie/221/umfrage/anzahl-der-studenten-an-deutschen-hochschulen/

Understanding the Role of Time on Task in Formative Assessment: The Case of Mathematics Learning

Dirk T. Tempelaar[1(✉)], Bart Rienties[2], and Bas Giesbers[3]

[1] School of Business and Economics, Maastricht University, Maastricht, The Netherlands
D.Tempelaar@MaastrichtUniversity.nl
[2] Open University UK, Institute of Educational Technology, Milton Keynes, UK
Bart.Rienties@open.ac.uk
[3] Rotterdam School of Management, Erasmus University, Rotterdam, The Netherlands
BGiesbers@rsm.nl

Abstract. Mastery data derived from formative assessments constitute a rich data set in the development of student performance prediction models. The dominance of formative assessment mastery data over use intensity data such as time on task or number of clicks was the outcome of previous research by the authors in a dispositional learning analytics context [1–3]. Practical implications of these findings are far reaching, contradicting current practices of developing (learning analytics based) student performance prediction models based on intensity data as central predictor variables. In this empirical follow-up study using data of 2011 students, we search for an explanation for time on task data being dominated by mastery data. We do so by investigating more general models, allowing for nonlinear, even non-monotonic, relationships between time on task and performance measures. Clustering students into subsamples, with different time on task characteristics, suggests heterogeneity of the sample to be an important cause of the nonlinear relationships with performance measures. Time on task data appear to be more sensitive to the effects of heterogeneity than mastery data, providing a further argument to prioritize formative assessment mastery data as predictor variables in the design of prediction models directed at the generation of learning feedback.

Keywords: Formative assessment · Computer assisted assessment · Dispositional learning analytics · Blended learning · E-tutorials · Student profiles

1 Introduction

This study is a follow-up of previous research [1–3], in which we demonstrated that formative assessment data and mastery data derived from e-tutorial practice systems play key roles in predicting student performance, when designing learning analytics (LA) based models (for further examples on the role of formative assessment, see [4, 5]). The type of LA models applied in our studies is that of dispositional LA [3, 6],

E. Ras and D. Joosten-ten Brinke (Eds.): CAA 2015, CCIS 571, pp. 120–133, 2015.
DOI: 10.1007/978-3-319-27704-2_12

which combines system generated track data with disposition data to design prediction models. Within rich data sets to base prediction models, as available in our research, we invariably find that formative assessment and tool mastery data outperform time on task data, or other use intensity data such as number of clicks, in the prediction of student performance. This outcome is in itself remarkable, since use intensity data is typically at the centre of LA based prediction models. In this follow-up study we explore potential causes of this large difference in predictive power between the two types of predictors. Heterogeneity of the sample may be one of these causes: the circumstance that the sample is constituted of different clusters of students, for whom online learning activities and its functions of practicing and self-assessment play different roles in the learning process. The existence of such diverse clusters may impact the relationships estimated in the full sample: parsimonious, linear relationships within clusters, can turn into nonlinear, even non-monotonic relationships when estimated in a sample containing diverse clusters.

2 Framework

2.1 Computer Assisted Formative Assessment

Computer assisted formative assessment (or formative e-assessment, feast: [7]) extends features of formative assessment, such as facilitating student-centred learning, by providing immediate and adequate learning feedback [8], and potentially adaptivity for each learner [7]. Maximal gain of these aspects of immediate feedback and adaptivity is achieved when formative assessment is embedded into digital learning platforms, such as e-tutorials [9].

2.2 Dispositional Learning Analytics

A broad goal of LA is to apply the outcomes of analysing data gathered by monitoring and measuring the learning process, whereby feedback plays a crucial part to assist regulating that same learning process. Several alternative operationalisations are possible to support this. In [10], six objectives are distinguished: predicting learner performance and modelling learners, suggesting relevant learning resources, increasing reflection and awareness, enhancing social learning environments, detecting undesirable learner behaviours, and detecting affects of learners. Traditional LA applications are based on process and output track data from learning management systems (LMS). Buckingham Shum and Deakin Crick [6] proposed a dispositional LA infra-structure that combines learning activity generated data with learning dispositions: values and attitudes measured through self-report surveys, which are fed back to students and teachers through visual analytics. In previous research of the authors [1–3], we demonstrated the power of integrating formative assessment and mastery track data into prediction models based on dispositional LA.

Heterogeneity in a sample may have a ‘heterogeneous’ impact on relationships constituting a prediction model. Previous research in LA has used cluster techniques to identify whether sub-groups of students engage differently in online settings. For example, in a study comparing 40 learning designs with student engagement and academic performance of 17 k students, [11] found four different clusters of learning design, which were significantly related to academic performance. In three MOOC environments, [11] found that learners could be categorised in four subgroups based upon their interactions in videos and online assessments. A follow-up study [12] amongst four FutureLearn MOOCs found seven subgroups of learner activity.

Although these studies provide important insights into the affordances of learning analytics approaches, most studies reported above have used linear modelling techniques, thereby potentially ignoring underlying heterogeneous effects in the sample and learning processes in particular. Perhaps, the use intensity data, such as time on task or number of clicks in learning activities, are much more sensitive to this heterogeneity than cognitive variables, such as mastery level in the practicing mode of e-tutorial systems. What in itself is a crucial factor in the endeavour of designing prediction models. Therefore, by investigating a large sample of 2011 students in a blended course on Mathematics who intensively used a computer-assisted e-tutorial environment, we will address the following two research questions:

1. To what extent is time on task a good linear predictor for academic performance?
2. To what extent are learning dispositions related in a linear manner to academic performance?

3 Method

3.1 Educational Context

Our empirical contribution focuses on freshmen students in a quantitative methods (mathematics and statistics) course of the Maastricht University School of Business & Economics. The course is the first module for students entering the program. It is directed at a large and diverse group of students. The population consists of 2011 freshmen students, in two cohorts (2013/2014 and 2014/2015), who have been active in the LMS: 1005 and 1006 students, respectively. The first cohort coincides with the sample used in previous studies [1, 2]; this study extends the sample with the second cohort.

The student population is highly diverse, first and for all in its international composition: only 23 % received their prior (secondary) education from the Dutch high school system. The largest group, 45 % of the freshmen, was educated according to the German Abitur system. The remaining 32 % are mainly from central-European and southern European countries. High school systems in Europe differ strongly, most particularly in the teaching of mathematics and statistics [1, 2]. Differences do not only exists between countries, but also within countries, where most high school systems differentiate between advanced levels, preparing sciences or technology studies, intermediate level, preparing social sciences, and basic level, preparing arts and humanities. Therefore it is crucial that the first module offered to these students is flexible and allows for individual learning paths.

The educational system in which students learn mathematics and statistics is best described as a ‘blended’ or ‘hybrid’ system. The main component is ‘face-to-face’: problem-based learning (pbl), in small groups (14 students), coached by a content expert tutor. Participation in these tutor groups is required, as for all courses based on the Maastricht pbl system. The online component of the blend, that is, the use of the two e-tutorials MyMathLab and MyStatLab, and participation in formative assessments, is optional. The reason for making the online component optional is that this best fits the Maastricht educational model, which is student-centred and places the responsibility for making educational choices primarily with the student. At the same time, due to the diversity in prior knowledge, not all students will benefit equally from using these environments; in particular for those at the high performance end, extensive practicing and testing will not be the most effective allocation of learning time. However, the use of e-tutorials is stimulated by making bonus credits available for good performance in the formative assessments, or quizzes, and for achieving good scores in the practicing modes of the MyLab environments (with a maximum of 20 % of the score in the final exam). Quizzes are taken every two weeks and consist of items that are drawn from the same or similar item pools applied in the practicing mode. We chose for this particular constellation, since it stimulates students with little prior knowledge to make intensive use of the MyLab platforms. They realize that they may fall behind other students in writing the exam, and therefore need to achieve a good bonus score both to compensate, and to support their learning. The most direct way to do so is to frequently practice in the e-tutorials and participate the quizzes in the assessment mode of both MyLab environments.

The instructional format was the same in the two subsequent implementations, with the exception of the composition of the quizzes: see [13] for more details. In the 2013 cohort, quiz items were randomly selected from the same pool of items students could access in the practicing mode of the e-tutorial. Thus by putting sufficient effort in practicing, students could achieve knowledge of all item types in the quiz (but not with the exact items themselves, since items are parametrized). To avoid stimulating students to repeat practicing over and over again, only to learn all different item types, we split all item pools into two non-overlapping sub-pools, one for independent practicing purposes, the other for quizzing, in the 2014 cohort [13].

In this study, we will focus the analysis of practicing and participation in formative assessment in the e-tutorials to the subject mathematics, and the tool MyMathLab, primarily since a crucial part of our disposition data is subject specific, that is, relates to mathematics.

3.2 E-tutorial MyMathLab

The e-tutorial system MyMathLab (MML) is a generic digital learning environment for learning mathematics developed by the publisher Pearson. Although MyLabs can be used as a learning environment in the broad sense of the word (it contains, among others, a digital version of the textbook), it is primarily an environment for test-directed learning, practicing and assessment. Each step in the learning process is initiated by submitting an item. Students are encouraged to (try to) answer each question (see Fig. 1

for an example). If they do not master a question (completely), the student can either ask for help to solve the problem step-by-step (Help Me Solve This), or ask for a fully worked example (View an Example). These two functionalities are examples of Knowledge of Result/response (KR) and Knowledge of the Correct Response (KCR) types of feedback; see Narciss [14, 15]. After receiving this type of feedback, a new version of the problem loads (parameter based) to allow the student to demonstrate his/her newly acquired mastery. When a student provides an answer and opts for 'Check Answer', Multiple-Try Feedback (MTF, [14]) is provided, whereby the number of times feedback is provided for the same task depends on the format of the task (only two for a multiple choice type of task as in Fig. 1, more for open type of tasks requiring numerical answers).

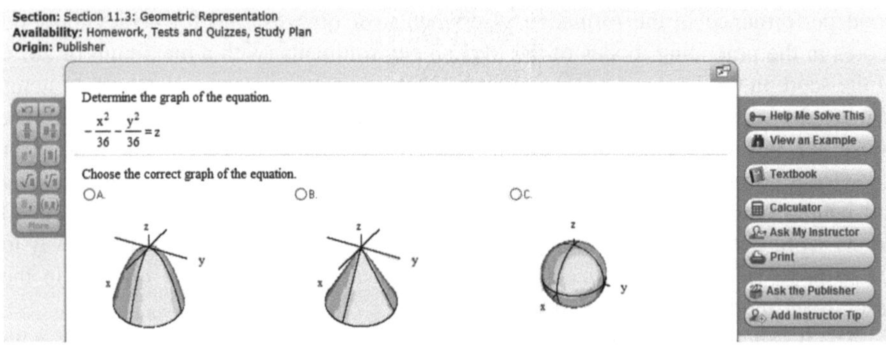

Fig. 1. Sample of MyMathLab item

In the two subsequent years, students average time on task is 37.9 h (2013) and 29.7 h (2014) in MML, which is 30 % to 40 % of the available time of 80 h for learning in both topics. All weekly assignments count a total of 245 items. The decline in time on task is in line with the instructional intervention of splitting practice and quiz item pools, in order to provide fewer stimuli to rehearse activities. In the present study, we use two different indicators for the intensity of the MyLabs usage: MLHours indicates the time a student spends practicing in the MyMathLab environment per week, and MLAttempts indicates the total number of attempts in the practicing mode. As the consequence of these two, MLMastery indicates the average final score achieved for the practice questions in any week.

3.3 LA Dispositions Instruments

In our application of dispositional LA [3], dispositions were operationalized with a broad range of self-report instruments based on contemporary social-cognitive learning theories. These instruments cover dispositions as learning styles, motivation and engagement constructs, goal setting, subject attitudes and learning emotions. In this study, we will restrict to two of these instruments: motivation and engagement scales, and learning emotions. Recent Anglo-Saxon literature on academic achievement and dropout assigns an increasingly important role to the theoretical model of Andrew Martin: the 'Motivation and Engagement Wheel' [16] (see also [17]). This model includes both behaviours and thoughts, or cognitions, that play a role in learning. Both are subdivided into adaptive and mal-adaptive (or impeding) forms. As a result, the four quadrants are: adaptive behaviour and adaptive thoughts (the 'boosters'), mal-adaptive behaviour (the 'guzzlers') and impeding thoughts (the 'mufflers'). Adaptive thoughts consist of Self-belief, Learning focus, and Value of school, whereas adaptive behaviours consist of Persistence, Planning, and Task management. Mal-adaptive or impeding thoughts include Anxiety, Failure avoidance, and Uncertain control, and lastly, maladaptive behaviours include Self-sabotage and Disengagement.

Learning emotions were measured through four scales of the Achievement Emotions Questionnaire (AEQ) developed by Pekrun [18]: Enjoyment, Anxiety, Boredom and Hopelessness (see also [17, 19]). Pekrun's taxonomy of achievement emotions provides a subdivision into three different contexts of academic settings where students can experience emotions: attending class, when studying, and while taking exams. For the purpose of our study, we have considered the four emotions just mentioned in study situations: the learning mathematics related emotions. The other assumptions underlying Pekrun's taxonomy are that achievement emotions have a valence, which can be either positive or negative, and an activation component, usually referred to as physiologically activating versus deactivating. Considering these dimensional perspectives, Enjoyment is a positive activating emotion, Anxiety is negative activating, and Hopelessness and Boredom are negative deactivating emotions.

Academic control was measured with the perceived Academic control scale of Perry [20]. The perceived academic control is a domain-specific measure of college students' beliefs of being 'in control' whilst learning mathematics. For a detailed description of the validity and response rates of these psychometric instruments, we refer to our previous study [17].

3.4 Procedures

Beyond disposition data, administered through digital self-reports in the very start of the module for the motivation and engagement data, and halfway the module for the learning emotions data, system data have been collected. System data refer to both data from concern systems as the student registration system (nationality, prior education, especially for mathematics, gender), and system track data from the MyLab system. Three main features we tracked in MML are:

- Mastery level, expressed as the proportion of the 245 MML items partially or completely mastered (MLMastery);
- Time on task, expressed as the number of hours students spend in practicing and self-assessment of the 245 MML items (MLHours);
- Number of attempts, to measure the number of trials and repetitions in practicing items (MLAttempts).

Two different performance measures are distinguished: score in exam (Exam) and total score in the three quizzes (Quiz).

To investigate whether relationships between the several variables, and in specific between time on task data and other data, are of linear type, we clustered students both on total time on task (MLHours), and average time on task per attempt (MLHours/MLAttempts), using an approximate quintile split. Clustering is in five clusters, based on standardized data: VeryLow (below 1 SD below the mean), Low (between 1 and 0.5 SD below the mean), Neutral (between −0.5 and 0.5 SD from the mean), High (between 0.5 and 1 SD from the mean) and VeryHigh (above 1 SD from the mean).

4 Results

4.1 Descriptive Statistics and Correlations

Student mastery in the e-tutorial MyMathLab is the stronger predictor of both performance types: exam score and quiz score, amongst the three MML based system track data: mastery, time on task, and number of attempts. However, all three instances of track data demonstrate positive correlations with both exam and quiz performance, as can be seen in Table 1, with cohort 2013 below the diagonal and 2014 data above the diagonal. E-tutorial mastery data signal r values of about .4 for exam performance, and about .7 for quiz performance. These findings are fully in line with our previous LA studies [1, 2], where we concluded MLMastery to be the dominant system track variable in prediction models explaining module performance.

Table 1. Correlation matrix for 2013 (left, bottom) and 2014 (right, top) of performance and MyLab variables (all correlations larger than .1 statistically significant at .001 level)

2013/2014	Exam	Quiz	MLMastery	MLHours	MLAttempts
Exam		.677	.400	.025	.119
Quiz	.716		.591	.144	.217
MLMastery	.406	.675		.506	.667
MLHours	.021	.201	.508		.447
MLAttempts	.061	.315	.647	.484	

MLMastery itself is strongly positively related to intensity of using the e-tutorial, measured in time on task, MLHours, as well as total number of attempts to solve an item, MLAttempts. The direct relationships between both use intensity variables, and both performance variables, is however rather weak, and in some cases not statistically significant. A last observation from the correlation matrix refers the intervention in instructional design. The largest differences between 2013 and 2014 correlations are in the two e-tutorial use intensity variables, and quiz performance, in the direction of a decrease in size, (from .2 and .3 to .0 and .1). Weakening those two relationships was indeed the main aim of the intervention described before (see also [13]).

Other descriptive outcomes refer to variables describing the composition of the sample. There is a weak gender effect: female students achieve higher mastery in the e-tutorial by spending more hours, but both performance measures, and number of attempts are gender invariant. There exists a strong nationality effect: international students strongly outperform Dutch students on both performance measures, and all three MyLab measures. Lastly, there is a strong prior education effect: students educated at advanced level outperform students educated at intermediate level with regard to exam and quiz performance, and MLMastery, but need both less time and less attempts to achieve these higher proficiency levels.

4.2 Partial Linear Prediction Models

The picture of all positive correlations changes crucially when we look at the same data from a multivariate perspective, deriving linear prediction models explaining the different types of module performance from a simultaneous regression model containing mastery in the e-tutorial, time on task and number of attempts as independent variables. These four prediction equations, for both cohorts 2013 and 2014, and for performance types exam and quiz, are as follows.

$$\text{Exam2013} = 0.66 \times \text{MLMastery} - 0.16 \times \text{MLHours} - 0.29 \times \text{MLAttempts} \quad (1)$$

$$\text{Quiz2013} = 0.81 \times \text{MLMastery} - 0.15 \times \text{MLHours} - 0.13 \times \text{MLAttempts} \quad (2)$$

$$\text{Exam2014} = 0.61 \times \text{MLMastery} - 0.18 \times \text{MLHours} - 0.19 \times \text{MLAttempts} \quad (3)$$

$$\text{Quiz2014} = 0.74 \times \text{MLMastery} - 0.11 \times \text{MLHours} - 0.25 \times \text{MLAttempts} \quad (4)$$

Estimated regression coefficients are beta's, that is, standardized regression coefficients, to allow comparison of different cohorts, and of different types of module performance. All coefficients are strongly statistically significant, with significance levels below .01.

The most notable feature of the four regression equations is the consistent, negative impact of both time on task, and number of attempts, for given mastery levels. In this, the multivariate outcomes are in contrast to the bivariate outcomes contained in Table 1. Its interpretation is that for a given mastery level, students who need more time on task to reach that mastery level, do less well in the exam, and in the quizzes. Similarly, for a given mastery level, students who need more attempts to reach that mastery level, do again less well in the exam, and in the quizzes. The fact that bivariate correlations are positive is explained by the positive relations between mastery and time on task as well as number of attempts. So in general, students with more time on task achieve higher mastery levels, as do students with more attempts, and these higher mastery levels contribute to higher performance levels. But when keeping mastery levels constant, the direct effect of use intensity on performance becomes visible, and this direct effect is negative.

When we compare exam with quiz performance, the stronger role of mastery in predicting quiz performance is evident. Since quizzes are administered in the e-tutorial and quiz items are similar to items encountered when practicing in the e-tutorial, this does not surprise. When comparing the two cohorts, the instructional intervention of distinguishing separate item pools for practicing and quizzing is visible in the decreased role of mastery in the prediction equation of quiz performance in the 2014 cohort: quizzes have become less predictable.

4.3 Time on Task and Academic Performance

Do these bivariate and multivariate relations together provide a full answer to the first research question on the role that time on task, and number of attempts, play in the prediction of module performance? Both correlations and regressions are based on the assumption of linear relationships. But when we allow for non-linear relationships, it is easy to see that in our case the assumption of linearity is not satisfied. When we cluster the populations of the two cohorts with regard to time on task, both in terms of total time, and time per attempt, we find relationships described in Fig. 2. These relationships between time on task as use intensity and exam score (range 0..20) are highly nonlinear, indicating that by far the worst performance is amongst students with lowest amount of time on task. But setting this cluster aside, we are left with a decreasing, rather than increasing relationship: exam performance deteriorates with more time on task. If we focus on time on task per attempt, rather than total time on task (as illustrated by the dashed lines), we find that best performance is now achieved in the middle of the time on task spectrum.

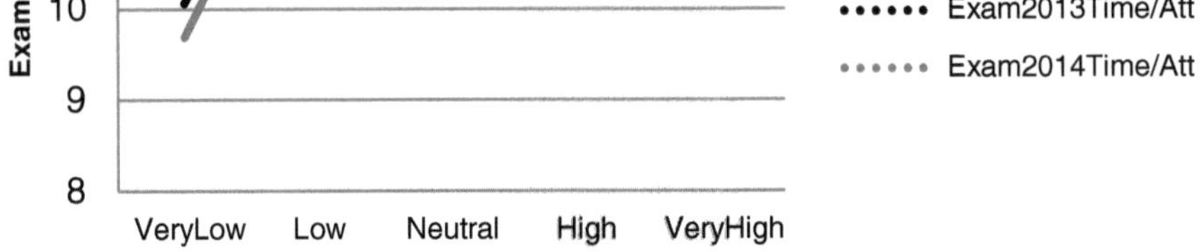

Fig. 2. Five clusters of time on task intensity, and exam performance

Inferential tests for differences in cluster means by analyses of variance (ANOVA), demonstrate the differences in cluster means to be strongly statistically significant (all four significance levels are below .01).

Redoing the same analysis for the second performance component, the quizzes (ranging in scores from 0..4), brings about two marked differences. The first is that quiz score is rather constant for increasing numbers of time on task, and in contrast to Fig. 2,

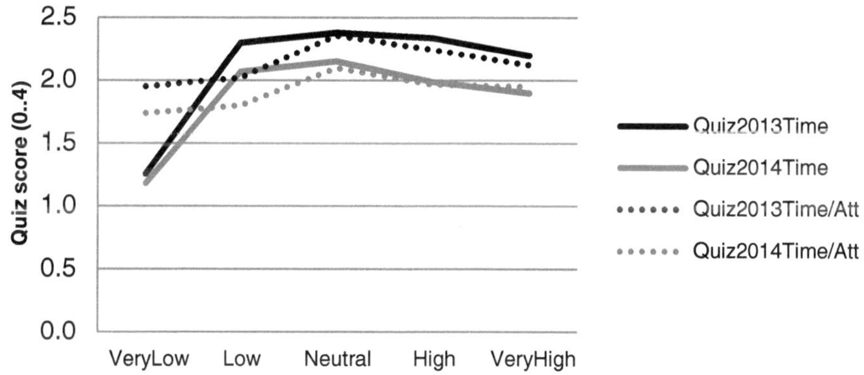

Fig. 3. Five clusters of time on task intensity, and quiz performance

does not deteriorate clearly. Second: the instructional intervention is clearly visible in Fig. 3 by the shift downwards of the two curves describing 2014 quiz performance.

Inferential tests for differences in cluster means of the quiz scores by analyses of variance again demonstrate differences in cluster means to be strongly statistically significant (all four significance levels are below .01).

4.4 Learning Dispositions and Academic Performance

In order to answer research question 2, from the broad selection of learning dispositions incorporated in the LA based study, we will report on two: motivation and engagement dispositions, and learning emotions. Figure 4 provides a breakdown of four motivation and engagement dispositions that demonstrate strong statistically significant cluster

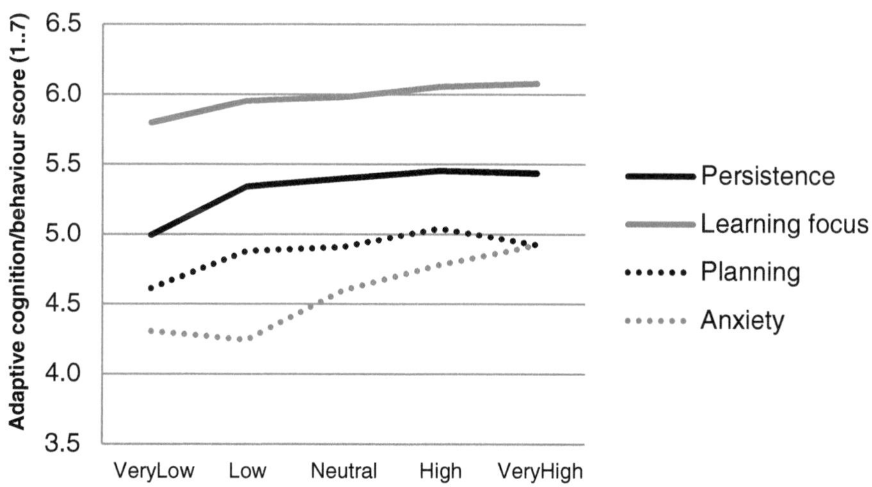

Fig. 4. Clusters of time on task intensity, and motivation and engagement dispositions

differences (at significance level .01): Persistence, Learning focus, Planning, and general Anxiety. Given the strong similarity of outcomes for the two time on task variables, we focus on total time on task, and data of the last cohort: that of 2014.

The three adaptive cognitions and behaviours Persistence, Learning focus, and Planning share a similar pattern: generally increasing with time on task. Relationships are approximately linear, with the exception of the cluster with very low time on task: that cluster scores less than expected in a linear model. The Anxiety variable demonstrates a clear nonlinear pattern: relative low levels of Anxiety amongst students with lower than average time on task, increasing Anxiety levels amongst students spending more than average time on task: see Fig. 4. Scores are from a Likert scale ranging (1..7).

Again, analyses of variance indicate strong statistically significant differences between cluster means (below .01 significance levels).

Further examples of nonlinear relationships are observed in the learning emotions variables depicted in Fig. 5. Learning emotions are measured in the context of learning mathematics, implying e.g. that the Anxiety variable in Fig. 5 plays a different role than that in the previous figure. The negative learning emotions Anxiety and Helplessness, as well as the antecedent variable Control, achieve their highest scores amongst students with low levels of time on task. Learning Boredom requires more time effort to reach its optimum: students with high levels of time on task are lowest on Boredom. The same pattern is visible in the positive learning emotion Enjoyment: students high in time on task achieve the highest levels. Again, learning emotions are measured using a Likert (1..7) scales, and in analyses of variance, all differences between cluster means are statistically significant (significance levels below .01).

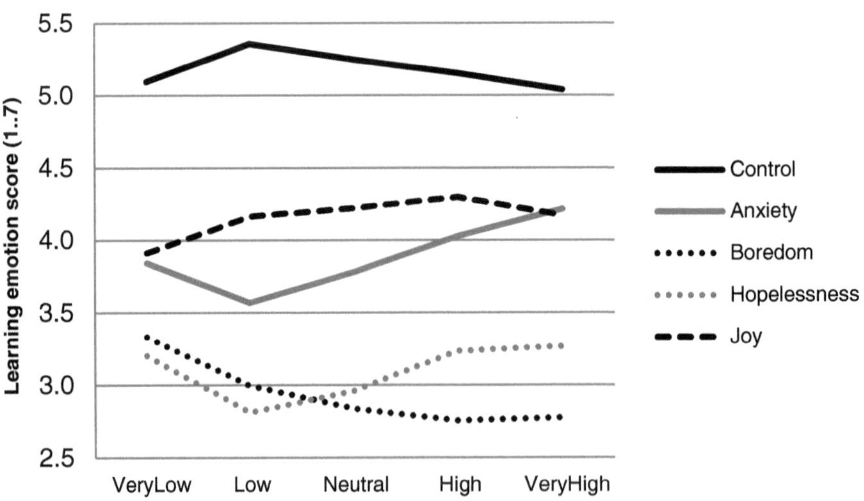

Fig. 5. Clusters of time on task intensity, and learning emotions dispositions

5 Conclusions and Implications

Our previous research [1–3] aimed at developing performance prediction models on the basis of process and output track data, and dispositions date, in order to generate learning feedback. Such prediction models were of linear type, and had adequate predictive power. As exemplified by research questions 1-2, the investigation into the role of time on task in module performance first and foremost signals that the assumption of linearity commonly used in LA approaches does not seem to be a reasonable assumption. In fact, most relationships with time on task were even not monotonic, as Figs. 2, 3, 4 and 5 make clear. Using linear prediction models containing prediction variables that are likely to be sensitive to heterogeneity is a dangerous expedition.

It is not difficult to see why linearity breaks down. As addressed in the descriptive part of the results section, students in this study are quite heterogeneous, and this will be even more so for the several cluster outcomes. To provide one clear example: whereas Dutch students are only 26 % of all students in the 2014 sample, they make up 48 % of the VeryLow cluster (with declining shares in the next clusters: 39 %, 23 %, 15 %, 11 %). Thus, more often than international students, Dutch students tend to opt out with regard to the e-tutorial practicing and formative assessment activities, being an optional component of the educational program. Their opting out is facilitated by an apparent lack of urgency: anxiety levels in cluster VeryLow are relatively low, both mathematics specific, and in general with regard to university.

Another piece of heterogeneity pops up in the second cluster: Low levels of time on task. Prior mathematics education of students in our sample is either at advanced level (39 %, such as German "Leistungskurs", or Dutch "WiB"), or at intermediate level (61 %, such as "Grundkurs", "WiA"). These students are unevenly spread over the five time on task clusters: 39 %, 53 %, 42 %, 31 %, and 25 % respectively. That is: in the Low cluster, more than half of the students are from an advanced track of mathematics education, explaining their high levels of being in control, and their low levels of anxiety. In contrast, the composition of the cluster at the very high end, with no more than 25 % of students from the advanced track, explains the combination of high levels of time on task, low levels of control, and high levels of anxiety.

Sensitivity to heterogeneity of the sample is a 'heterogeneous phenomenon' in itself: different prediction variables are more or less influenced by differences between subgroups in the sample. Stable prediction models are best based on predictors least sensitive to heterogeneity. That was visible from our previous research, where the automatic generation of most predictive models lead to models dominantly based on formative assessment outcomes, and tool mastery variables, rather than on time on task variables, or click variables [1–3]. Other studies point into the same direction: Babaali and Gonzalez [21] e.g. demonstrate that in their empirical research, the availability of e-tutorial systems to students is highly predictive for performance, but time on task in these e-tutorial systems is not. For reasons very similar as in our case, and labelled as the divide between prepared and underprepared students in their study. Heterogeneity of such type will generally impact all types of intensity of use kind of variables, so not only time on task, but also number of clicks. The paradox is that these types of data are most easily available in the development of (LA based) prediction models. It is not only the search for most predictive models, which strongly suggest to focus on the collection on formative assessment and mastery data [1–3], but also the aim to achieve so with parsimonious and robust (linear) prediction model types.

Acknowledgements. The project reported here has been supported and co-financed by SURF-foundation as part of the Learning Analytics Stimulus and the Testing and Test-Driven Learning programs.

References

1. Tempelaar, D.T., Rienties, B., Giesbers, B.: Computer assisted, formative assessment and dispositional learning analytics in learning mathematics and statistics. In: Kalz, M., Ras, E. (eds.) CAA 2014. CCIS, vol. 439, pp. 67–78. Springer, Heidelberg (2014). doi:10.1007/978-3-319-08657-6_7
2. Tempelaar, D.T., Rienties, B., Giesbers, B.: In search for the most informative data for feedback generation: learning analytics in a data-rich context. Comput. Hum. Behav. (Spec. Issue Learn. Analytics) (2015). doi:10.1016/j.chb.2014.05.038
3. Tempelaar, D.T., Cuypers, H., Van de Vrie, E.M., Heck, A., Van der Kooij, H.: Formative assessment and learning analytics. In: Proceedings LAK2013: 3rd International Conference on Learning Analytics and Knowledge, pp. 205–209. ACM Press: New York (2013). doi:10.1145/2460296.2460337
4. Calvert, C.E.: Developing a model and applications for probabilities of student success: a case study of predictive analytics. Open Learn. J. Open Distance e-Learn. **29**(2), 160–173 (2014). doi:10.1080/02680513.2014.931805
5. Kuzilek, J., Hlosta, M., Herrmannova, D., Zdrahal, Z., Wolff, A.: OU Analyse: Analysing at-risk students at The Open University, Learning Analytics Review, Paper LAK15-1, ISSN 2057-7494, March 2015. http://www.laceproject.eu/learning-analytics-review/analysing-at-risk-students-at-open-university/
6. Buckingham Shum, S. Deakin Crick, R.: Learning dispositions and transferable competencies: pedagogy, modelling and learning analytics. In: Proceedings LAK2012: 2nd International Conference on Learning Analytics and Knowledge, pp. 92–101. ACM Press: New York (2012)
7. Pachler, N., Mellar, H., Daly, C., Mor, Y., Wiliam, D.: Scoping a vision for formative e-assessment: a project report for JISC, version 2, April (2009). http://www.wlecentre.ac.uk/cms/files/projectreports/scoping_a_vision_for_formative_e-assessment_version_2.0.pdf
8. Black, P., Wiliam, D.: Developing the theory of formative assessment. Assess. Eval. Accountability **21**(1), 5–31 (2009)
9. Tempelaar, D.T.; Kuperus, B., Cuypers, H., Van der Kooij, H., Van de Vrie, E., Heck, A.: The role of digital, formative testing in e-Learning for mathematics: a case study in the Netherlands. In: "Mathematical e-learning" [online dossier]. Universities and Knowledge Society Journal (RUSC). vol. 9, no 1, UoC (2012). doi: 10.7238/rusc.v9i1.1272
10. Verbert, K., Manouselis, N., Drachsler, H., Duval, E.: Dataset-driven research to support learning and knowledge analytics. Educ. Technol. Soc. **15**(3), 133–148 (2012)
11. Rienties, B., Toetenel, L., Bryan, A.: "Scaling up" learning design: impact of learning design activities on LMS behavior and performance. In: Proceedings LAK 2015: 5th International Conference on Learning Analytics and Knowledge, pp. 315–319. ACM Press, New York (2015). doi:10.1145/2723576.2723600

12. Ferguson, R., Clow, D.: Examining engagement: analysing learner subpopulations in massive open online courses (MOOCs). In: Proceedings LAK 2015: 5th International Conference on Learning Analytics and Knowledge, pp. 51–58. ACM Press, New York (2015). doi:10.1145/2723576.2723606
13. Tempelaar, D.T., Rienties, B., Giesbers, B.: Stability and sensitivity of Learning Analytics based prediction models. In: Helfert, M., Restivo, M.T., Zvacek, S., Uhomoibhi, J. (eds.) Proceedings CSEDU 2015, 7th International Conference on Computer Supported Education, vol. 1, pp. 156–166. SCITEPRESS, Lisbon (2015)
14. Narciss, S.: Feedback strategies for interactive learning tasks. In: Spector, J.M., Merrill, M. D., van Merrienboer, J.J.G., Driscoll, M.P. (eds.) Handbook of Research on Educational Communications and Technology, 3rd edn, pp. 125–144. Lawrence Erlbaum Associates, Mahwah (2008)
15. Narciss, S., Huth, K.: Fostering achievement and motivation with bug-related tutoring feedback in a computer-based training on written subtraction. Learn. Instr. **16**, 310–322 (2006)
16. Martin, A.J.: Examining a multidimensional model of student motivation and en-gagement using a construct validation approach. Br. J. Educ. Psychol. **77**, 413–440 (2007)
17. Tempelaar, D.T., Niculescu, A., Rienties, B., Giesbers, B., Gijselaers, W.H.: How achievement emotions impact students' decisions for online learning, and what precedes those emotions. Internet High. Educ. **15**, 161–169 (2012). doi:10.1016/j.iheduc.2011.10.003
18. Pekrun, R., Goetz, T., Frenzel, A.C., Barchfeld, P., Perry, R.P.: Measuring emotions in students' learning and performance: the achievement emotions questionnaire (AEQ). Contemp. Educ. Psychol. **36**, 36–48 (2011)
19. Rienties, B., Rivers, B.A.: Measuring and understanding learner emotions: evidence and prospects. Learning Analytics Review, no. 1, December 2014, ISSN 2057-7494. http://www.laceproject.eu/learning-analytics-review/measuring-and-understanding-learner-emotions/
20. Perry, R.P., Hladkyj, S., Pekrun, R.H., Clifton, R.A., Chipperfield, J.G.: Perceived academic control and failure in college students: a three-year study of scholastic attainment. Res. High. Educ. **46**, 535–569 (2005)
21. Babaali, P., Gonzalez, L.: A quantitative analysis of the relationship between an online homework system and student achievement in pre-calculus. Int. J. Math. Educ. Sci. Technol. (2015). doi:10.1080/0020739X.2014.997318

Towards Policy on Digital Summative and Formative Assessment

Ludo W. van Meeuwen(✉), Migchiel R. van Diggelen, and Bianca van der Aalst

Eindhoven University of Technology, De Rondom 70, 5612 AP Eindhoven, The Netherlands
L.W.v.Meeuwen@TUe.nl

Abstract. In line with other institutions, Eindhoven University of Technology is in need of developing policy on digital assessment that should cover the entire assessment process for summative and formative assessments. This paper discusses the use of the assessment cycle as a framework for that policy. The use of the assessment cycle resulted in a useful overview of the summative assessment process although not enough on formative assessment. To ensure the inclusion of formative assessment, we discuss the evidence for the effectiveness of ICT-functionalities in formative assessment. We conclude that an exploration of best practices and scientific evidence on the specific outcomes and effectiveness of digitalizing summative and formative assessment is a necessary step towards a well-founded policy on digital assessment. In the light of that direction, we developed an extended assessment cycle based on our findings as a framework for policy on digital assessment including formative assessment.

Keywords: Digital assessment · Efficient assessment · Assessment policy · Formative assessment

1 Introduction

Feedback and assessment can have powerful effects on learning (cf. [1]). However, providing feedback and assessment processes can also be time-consuming and difficult to perform in nowadays need for personalized education for increasing numbers of students [2]. Technology is frequently seen as a tool to effectively manage feedback and assessment processes [3, 4]. Systematic use and support of technology when providing feedback and organizing assessment asks for policy development. Little is known about how policy is developed for supporting the assessment practice with ICT towards more efficiency and assessment quality. Therefore the main question is: how can policy for digital assessment be developed?

This paper reports on the first steps towards policy on digital assessment at the Eindhoven University of Technology (TU/e). More particularly, this paper explores a framework for digital assessment policy and elaborates on formative assessment. Chapter 2 shortly presents related work and introduces the research questions. Chapter 3 describes

E. Ras and D. Joosten-ten Brinke (Eds.): CAA 2015, CCIS 571, pp. 134–141, 2015.
DOI: 10.1007/978-3-319-27704-2_13

the methods. Chapter 4 outlines the main results. Finally, conclusions are drawn and discussed.

1.1 Theoretical Framework

Both the TU/e educational vision [2] and the TU/e vision on blended learning [1] emphasize the important role for digital education as a tool to support the continuation of small scale education in growing numbers of students. Together these visions underlie need for policy on digital assessment. Policy is required as foundation for investments in the ICT-landscape, supporting the assessment processes.

Policy on digital assessment should focus on the procedures during formal assessment moments. This paper focuses on formal assessment only. Formative assessment can be classified on a continuous scale that ranges from informal to formal [5]. Hence this paper only includes all summative and formal formative assessments. Policy on digital assessment should consider the entire assessment process from design to quality assurance for both (formal) formative and summative assessment. Policy should focus on digitalizing elements in the assessment processes that will result in an improvement of quality, efficiency and/or effectiveness of the assessment organization and students' learning. Regarding digitalization, digital exams are required to be administered on students' own devices (i.e., laptop) instead of using a preset device from the university (e.g., desktops, Chromebooks). In short, policy should be structured in a way that covers the management of the digital assessment landscape.

The authors see several advantages to approach assessment as a process comprising several sub-processes. This approach gives guidance to the arrangement of organizational processes, it supports development of a shared conceptual framework among stakeholders and helps them to structure their tasks and responsibilities. Thus providing a structure to monitor and regulate all aspects of assessment.

Several process models are mentioned in literature. For example the model of Ferrell [6] comprises the elements from her 'assessment and feedback lifecycle' (i.e., specifying, setting, supporting, submitting, marking and production of feedback, recording grades, returning marks and feedback, and reflecting). The model of Geloven [7], and Joosten-ten Brinke and Sluijsmans [8] as shown in Fig. 1, comprises the logistic steps of the assessment process (i.e., steps prior to administering a test, the administering phase itself, and the post administering phase).

The reason for this paper is the desire to digitalize elements of the current assessment processes in order to increase effectiveness (particularly in formative aspects of assessment) and efficiency within the complete assessment process. Underlining the effectiveness of formative assessment for learning, insight is needed in specific ICT-functionalities that can effectively be used in supporting assessment processes in general and formative assessment in particular.

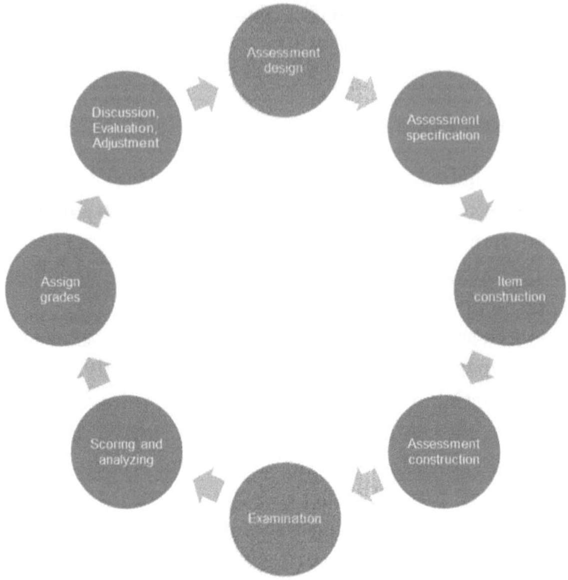

Fig. 1. Assessment cycle [7, 8]

1.2 Research Questions

This paper addresses two separate research questions. The first question is: Does the assessment cycle as shown in Fig. 1 provide a sufficient framework for policy on the entire digital assessment process within the TU/e? The second question is: Which ICT-functionalities are effective for formative assessment according to literature?

2 Method

To answer the first question, the assessment cycle ([7, 8], Fig. 1) has been used as starting point for concept mapping. Post-It's were used by members of the TU/e Digital Assessment Project team to assign all kinds of assessment-related concepts to elements of the assessment process. These concepts varied from specific activities (e.g., calculating cutting-off points) to the use of ICT-functionalities in current and/or future situations (e.g., students bring their own device). Next, the concepts have been clustered into three categories: the phase prior to the exam, the phase of administering the exam, the phase after the exam (Fig. 2). The clusters have been evaluated qualitatively, to get insight in all assessment-related concepts within the assessment cycle.

Fig. 2. Concept mapping on digital assessment policy

To answer the second question, which ICT-functionalities are effective for formative assessment according to literature? A study was conducted via Google Scholar. The search terms digital formative assessment and review were used. The search led to 51.600 results. The first hit provided a review article about online formative assessment in higher education [9]. This was the only available review study about online formative assessment in higher education. Therefore, we decided to compare findings from Gikandi et al. [9] with literature that combines a process approach to assessment and feedback.

3 Results

To answer RQ1, the mind-map (Fig. 3) shows the three phases: the phase prior to the exam, the phase of administering the exam, the phase after the exam and shows the categories defined as requirements (i.e., system and user) and process. These two categories emerged as categories that overarch the individual phases for efficient and effective digital assessment. Next, the mind-map shows the subdivision per main category in order to provide an overview of subjects that are related to an effective and efficient assessment process. This provided insight in specific requirements needed for ICT-functionalities during digital summative assessment. For example the concept of Bring Your Own Device (BYOD), requires an equally safe exam administration compared to an analogue process. For formative use, the digital assessment system should be equipped with possibilities to provide students with individual feedback, feed-up, and feed-forward. The assessment cycle however pays little attention to providing individual feedback, feed-up, and feed-forward. These possibilities should not be neglected in policy on digital assessment.

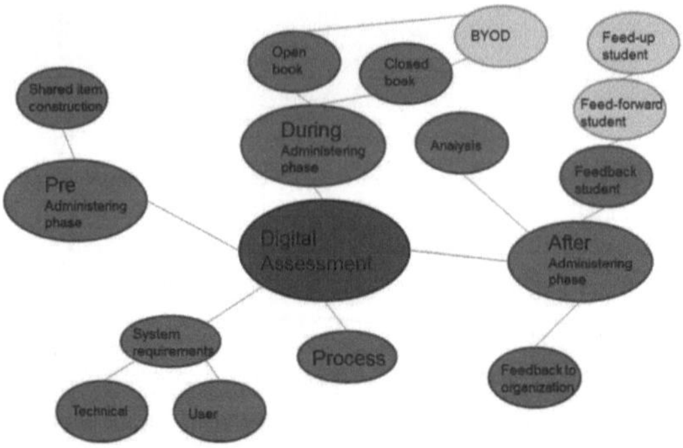

Fig. 3. Concept map on digital assessment policy

After an initial search of relevant literature for answering research question two, Gikandi et al. [9] concluded that no review had been undertaken about online formative assessment. Starting from this observation the authors performed a systematic narrative review to distinguish key findings and themes in the domain. Initially, the authors found 91 potentially relevant articles and selected 18 core articles. The authors distinguished various techniques on formative assessment by individuals, peers and teachers. These techniques were related to online tools with functionalities such as self-test quizes, discussion forums and e-portfolios. According to the authors the review provided evidence that online formative assessment has potential to engage both teachers and students in meaningful educational experiences. Also, the authors were of the opinion that online formative assessment can support higher education to meet the needs of the 21st century students. In a landscape review on electronic management of assessment, Ferrell [6] devotes attention to marking and producing feedback as a step in the assessment process. These findings can be translated to formative assessment. Ferrell [6] considers assessment and feedback as the most problematic component of assessment. This area shows variety in pedagogic practice and results in situations where institutional processes and functionalities of commercial systems least well match. Her review does not provide further evidence on the effectiveness on formative assessment in this part of the assessment cycle. Ferrell emphasizes that grades and feedback are different things but this proposition is hardly recognized and visible in practice [6]. She reveals that there is little support to separate grades from feedback in existing systems. The final component of the assessment process Ferrell distinguishes, is reflecting. She considers this the phase where actual learning takes place. Therefore, findings from this phase in the assessment cycle are applicable to formative assessment as well. Ferrell notes that this phase is least well supported by existing commercial systems. Furthermore, the author states that there are many good practices but a commonly heard issue is the small number of students that took part in studies proving these examples.

4 Conclusion

Concerning question 1, the assessment cycle did provide a basic framework for the outline of policy on digital assessment in a university of technology. However, two points of attention emerged. First, there turned out to be additional requirements (e.g., usability and system safety) and processes (e.g., professionalization) that were more generic and emerged in al steps of the cycle. These requirements and processes should get extra attention in the design phase of an assessment cycle for digital assessment. The second addition relates to formative function of assessment. For this function the feedback process is essential. In our definition, this should entail the steps from the 'assessment and feedback cycle' as defined by Ferrell [6]. She provides a framework to support this process with ICT-functionalities. Figure 4 shows a simplification of this process that fits the TU/e practice. *Specifying* the assessment is similar to the summative process and takes place at point A. *Setting* as specified, takes place at situation B. *Support* is given during the product creation or performance at point C. The step from product to review (D.) shows the *Submission* process in case of (written) products. The *production of feedback* takes place in the reviewing process E. The process of *Returning feedback* is shown as the up-going arrow F. In case the student can reflect and use feedback G in the setting for starting an iteration of the product/performance development process, students (and teachers) decide to make the product of performance formal for summative *Examination* which continues the process in the original assessment cycle. *Grading* and *Returning* Grades takes place outside the formative process H. by supporting, submitting, grading and production of feedback, recording grades, returning grades and feedback, and reflecting.

Fig. 4. Iterative process in TU/e formative assessment that finally can lead to a grade

Concerning the second question, we conclude that a landscape of online digital formative assessment functionalities seems promising but remains limited to mainly small scale and isolated functionalities. Consequently, we conclude that more empirical evidence and quantitative comparison of different studies is needed to support this promising nature of formative assessment functionalities. Thus, although promising it cannot be stated that online or digital formative assessment is more effective than offline.

5 Discussion

There is a need of research to specify the user and technical requirements and define the roles and processes for digital assessment. Studying the best practices can be of major importance. While studying best practices in the organization will provide the project team with insights on effectiveness of functionalities of digital tools for assessment, the potential laggards (lecturers who are reluctant to go digital) should be included in the research as well, to discover how they can be facilitated by digital assessment functionalities. This might be useful to get a complete overview of the current situation regarding digital assessment and provide potential input for increasing efficiency and effectiveness. It might also support non-users in getting used to the idea of digital assessment and make them more willing to use the functionalities in ICT when implementing a new digital assessment system. The literature search showed that online digital formative assessments seems promising, but that effectiveness cannot be affirmed yet. Feedback and formative assessment form the core of learning and are the most difficult parts of the assessment process for using technological support. Most existing systems are based on the proposition that grading and feedback are similar things [6]. Whereas pedagogy, and therefore feedback and formative assessment, varies considerably between institutes, departments and even between teachers and students. As consequence, there are isolated and small-scale functionalities available for practitioners which are developed based on specific needs of individual teachers or institutes.

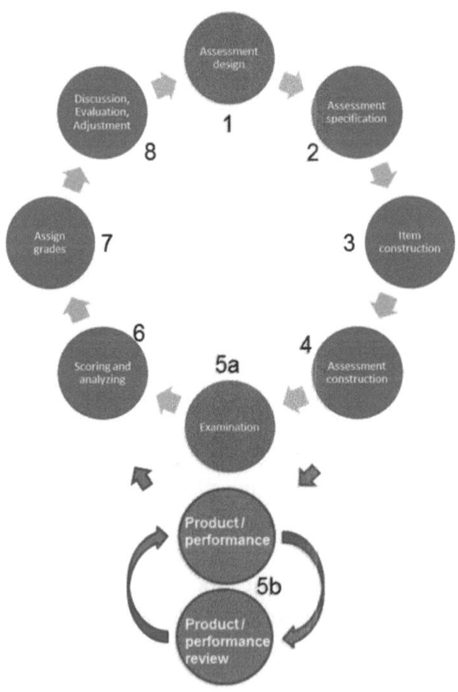

Fig. 5. The iterative process of feedback added to the classical assessment cycle

Nevertheless, many of these tools are considered as good practices [6, 9]. Therefore, more insight is needed in the specific outcomes of particular functionalities in ICT-tools and the specific outcomes when used in particular domains. Logical next steps would be: 1. Explore best practices in literature and practice and 2. Theorize the specific outcomes and effectiveness. Formulated hypotheses can be subjected to further research. In this study, the classic assessment cycle turned out to be too focused on summative assessment only. The classic cycle is missing a feedback loop. This loop however is relevant even in the narrow definition of formative assessment as presented above. We therefore propose the cycle as presented in Fig. 5 where the classic version is extended with elements and relations that are necessary for including feedback.

Acknowledgements. We thank Desirée Joosten- ten Brinke for reviewing an earlier version of this manuscript.

References

1. Taskforce ICTO 2.0: Blended Learning TU/e. Eindhoven, The Netherlands (2015)
2. Meijers, A., den Brok, P.: Engineers for the Future; An Essay on Education at TU/e in 2030. Eindhoven University of Technology, Eindhoven, The Netherlands (2013)
3. Geloven, M.: De Business Case van Digital Toetsen [The Business case of Digital Assessment]. Surf, Utrecht, The Netherlands (2014)
4. Van Berkel, H., Bax, A., Joosten-ten Brinke, D.: Toetsen in het Hoger Onderwijs [Assessment in Higher Education], Bohn Stafleu van Loghum, Houten, Utrecht, The Netherlands (2014)
5. Shavelson, R.J., Young, D.B., Ayala, C.C., Brandon, P.R., Furtak, E.M., Ruiz-Primo, M.A.: On the impact of curriculum-embedded formative assessment on learning: a collaboration between curriculum and assessment developers. Appl. Measur. Educ. 295 314 (2008). doi: 10.1080/08957340802347647
6. Ferrell, G.: Electronic Management of Assessment (EMA): A Landscape Review. Jisc, Bristol, UK (2014)
7. Geloven, M.: Begrippenkader voor Digitaal Toetsen [Conceptual Framework for Digital Assessment]. Surf, Utrecht, The Netherlands (2013)
8. Joosten-ten Brinke, D., Sluijsmans, D.: Tijd voor toetskwaliteit: het borgen van toetsdeskundigheid van examencommissies [Time for Assessment Quality: Safeguarding the Assessment Competences]. TH&MA, **19**(4), 16–21 (2012). doi:http://hdl.handle.net/1820/4759
9. Gikandi, J.W., Morrom, D., Davis, N.E.: Online formative assessment in higher education: a review of the literature. Comput. Educ. **57**, 2333–2351 (2011). doi:10.1016/j.compedu.2011.06.004

Maximising Student Success with Automatic Formative Feedback for Both Teachers and Students

Denise Whitelock(✉)

The Open University, Walton Hall, Milton Keynes, MK7 6AA, UK
Denise.whitelock@open.ac.uk

Abstract. This paper discusses the outcomes from the building and empirical investigation of two automatic feedback systems, namely OpenMentor and OpenEssayist that can support student learning. The findings from OpenMentor and OpenEssayist usage suggest that prompt targeted feedback for time poor students can maximise student success. Both systems facilitate the users to take ownership and reflect on their own work, through provision of feedback at a point where they can build on it in subsequent tasks. This should have the most impact on the users' understanding of the requirements of academic writing and the tutors' understanding of feedback for academic writing. The systems are also starting to be used as research tools that allow pedagogical strategies to be open to test.

Keywords: Formative feedback · Automatic feedback · Essay feedback · Natural Language Processing · Opensource

1 Introduction

Full time students in Higher Education are even more time poor and less prepared than their predecessors [1]. They often undertake paid employment during their studies. This means their time to write assignments is concentrated in smaller bursts of activity and mastering the art of essay writing can become a more onerous task [2]. Meaningful feedback is essential to gaining good writing skills, which illustrate the subject knowledge gained. One approach to this problem adopted by The Open University UK was to build an automatic feedback system to assist tutors in providing "advice for action" [3] so that students can improve their grade and open a dialogue with their tutor and improve their grade on the next assignment.

This paper discusses the role OpenMentor can play in assisting to improve their tutors' feedback, together with the findings from another tool called OpenEssayist that gives students automatic feedback on draft essays. Students can, therefore, start to judge for themselves how to improve their assignment within the time they have left before summative submission.

This two pronged approach has been adopted at The Open University and beyond to assist tutors and students in giving and receiving meaningful feedback. With each system all the users, whether they are tutors or students, are given the opportunity to test out the boundaries of their skills or knowledge in a safe environment, where their

E. Ras and D. Joosten-ten Brinke (Eds.): CAA 2015, CCIS 571, pp. 142–148, 2015.
DOI: 10.1007/978-3-319-27704-2_14

predictions may not be correct, without expecting to be penalised for it. Feedback does not always imply guidance (i.e. planning for the future) and this is the type of support incorporated into the two systems described below.

2 OpenMentor

Feedback can sometimes be the only contact students have with their tutors [4]. It plays an essential role in assessment for learning which can assist with maximising student success with their higher education studies. In order to achieve this goal, assessment has to be accompanied by appropriate meaningful feedback [5–8]. Feedback also needs to be commensurate with the marks awarded and this was one of the main drivers for the building of OpenMentor. The main function of OpenMentor is to support tutors' feedback practices and in order to do this it has to analyse the tutor comments.

A classification system is employed to implement this task and the one chosen for use in OpenMentor is based on that of [9]. Bales's category system was originally devised to study social interaction, especially in collaborating teams; its strength is that it brings out the socio-emotive aspects of dialogue as well as the domain level. In previous work, [10] found that the distribution of comments within these categories correlates very closely with the grade assigned.

Bales' model provides four main categories of interaction: positive reactions, negative reactions, questions, and answers (see Table 1). These interactional categories illustrate the balance of socio-emotional comments that support the student. We found [10] that tutors use different types of questions in different ways, both to stimulate reflection, and to point out, in a supportive way, that there are problems with parts of an essay. These results showed that about half of Bales's interaction categories strongly correlated with grade of assessment in different ways, while others were rarely used in feedback to learners. This evidence of systematic connections between different types of tutor comments and level of attainment in assessment was the platform for the current work.

The advantage of the Bales model is that the classes used are domain-independent – this model was used to classify feedback in a range of different academic disciplines, and it has proven successful in all of them. An automatic classification system, therefore, can be used in all fields, without needing a new set of example comments and training for each different discipline.

Others (e.g., [11]) have looked at different classification systems, including Bales, and from these developed their own to bring out additional aspects of the tutor feedback, bringing back elements of the domain. In practice, no (useful) classification system can incorporate all comments. Bales was selected and preferred because of its relative simplicity, its intuitive grasp by both students and tutors, and because it brings out the socio-emotive aspects of the dialogue, which is the one aspect tutors are often unaware of.

A second point is that Bales draws out a wider context: we bring in to question the notion of feedback itself. When building OpenMentor the concept seemed to divide naturally into two different aspects: learning support and learning guidance. Support

Table 1. Bales categories

Categories		Specific Examples
Positive Reactions		
A1	1. Shows solidarity	Jokes, gives help, rewards others
A2	2. Shows tension release	Laughs, shows satisfaction
A3	3. Shows agreement	Understands, concurs, complies, passively accepts
Attempted Answers		
B1	4. Gives suggestion	Directs, proposes, controls
B2	5. Gives opinion	Evaluates, analyses, expresses feelings or wishes
B3	6. Gives information	Orients, repeats, clarifies, confirms
Questions		
C1	7. Asks for information	Requests orientation, repetition, confirmation, clarification
C2	8. Asks for opinion	Requests evaluation, analysis, expression of feeling or wishes
C3	9. Asks for suggestion	Requests directions, proposals
Negative Reactions		
D1	10. Shows disagreement	Passively rejects, resorts to formality, withholds help
D2	11. Shows tension	Asks for help, withdraws
D3	12. Shows antagonism	Deflates others, defends or asserts self

encourages and motivates the learner, guidance shows them ways of dealing with particular problems.

OpenMentor also set out to solve one of the problems with tutor feedback to students and that is a balanced combination of socio-emotive and cognitive support is required from the teaching staff and the feedback also needs to be relevant to the assigned grade.

[12] found that students expect to receive feedback that is appropriate to the assigned grade. This feedback provides them with the supportive comments they need to feel confident about their level of work and where to improve in future assignments.

2.1 Transferring OpenMentor to Other UK Universities

The OpenMentor system which had proved successful in training tutors to give feedback at The Open University UK was then transferred for use at King's College London and Southampton University. The empirical studies and system update that resulted in the OMtetra project [13, 14] was supported by JISC funding.

The system was trialled with tutors from both Universities. All appreciated the opportunity they were given to receive comments on their feedback. This was because feedback is received, but not always systematically, at Faculty level, at tutor team meetings and sometimes at programme exam boards.

A series of recommendations for improvement to the system were implemented. Mainly system access from networks external to the institution and the enhancement of narrative in reports as the graphical output was not always easy to interpret, without supporting explanations. This also meant that the system was migrated to Grails[1]. The OMtetra project was successful in completing its transfer to two Higher Education Institutions in the UK and is assisting with the delivery of quality feedback to support the teaching and learning process.

2.2 Further Empirical Studies

Since the upgrade of OpenMentor, after the OMtetra project, a further study was undertaken with 48 tutors at The Open University. The tutors were asked to upload three of the assignments they had marked and then to answer a questionnaire. The majority of the tutors involved in the study judged themselves to be experienced tutors. All tutors agreed that comments should reflect the grade awarded, which is a basic premise of the OpenMentor system. Over two-thirds of tutors believed that new tutors provide students with the greatest amount of written feedback. With respect to the quality of feedback most tutors felt that experienced tutors provided higher quality than new tutors (Chi Square = 10.878 $p < 0.004$).

A significant majority of tutors also reported that OpenMentor would assist with Quality Assurance (Chi Square = 18 $p < 0.01$). A significant number were surprised by the lack of praise they had given to students (Chi Square = 19.0 $p < 0.01$). They also gave a strong indication that they expected assessments with low grades to attract more negative comments (Chi Square = 22.638 $p < 0.001$).

OpenMentor is becoming successful, both within The Open University UK and beyond. However the key factor is still institutional integration, which has more chance of success with the use of open frameworks that are enabled by the use of open-source applications.

OpenMentor has also been used to extract and analyse tutor comments received by 470 ethnic minority and 470 matched white students following a distance learning course [15]. Although the black students and students of mixed ethnicity obtained lower marks for their assignments than the white students, there were only small differences between the pattern of feedback each group received. It was concluded that students from all ethnic groups received feedback that was commensurate with their mark. The study revealed the under-attainment of ethnic minority students was not due to the nature of the feedback they received. This example illustrates how OpenMentor can also be used as a research tool to identify and analyse large numbers of assignments with tutor feedback.

3 Automated Feedback Direct to Students

Another approach to maximising student success at The Open University was to construct a natural language analytics engine to provide feedback to students when preparing an essay for summative assessment [16].

OpenEssayist was developed as a web application and consists of two components. The first component, EssayAnalyser, is the summarization engine, implemented in

[1] Grails is an open source web application framework.

Python with NLTK[2] [17] and other toolkits. It is designed as a stand-alone RESTful web service, delivering the basic summarization techniques that will be consumed by the main system. The second component is OpenEssayist itself, implemented on a PHP framework. The core system consists of the operational back-end (user identification, database management, service brokers, feedback orchestrator) and the cross-platform, responsive HTML5 front-end.

The flow of activities within the system meant that firstly, students are registered as users. Once they have prepared a draft offline and want to obtain feedback, they log on to the OpenEssayist system and submit their essay for analysis, either by copy-and-pasting or by uploading their text document. OpenEssayist submits the raw text to the EssayAnalyser service and, once finished retrieves and stores the summarization data. From that point on, the students can then explore the data at their own pace. Using the various external representations available to them, they can follow the prompts and trigger questions that the Feedback Orchestrator generates from the analysis and can start planning their next draft accordingly.

This rewriting phase takes place offline, the system simply offering repeated access to the summarization data and feedback, as a resource, until the students are prepared to submit and explore the summarization feedback on their second draft, and on subsequent changes between drafts. This cycle of submission, analysis and revision continues until the students consider their essays are ready for summative assessment. A major challenge is to provide feedback to the student that can be acted upon to improve the draft essay. In other words, to provide both textual and visual representations that can be used as cognitive tools.

OpenEssayist was used in anger by a cohort of Masters students following H817 “Openness and Innovation in eLearning”. It was designed to introduce students to the latest developments in educational technological developments and open learning. Therefore the adoption of OpenEssayist was a suitable addition to the course. 41 students who were studying H817 accessed OpenEssayist at least once during the course and 30 students made use of the system to practice their essay writing skills. However [18] found a significant correlation between students’ grades for Essay 1 and the number of drafts they submitted. The students from this cohort, who had access to OpenEssayist, achieved significantly higher overall grades than the previous cohort who had no access to OpenEssayist.

3.1 Implications

OpenEssayist was designed as a tool for student reflection on their draft essays. Students reported it took time to learn how to use the system but some were disappointed that it would not be available for their subsequent course of study. Hence these students appreciated that initial cognitive overload of mastering the system could have continual benefits throughout their studies. Some mentioned that using OpenEssayist gave them the confidence to submit a rough draft for feedback and the second draft was easier to complete. Others felt the feedback about the structure of the essay from OpenEssayist

[2] Natural Language Processing Toolkit, see http://nltk.org/.

complemented the feedback from their tutors. The latter mainly focussed feedback about the specific content of the essay they had written. Therefore feedback from the tutor combined with OpenEssayist's advice presented the student with an excellent combination of "advice for action" [3].

4 Conclusions

Feedback has been a popular topic of educational research for some decades and it is widely acknowledged that feedback is central to learning [19]. Both OpenMentor and OpenEssayist implement two of the principles of good practice for undergraduate education as described by [20] which are:

- The giving of prompt feedback and
- Encouraging active learning

However it must be acknowledged that students may also need to receive a form of training to interpret their tutors' feedback in order to benefit from receiving good quality feedback [21]. Time poor students require prompt feedback and automated systems that elicit and capture higher order thinking skills can move some way towards that goal.

Acknowledgements. The OpenEssayist Research was supported by the Engineering and Physical Sciences Research Council (EPSRC, grant numbers EP/J005959/1 & EP/J005231/1). Thanks are also due to the SAFeSEA team who produced OpenEssayist, namely John Richardson, Alison Twiner, Debora Field and Stephen Pulman. I would also like to thank Stuart Watt and the JISC for their support in the development of OpenMentor.

References

1. Nonis, S.A., Hudson, G.I.: Academic performance of college students: influence of time spent studying and working. J. Educ. Bus. **81**(3), 151–159 (2006). doi:10.3200/JOEB.81.3.151-159
2. Metcalf, H.: Increasing inequality in higher education: the role of term-time working. Oxford Rev. Educ. **29**(3), 315–329 (2003). doi:10.1080/03054980307447
3. Whitelock, D.: Activating assessment for learning: are we on the way with web 2.0? In: Lee, M.J.W., McLoughlin, C. (eds.) Web 2.0-Based-E-Learning: Applying Social Informatics for Tertiary Teaching, pp. 319–342. IGI Global (2011)
4. Gibbs, G., Simpson, C.: Conditions under which assessment supports students' learning? Learn. Teach. High. Educ. **1**, 3–31 (2004)
5. Evans, C.: Making sense of assessment feedback in higher education. Rev. Educ. Res. **83**(1), 80–120 (2013)
6. Hattie, J., Timperley, H.: The power of feedback. Rev. Educ. Res. **77**(1), 81–112 (2007)
7. Nicol, D.J., Macfarlane-Dick, D.: Formative assessment and self-regulated learning: a model and seven principles of good feedback practice. Stud. High. Educ. **31**(2), 199–218 (2006)
8. Price, M., Handley, K., Millar, J.: Feedback: focusing attention on engagement. Stud. High. Educ. **36**(8), 879–896 (2011)
9. Bales, R.F.: A set of categories for the analysis of small group interaction. Am. Sociol. Rev. **15**, 257–263 (1950)

10. Whitelock, D., Watt, S.N.K., Raw, Y., Moreale, E.: Analysing tutor feedback to students: first steps towards constructing an electronic monitoring system. ALT-J **1**(3), 31–42 (2004)
11. Brown, E., Glover, C.: Evaluating written feedback. In: Bryan, C., Clegg, K. (eds.) Innovative Assessment in Higher Education, pp. 81–91. Routledge (2006)
12. Whitelock, D., Watt, S.: e-Assessment: how can we support tutors with their marking of electronically submitted assignments? Ad-Lib J. Continuing Liberal Adult Educ. (32), 7–9 (2007). ISSN: 1361-6323
13. Whitelock, D.M., Gilbert, L., Hatzipanagos, S., Watt, S., Zhang, P., Gillary, P., Recio, A.: Addressing the challenges of assessment and feedback in higher education: a collaborative effort across three UK universities. In: Proceedings of the INTED 2012, Valencia, Spain (2012). ISBN: 978-84-615-5563-5
14. Whitelock, D., Gilbert, L., Hatzipanagos, S., Watt, S., Zhang, P., Gillary, P. Recio, A.: Assessment for learning: supporting tutors with their feedback using an electronic system that can be used across the higher education sector. In: Proceedings 10th International Conference on Computer Based Learning in Science, CBLIS 2012, Barcelona, Spain, 26–29 June (2012)
15. Richardson, J.T.E., Alden Rivers, B., Whitelock, D.: The role of feedback in the under-attainment of ethnic minority students: evidence from distance education. Assess. Eval. High. Educ. **40**(4), 557–573 (2014). doi:10.1080/02602938.2014.938317
16. Van Labeke, N., Whitelock, D., Field, D., Pulman, S, Richardson, J.: OpenEssayist: extractive summarisation & formative assessment of free-text essays. In: Workshop on Discourse-Centric Learning Analytics, 3rd Conference on Learning Analytics and Knowledge (LAK 2013), Leuven, Belgium (2013)
17. Bird, S., Klein, E., Loper, E.: Natural Language Processing with Python. O'Reilly Media, Inc., Sebastopol (2009)
18. Whitelock, D., Twiner, A., Richardson, J.T.E., Field, D., Pulman, S.: OpenEssayist: a supply and demand learning analytics tool for drafting academic essays. In: The 5th International Learning Analytics and Knowledge (LAK) Conference, Poughkeepsie, New York, USA, 16–20 March 2015 (2015). ISBN: 978-1-4503-3417-4
19. Black, P., Wiliam, D.: Assessment and classroom learning. Assess. Educ. **5**(1), 7–74 (1998). doi:10.1080/0969595980050102
20. Chickering, A.W., Gamson, Z.F.: Seven principles for good practice in undergraduate education. Am. Assoc. High. Educ. Bull. **39**(7), 3–7 (2015). http://www.aahea.org/aahea/articles/sevenprinciples1987.htm. Accessed 12 May 2015
21. Buhagiar, M.A.: Mathematics student teachers' views on tutor feedback during teaching practice. Eur. J. Teach. Educ. iFirst Article, 1–13 (2012)

Formative Quizzing and Learning Performance in Dutch First-Year Higher Education Students

Sjirk-Jan J. Zijlstra[1(✉)], Eva J. Sugeng[1(✉)], Silvester Draaijer[2], and Margot van de Bor[1]

[1] Health and Life Sciences, Faculty of Earth and Life Sciences, VU University, Amsterdam, The Netherlands
{s.zijlstra,e.j.sugeng,margot.vande.bor}@vu.nl

[2] Faculty of Education and Psychology, VU University, Amsterdam, The Netherlands
s.draaijer@vu.nl

Abstract. In this research paper, a cross-sectional study into the effects of formative quizzing in higher education and its relation to learning performance is presented. For the current study, six online Formative Quizzing modules, consisting of texts, graphics and video clips followed by two or more test questions to reiterate the material, were provided to students. Students could not earn marks and were free to use the material, but were informed that in the final examination, questions relating to the material would be asked. Data analysis showed that students who completed all six modules had a statistical significant higher chance to score better on the final examination. This was true for high achieving students, but also, and even stronger, for low achieving students. The results therefore show in this particular set-up a potential causal relationship of online formative quizzing on learning performance in higher education.

Keywords: Online quizzing · Formative assessment · Formative quizzing · Learning performance · Deep learning · Self-study

1 Introduction

Formative assessment or quizzing is widely used in higher education, both in the more traditional classroom settings and online. Online formative assessment offers several opportunities such as (formative and) immediate feedback, student (and teacher) engagement in critical learning processes and personalized education [1]. Although these opportunities offer the possibility to enhance student performance, research regarding the extent of learning performance of using (online) formative quizzes is not conclusive [2]. Various studies have demonstrated one or several factors contributing to this testing effect such as time on task [3], question type [4] and feedback [5]. However, regardless of the type of factor studied, some studies report a negative effect or no effect of formative assessment [6, 7], other report a positive effect [5, 7, 8]. This difference in outcome that can be explained, among others, by the fact that laboratory studies often find effects that cannot be reproduced in the classroom, and therefore require careful interpretation [9, 10].

In this research paper, a cross-sectional study into the effects of formative quizzing in higher education and its relation to learning performance is presented. The aim of the

E. Ras and D. Joosten-ten Brinke (Eds.): CAA 2015, CCIS 571, pp. 149–154, 2015.
DOI: 10.1007/978-3-319-27704-2_15

study was to investigate if formative quizzing results in better learning performance among Dutch first-year higher education students.

2 Methods

This study was conducted in the first-year Bachelor course Human Life Cycle II, within the Health and Life Sciences Program, at the VU University, Amsterdam, The Netherlands. The Bachelor program compromises both a biomedical and a health sciences view on human health and disease. The course Human Life Cycle II, which is the fifth and final course of the first semester, covers an overview of human development, health and disease from early childhood until senescence, which includes topics such as psychomotor development of children, puberty and diseases of aging. Students were able to participate in lectures, practical's, group meetings and online quizzing. For the topic puberty, six online Formative Quizzing modules were designed to improve student's deep learning.

The six online Formative Quizzing modules compromised online instructional material regarding the topic and consisted of texts, graphics and video clips followed by two to nine (on average six) multiple choice and fill-in-the-blanks questions to reiterate the material. The students were free to use the modules at their own time and place and could not earn marks for completing them. The information in the modules was not covered by tutors in face-to-face meetings. The modules were available during the course until the final examination. To create the Formative Quizzing modules Easy-Generator was used, which allowed the design of easy accessible and attractive online modules.

Data on the completion of each of the six online Formative Quizzing modules and examination grades and scores were collected. Data on the completion of the online Formative Quizzing modules were coded 'not completed' (none of the six modules completed) or 'completed' (all six modules completed). For the examination, a total of 225 points could be earned with a passmark of 145 points. The examination included four test items that covered the topics assessed in the Formative Quizzing modules ('topic-covering questions') for a total of 13 points. These four topic-covering questions included both multiple choice questions as fill-in-the-blanks questions and were therefore similar to the type of questions in the Formative Quizzing modules. A passmark for the four topic-covering questions was set at three or four correct questions.

The data were processed and analyzed in IBM SPSS Statistics (version 21). Chi-square tests were used to study the relationship between Formative Quizzing completion (not-completed or completed) and the examination (pass or fail) and topic-covering questions (pass or fail).

3 Results

In total 319 students participated in the course Human Life Cycle II and completed the final examination. Information regarding demographic factors was unavailable for privacy reasons. Data on the completion of the six modules showed that 92 students (29 %) did not complete any Formative Quizzing modules, 105 students (33 %)

completed one to five modules and 122 (38 %) completed all six Formative Quizzing modules. Within the group that completed one to five modules, no pattern was found on which modules were always or never completed. In this study, students who did not complete any Formative Quizzing module were compared to students who completed all modules.

The Chi-square test showed that students who completed all Formative Quizzing modules had 3.7 (CI: 1.6–8.4) higher odds to pass the examination compared to students who completed no Formative Quizzing modules at all (Table 1).

Table 1. Formative quizzing modules (none-completed versus all-completed) and failed or passed examination (OR = 3.7 (CI: 1.6–8.4) (N = 214))

Formative quizzing modules	Number of students (%)		
	Failed examination	Passed examination	Total
None	40 (43)	52 (57)	92 (100)
All	21 (17)	101 (83)	122 (100)
Total	61 (28)	153 (72)	214 (100)

The Chi-square test showed that students who completed all six Formative Quizzing modules had 4.9 (CI: 2.6–9.2) higher odds to successfully pass all four topic-covering questions compared to students who completed no Formative Quizzing modules at all (Table 2).

Table 2. Formative quizzing modules (none-completed versus all-completed) and failed or passed topic-covering questions (OR = 4.9 (CI: 2.6–9.2) (N = 214))

Formative quizzing modules	Number of students (%)		
	Failed topic-covering questions	Passed topic-covering questions	Total
None	45 (49)	47 (51)	92 (100)
All	20 (16)	102 (85)	122 (100)
Total	65 (30)	149 (70)	214 (100)

An analysis on topic-covering questions was made by comparing students who passed or failed the examination. Of the students who passed the examination, those who completed all six Formative Quizzing modules had 3.0 (CI:1.4–6.6) higher odds to successfully answer all four topic-covering questions compared to those who completed no Formative Quizzing modules at all (Table 3). Of the students who did not pass the examination, those who completed all six Formative Quizzing modules had 6.7 (CI: 2.0–22.3) higher odds to successfully answer four topic-covering questions compared to those who completed no Formative Quizzing modules at all (Table 4).

Table 3. Formative quizzing modules (none-completed versus all-completed) and failed or passed topic-covering questions for students who passed examination (OR = 3.0 (CI:1.4–6.6) (N = 153))

Formative quizzing modules	Number of students who passed examination (%)		
	Failed topic-covering questions	Passed topic-covering questions	Total
None	18 (35)	34 (65)	52 (100)
All	15 (15)	86 (85)	101 (100)
Total	33 (22)	120 (78)	153 (100)

Table 4. Formative quizzing modules (none-completed versus all-completed) and failed or passed topic-covering questions for students who failed examination (OR = 6.7 (CI: 2.0–22.3) (N = 61))

Formative quizzing modules	Number of students who failed examination (%)		
	Failed topic-covering questions	Passed topic-covering questions	Total
None	27 (67)	13 (33)	40 (100)
All	5 (24)	16 (76)	21 (100)
Total	32 (52)	29 (48)	61 (100)

4 Discussion

The results show a possible causal relationship of online formative quizzing on learning performance in higher education. It demonstrates that students who completed all Formative Quizzing modules, had a higher change to pass the examination and the four questions that covered the topic in the Formative Quizzing modules. Moreover, students who failed the examination but completed all Formative Quizzing modules, had a higher chance to pass topic-covering questions compared to the students who failed the examination and did not complete any Formative Quizzing module.

In this study, a positive effect of the Formative Quizzing modules is therefore less related to overall performance. That is, a significant finding as overall performance is in general an underlying variable expressing motivation and persistence, which therefore explains much of the variance between performance on course related activities and achievement. The positive effect of the Formative Quizzing modules on achievement found in this study is likely to be explained by the fact that the actual engagement of the students with the formative quizzing resulted in better retention and deeper learning.

Of interest regarding this study is the participation (69 %) of students in Formative Quizzing without an incentive (e.g. grade mark for completion). Although previous research demonstrated that student participation increases when incentives are offered [11, 12], it was also shown that students can use questionable methods to achieve these credits [12]. More recently it is recommended to boost voluntary participation in online formative quizzing [13]. In this study, the Formative Quizzing modules were designed to engage students and thereby increasing the participation without the need for incentives. Additional focus groups and questionnaires (not reported) showed that students were indeed positively engaged by the design of the Formative Quizzing modules, highlighting the design of formative quizzing modules as an opportunity to increase participation.

The findings are supported by other studies [5, 8], although literature is not conclusive [2, 6]. However, comparing studies is difficult because of the use of different methodology (laboratory- versus classroom-based). A standardized methodology could aid in a better understanding of the complexity of this relationship and could explain differences found in this and other studies.

The strength of this study lies in the fact that data collection and registration were executed objectively and anonymously, which limits the chance on selection bias. Data were derived directly from Blackboard and examination grades were derived from the digital examination.

Although this study was able to distinguish between good and poor performance based on the examination grade, the effects that were found may still be partially influenced by the effect of students with a good study performance who study all materials offered. The conclusions of this study would gain strength by including students overall study performance as a covariate.

A limitation is that the current study did not include the moment at which the quizzes were taken and the amount of time spent on the task due to technical difficulties. It is known that formative quizzes can have a beneficial as well as detrimental effect on performance, depending on the moment of the quizzes in relation to the final test [8, 14]. Furthermore, research has shown that more time on task correlates with learning performance [3]. Therefore, further analyses that would include the moment of quizzing and amount of time spent, would provide a more thorough understanding of the relationship between formative quizzes and final test outcome.

Another limitation is the exclusion of the group of students that completed 1 to 5 modules. Future analysis of this group would offer a better understanding of the relation between online formative assessment and student performance.

Regarding the positive results presented in this paper, it is recommended to use Formative Quizzing in higher education. However, in the current study, the Formative Quizzing modules were related to only one topic of the course. Future research is needed to show what would happen with students engagement and learning performance with online materials if larger parts of the course, or the whole course, were provided to students in this manner. It is by studying formative quizzing that we aim to address the value of adding this type of education to higher education curricula.

This study showed a significant and most likely causal positive effect of providing online instructional materials with formative quizzes to higher education students reinforcing learning. This study shows that this instructional method is viable to be incorporated in higher education curricula.

References

1. Gikandi, J.W., Morrow, D., Davis, N.E.: Online formative assessment in higher education: a review of the literature. Comput. Educ. **57**, 2333–2351 (2011)
2. Nguyen, K., Mcdaniel, M.A.: Using quizzing to assist student learning in the classroom: the good, the bad, and the ugly. Teach. Psychol. **42**, 87–92 (2014)
3. Cook, D., Levinson, A., Garside, S.: Time and learning efficiency in Internet-based learning: a systematic review and meta-analysis. Adv. Health Sci. Educ. **15**, 755–770 (2010)
4. Karpicke, J.D., Blunt, J.R.: Retrieval practice produces more learning than elaborative studying with concept mapping. Science **331**, 772–775 (2011)
5. Bouwmeester, R.A.M., De Kleijn, R.A.M., Freriksen, A.W.M., et al.: Online formative tests linked to microlectures improving academic achievement. Med. Teach. **35**, 1044–1046 (2013)
6. Bol, L., Hacker, D.J.: A comparison of the effects of practice tests and traditional review on performance and calibration. J. Exp. Educ. **69**, 133–151 (2001)
7. Herring, W.: Use of practice tests in the prediction of GED test scores. J. Correctional Educ. **50**, 6–8 (1999)
8. Roediger, H.L., Karpicke, J.D.: Test-enhanced learning: taking memory tests improves long-term retention. Psychol. Sci. **17**, 249–255 (2006)
9. Black, P., Wiliam, D.: Assessment and classroom learning. Assess. Educ. Principles Policy Pract. **5**, 7–74 (1998)
10. Mcdaniel, M.A., Anderson, J.L., Derbish, M.H., et al.: Testing the testing effect in the classroom. Eur. J. Cogn. Psychol. **19**, 494–513 (2007)
11. Dobson, J.L.: The use of formative online quizzes to enhance class preparation and scores on summative exams. Adv. Physiol. Educ. **32**, 297–302 (2008)
12. Kibble, J.: Use of unsupervised online quizzes as formative assessment in a medical physiology course: effects of incentives on student participation and performance. Adv. Physiol. Educ. **31**, 253–260 (2007)
13. Kibble, J.D.: Voluntary participation in online formative quizzes is a sensitive predictor of student success. Adv. Physiol. Educ. **35**, 95–96 (2011)
14. Karpicke, J.D., Roediger, H.L.: The critical importance of retrieval for learning. Science **319**, 966–968 (2008)

Author Index

MIX
Papier aus verantwortungsvollen Quellen
Paper from responsible sources
FSC® C105338

If you have any concerns about our products,
you can contact us on
ProductSafety@springernature.com

In case Publisher is established outside the EU,
the EU authorized representative is:
Springer Nature Customer Service Center GmbH
Europaplatz 3, 69115 Heidelberg, Germany

Printed by Libri Plureos GmbH
in Hamburg, Germany